Heath O'Loughlin is the son of a former member and 'Sons of God' Chief Inspector. Having earned  Special Operations Group, he is r stories for the first time.

Heath began his journalism cad in Melbourne in 2001. In his tim Melbourne's most infamous crimes including underworld killings and other high-profile cases. He crossed to the Nine Network in 2006 to report on sport and co-anchor the weekend bulletin. After eight years in television news, he became General Manager of Media, Communications and Marketing at the North Melbourne Football Club in the Australian Football League (AFL), where he has been since 2008. Under his lead, the club's media department has become an industry trailblazer, winning several nationwide awards for excellence and innovation.

In 2016, Heath collaborated with NMFC legend Brent Harvey on his acclaimed autobiography, *Boomer* (Macmillan). *Sons of God* is Heath's first book.

INSIDE THE SECRET WORLD OF OUR
= SPECIAL OPERATIONS =
GROUP

SONS OF GOD

HEATH O'LOUGHLIN

MACMILLAN
Pan Macmillan Australia

Some of the people in this book have had their names changed to protect
their identities.

First published 2017 in Macmillan by Pan Macmillan Australia Pty Ltd
1 Market Street, Sydney, New South Wales, Australia, 2000

Copyright © Heath O'Loughlin 2017

The moral right of the author to be identified as the author of this work has
been asserted.

All rights reserved. No part of this book may be reproduced or transmitted
by any person or entity (including Google, Amazon or similar organisations),
in any form or by any means, electronic or mechanical, including
photocopying, recording, scanning or by any information storage and retrieval
system, without prior permission in writing from the publisher.

Cataloguing-in-Publication entry is available
from the National Library of Australia
http://catalogue.nla.gov.au

Typeset in 12/17 pt Fairfield LH Light by Midland Typesetters
Printed by McPherson's Printing Group

The author and the publisher have made every effort to contact copyright
holders for material used in this book. Any person or organisation that may
have been overlooked should contact the publisher.

Aboriginal and Torres Strait Islander people should be aware that this book
may contain images or names of people now deceased.

MIX
Paper from
responsible sources
FSC® C001695

The paper in this book is FSC® certified.
FSC® promotes environmentally responsible,
socially beneficial and economically viable
management of the world's forests.

Being a member of the Special Operations Group takes great courage, bravery and commitment, but away from all the raids, arrests, gunfire and risk-taking other heroes are found.

To my amazing mum, Linda, I dedicate this book to you and all your sacrifices, selfless acts, shot nerves and heartache. You kept our family together through the toughest times and, to this day, we still get our strength from you.

To my dad, Doug, you were born to protect and shield those around you from danger. You have always been a solid rock for your family and the one everyone looks to in times of need. You're always more than willing to help people in trouble with your level-headedness and wise counsel – I don't know what I'd do without you. Thank you for working closely with me on this book – I will treasure the experience forever.

To my amazing brother Ben and all those who dedicate their lives to serve and protect in our emergency services organisations, especially uniformed police who confront unknown danger on a regular basis, thank you for looking out for us.

To the incredible members of the SOG, past and present, may this book add to your lasting legacy of bravery, courage and selflessness. I have nothing but the highest level of respect for you all.

CONTENTS

Blessed are the peacemakers, for they shall be called the Sons of God.

Matthew 5:9

FOREWORD

by John Silvester

It was at the Special Operations Group thirtieth anniversary dinner that I saw first-hand how the 'Soggies' demand excellence and find it difficult to compromise on even the smallest detail.

The hired comedian was performing a forty-minute monologue, which began slowly and then tailed off quickly. Much of his material was delivered in a fake subcontinental accent, which entertained neither the audience nor the waiters – the latter of whom were of Indian descent.

Anyone who tells jokes for a living knows that some days you just die on stage, although it is probably advisable not to do so in front of an audience trained to kill.

I was sitting on the organisers' table that night and saw a mobile phone light up with a text. 'Get him off or we'll shoot him.' It came from the snipers' table. These people can hit you between the eyes from a distance of more than one kilometre. Best to keep them onside.

It is fitting this insider's account of one of the most secret police units in Australia should be written by Heath O'Loughlin – as his family is part of the very fabric of the SOG, with his father Doug and uncles Neil and Robert all former officers in charge. While Heath chose journalism ahead of the family business of policing, he's had unique access for this book.

But there is irony there too for Neil (who rose to the rank of deputy commissioner), who was one of a number of senior officers that for years refused to allow individual acts of extreme courage by members of The Group to be recognised with valour awards. They argued that what was considered exceptional elsewhere was simply expected at the SOG. This was later relaxed, with the names of many now on the Honour Board at police headquarters.

Such as when Fawkner gunman Fotios Diakonidis killed two people and fired more than one hundred shots into local cars and homes, in a siege in 1994. Police had set up a kilometre exclusion zone with the SOG prepared to wait him out, when a woman with her two children, who were inside the zone and unaware of the danger, drove straight towards him and what would have been certain death.

Without hesitation three Soggies broke cover, two drawing fire on themselves while the third ran to stop the woman. Diakonidis came out in the open to shoot at the police. They shot him dead.

Another on the Honour Board is the member who after a colleague was shot (saved only by his ballistic vest) ignored a fusillade of bullets to return fire and kill the neo-Nazi gunman.

While the operations that result in shootings draw the headlines, in most cases the SOG live up to their nickname of the Sons of God (Blessed are the Peacemakers), for the unit routinely saves the lives of members of the public and the suspects they are sent to arrest.

The SOG complete around four hundred operations a year with more than a hundred considered high risk and life threatening. These jobs include sieges, forced entries, cordon-and-contain operations, mobile intercepts, and arresting violent local criminals and terror suspects.

During Melbourne's underworld war, some of the major players were relieved to find the armed masked men ordering them to surrender were the SOG and not gangland rivals. At least then they knew they weren't going to be shot.

The Soggies' philosophy has always been to overprepare when they can to avoid violent confrontations. Speed and stealth are valued over brawn.

Which is why, as Heath captures perfectly in this book, the training is mentally and physically brutal, where some of the fittest applicants wash out quickly. The SOG needs to know every member can be relied upon not to crack under extreme pressure.

A perfect example of how the SOG use fatal force only as a last resort was the 2012 East Keilor siege involving notorious gunman and armed robber Christopher Dean Binse.

For forty hours 'Badness' Binse kept police at bay, occasionally venturing out to fire shots before seeking cover in the house. He was convinced the siege would end in his death and was determined to take as many police with him in the final gunfight.

When police finally hit the house with stun grenades and tear gas, 'Badness' emerged carrying a gun and wearing a bulletproof vest. If he had confronted any other police, he almost certainly would have been shot dead but the SOG shot him with non-fatal (but painful) beanbag shots.

Dazed but otherwise unhurt, he was taken alive.

Much later, Binse wrote to the SOG to critique the operation and ask for a beanbag shot as a memento.

It seems even the crooks are fans.

Heath O'Loughlin's book *Sons of God* gives us a unique insight into one of the most secretive, feared (by some) and trusted (by others) police units in Australia.

Thank God they are on our side.

John Silvester
Senior Crime Reporter, *The Age*

INTRODUCTION

I sat in the back of the four-wheel drive with the hood of my jumper pulled over my head and eyes. It had been tied tightly in front of my face by the drawstrings and I couldn't see a thing. I knew we were on an unmade road because the car was vibrating violently and I could feel the jolting bumps as the tyres ploughed into potholes. The cage in the back of the vehicle was rattling loudly and the padlock that secured its doors was constantly bashing against the steel frame. Each time we hit a bump in the road, I was thrust sideways into one of the armed men who sat on both sides of me. They were little comfort and would just shove me back into an upright, seated position with a heavy elbow. They were there to ensure I couldn't grab a door handle and escape the moving vehicle. At one point, I asked where we were going and was met with a sharp 'Shut the fuck up!' from one of the men in the front.

As the car gathered speed, I could hear the sound of thunder approaching. 'They're coming! Here they come!' one of the men next to me shouted with a hint of nervousness. I could feel his body turn towards the rear of the car and assumed he was trying to look out the back window. I then heard the clicks of their guns as they locked and loaded. 'You know the drill,' the man driving said. 'No surrender!'

The thunder got louder. My stomach was bunched up in knots. I had no idea what was about to happen, but I was frightened and excited at the same time. The thunder passed over the roof of the car and I fell forwards as the driver slammed on the brakes and caused the car to skid to a halt. My seatbelt dug into my shoulder and neck as it tightened to hold me back. 'Fuck! Go! Go! Go!' one of the men shouted. The doors sprung open and thick dust filled the car. I could hear the sound of helicopter blades slapping the air outside – my eardrums were being buffeted but I couldn't cover them because my hands were bound behind my back.

There were lots of men yelling, 'Police! Don't move! Police! Don't move!' Then someone shouted, 'Fuck you, pig!' and another screamed aggressively, 'Die, motherfuckers!' all before the sounds of gunfire rang out: CRACK! CRACK! CRACK! CRACK! CRACK! CRACK! CRACK! CRACK! CRACK!

I buried my head between my knees to try to shield myself from the mayhem. Suddenly, someone grabbed my arm and pulled me from the vehicle. 'Come with me, little fella, quickly!' The hood was ripped off my head and the sunlight blinded me as I was dragged from the car. No sooner had I stepped out than another hand firmly gripped my other arm and I was virtually walking on air. I was still trying to open my eyes and adjust to the light. As I was being whisked away towards the chopper, I could see several men in black with heavy-duty machine guns pointing at a group of other men who were lying on the ground, face down. 'Let's go!' one of the men who was carrying me ordered. I looked up at him and saw that he was wearing a black helmet, protective goggles and gasmask. I couldn't make out who he was. I had to turn my head to the ground and keep my mouth closed because of all the dust that was being whipped up by the rotors.

I was thrown into the back of the chopper and was able to open my eyes properly for the first time as several armed men, all dressed in black, piled in. When the last one got aboard, the order was given to the pilot, 'Go! Go! Go!' and the aircraft rose from the ground a few feet, tipped its nose forwards and flew away. 'Whoo!' one of the men yelled with delight as he high-fived another sitting directly across from him. 'And that's how it's done!'

Being the son of the man in charge of the Special Operations Group (SOG) in the Victoria Police Force had its perks, that is for sure. The scene I just described to you happened during week one of my high school work-experience placement. While all my mates were bored out of their minds stacking supermarket shelves or repetitiously stuffing filing cabinets full of alphabetised documents at medical clinics or accountancy firms, at fifteen years of age I was pretending to be a hostage as part of a highly confidential counter-terrorism exercise conducted especially for police command and powerful state government ministers.

This was back in 1995, and health and safety wasn't quite as stringent as it is now, but it did still exist. My father signed off on it all, relying on the professionalism of his men to keep me safe and reassuring the school that I'd mainly be doing paperwork at SOG headquarters. What I got instead were among the most thrilling moments of my life. Not only did I get to re-enact the hostage scenario five times but I also took part in a whole range of other role-plays.

In some of the other exercises, I wasn't one of the good guys. In the back room of a house with no roof and walls made out of used tyres, I paced up and down and waited for the door in front of me to burst open. 'Come and get me!' I yelled. 'I'll take every last one of you down with me if you come through that door!' This time, I was acting as an armed offender who had barricaded himself inside with a weapon. I was told to threaten and taunt the Soggies (as the SOG members referred to themselves), who were shouting at me to 'surrender peacefully' and come out with my 'hands in the air'. I knew it was only a drill, but I was still scared at the thought of the SOG about to 'arrest' me. I knew they were coming, but I didn't know what tactics they'd employ, and the suspense was eating me up inside. Would they come in from above? Would they use tear gas or distraction grenades on me? How many of them would there be? Why did they make me put on a safety mask, helmet and bulletproof vest? Those experiences should be reserved for the worst and most dangerous criminals, not Year Nine school students! I'd put on a brace face when the Soggies had asked me to be involved, but I'm sure they'd seen right through the facade.

'This is your last chance. Come out with your hands up!' The clock was ticking and my time alone in that room was coming to an end. I looked over to the table in the corner and saw a rubber knife. It was left there for a reason, so I grabbed it and backed myself into the corner furthest from the door.

Everything went eerily quiet. They stopped calling on me to give up, and I felt extremely isolated and began reconsidering my options. Maybe I should put down the knife so they'll go easier on me . . . Maybe I should tell them I've decided to surrender . . . Maybe I should tell Dad I don't want to be involved anymore. It was too late.

What happened next was a blur. One minute I was standing alone in the room and then all hell broke loose. BANG! BANG! BANG! BANG! BANG! BANG! BANG! BANG! BANG! Flashes of bright lights and a thick smoke filled the room as the nine-banger stun grenade exploded over and over again. I buried my head in my arms and looked away to shield my eyes from the blinding lights. I then shuffled forwards to the middle of the room with the knife still in my right hand.

'Police! Don't move! Police! Don't move!' one of the Soggies yelled with a booming voice that shook me to the core. 'Drop the knife! Drop the knife! Get on the ground! Get on the ground!' Stunned and disorientated, I let go of the knife. I can only assume it hit the floor at the same time I did – the heavy tackle laid on me by one of the SOG seemed to have occurred simultaneously with the release of the blade from my hand.

Before I knew it, I was face down on the floor with my arms twisted behind my back and a knee buried between my shoulder-blades. The pain was intense but thankfully it only lasted a few seconds. My hands were zip-tied together and I was placed under 'arrest'. It was such a surreal experience. 'Clear!' one of the men yelled to indicate the drama was now over and the other rooms of the house were empty of danger. He radioed to the command post, 'Rogue to Kek. We have one male in custody. No injuries to report. The house is clear, over.'

My intentions were to rush at the men in black when they burst through that door, and I thought I was ready for them, but I simply didn't have a chance to go on the attack. The power, skill and speed they displayed during the mock raid seemed super-human. I was left shocked and in utter awe of their abilities. I have never felt so helpless and insignificant in my entire life.

In week two of my work experience, I went sniper training with some of the best marksmen in the country. On the secret SOG shooting range in the bush, I learnt how to fire just about every gun in the group's armoury. From sniper rifles to semi-automatic machine guns, shotguns and handguns, I 'unloaded' with them all.

I was given my own sniper rifle for the day during target practice with the group's best shooters. On the range, I set up a big yellow target about 300 metres away, lay on my stomach, stared down the high-tech telescopic sight and spat out round after round in quick succession. The high-powered weapon repeatedly recoiled into my bony right shoulder and left a giant, dark-purple bruise for several days after.

I had a few magazines on rotation, and after I'd emptied them I got up and walked over to the large ammunition crate that was about ten metres away, to reload. This soon became a hassle for me, though, as I was churning through each supply of sixty bullets and having to retrace my steps. The men decided to take action to ease the burden on me. As I emptied another magazine and prepared to collect more bullets, two Soggies set the ammo crate down right next to me. 'Here you are,' one of them said. 'Now you can go for your life, mate!'

There was no stopping me, and for the next thirty or so minutes I unleashed hell on that target. I was like a man possessed, pulling the trigger again and again, merely hoping that I'd hit something. From that distance, I couldn't really tell whether I was landing my shots or dropping them. All I could see was a puff of dust billow up from the mountain of dirt piled behind the target after a bullet impacted. I couldn't help but think about the story of one of the men hitting a rabbit at almost a kilometre away. It was incredible how good these guys were.

About an hour later, the call came to 'Cease fire!' and it was time to inspect our targets and assess our accuracy. This was where the fun ended and the embarrassment began for me.

After being drilled by about 500 bullets, my target looked like a block of Swiss cheese, but to my horror the snipers' targets were very different to mine. Theirs had only about ten holes punched through each cardboard cut-out, and their shots were all grouped together in neat little bunches. Somewhere along the line, I had missed the point of the exercise. I must have been distracted by all the excitement when the instructions were given out. The opportunity to fire such an amazing weapon simply overwhelmed me. Apparently, we were supposed to display deadly accuracy by grouping our shots together as tightly as possible on the target. Someone (me) didn't get the message and was left a little red-faced. I was allowed to take the target home as a souvenir, and it also served as a reminder to always listen to instructions, especially when you're trying to impress.

While I felt my efforts as a stand-in hostage and would-be sniper were up to scratch considering my age and lack of experience, my dad disagreed and thought I could have done better – a lot better. When he filled out my work-experience evaluation, I was left disappointed, to put it mildly. One question on the form was: How would you rate the student's overall performance? It was rare for anyone to receive anything below the top answer of 'Excellent', as work experience was designed to encourage students to think positively about the workforce and look back fondly on the fortnight of mostly slave labour. But Dad instead gave me the mediocre rating of 'Satisfactory', and I was the only student at school to come back with such a substandard result. Dad was a hard marker and said I would have needed to do something 'extraordinary' in order to receive the top mark. To this day, he still refuses to concede that he was a little harsh.

There are three photographs kept in a family album at my parents' house that best sum up my early childhood. They were taken when I was just a toddler, and my dad is in all of them, wearing his trademark black jumpsuit for work. Crying, with my arms outstretched, I'm pictured stumbling towards him on the landing from the lounge room to the front door, desperately hoping he will save me from face-planting into the slate-tiled floor by scooping me into his arms. It's obvious I can barely stand on my own two feet without toppling over. In the second picture, Dad has reached out and grabbed my hand. But he only steadied me and didn't lift me up like I would have wanted him to. Instead, I'm told, he unsuccessfully tried to redirect my attention behind me towards Mum and hoped I'd head in her direction for some comfort. It's at that moment that I realised he was about to leave me, again. Determined not to let him out of my sight, I tried to cling on to his hand.

In the final photo, he bends down in an effort to placate me. He would have said something like, 'You be a good boy for Mummy, okay? Daddy will be home soon, mate,' as he edged closer to the door.

Despite the endless stream of tears that rolled down my face in this familiar scenario and the ear-piercing screams I always managed to generate, nothing I ever did would stop him from heading out that door. I simply didn't know there were others out there that need my dad much, much more than I did.

I'll never forget the smell of his uniform. It was very musty – a combination of gunpowder and grease with a smearing of oil, metal, petrol and dirt. That's about the only way I can describe it. It was such a distinct smell. I know it so well because I spent so much time with my nose pressed hard against his pants. I would mash my face into his leg and grab on to it like a tiny koala would to its mother, hoping all twelve kilograms of me would be too much weight for him to step out the door with. I used to think if I could hold on long enough, it might convince him to stay.

Mum says it used to break my heart every time he left – which was all too often. 'It's okay, Mummy's here,' she'd say as I stared out the small window beside the door, still crying as Dad's unmarked police car reversed out of the driveway and disappeared up the road. We never knew where he was headed and he wouldn't have had much of an idea either. They never used to give him too much information over the pager or phone initially. If time permitted, he'd usually have to go to police headquarters in the city to pick up other men before heading to the job in question. All we knew was that it could be days or even weeks before we'd see him again. Each time he walked out that door, there was a chance he'd never come back. Maybe that's why I was always so upset. Although I was too young to comprehend it at the time, I probably reacted to Mum's fear and anxiety. While she tried to hide her feelings from my older brother, Benjamin, and me, I knew she was terrified by what Dad was potentially walking into. Deep down, she always feared the worst but had to put on a brave face to protect us.

My father, Douglas O'Loughlin, was a member of the Victoria Police Force's elite SOG for eighteen years from 1981 to 1998. He joined 'The Group' just after I was born and when Ben was about three. Our way of life was much different to other families', and the older I get, the more I've come to realise it.

Even in the days before mobile phones, text messages and emails, Dad was always on call and had to be contactable and available 24/7. He used to have a pager, and it was permanently attached to his hip by day and placed on his bedside table at night. When that little black device beeped loudly and started vibrating, it felt like our world stopped revolving. It didn't matter where we were at the time or what we were doing, Dad's work always came first. That meant that, as a family, we dropped everything, cancelled plans, left special occasions and birthday parties early or just missed them altogether when he was called out.

Initially, Dad was a tactical operator and specialist bomb technician in the group. His job, like all the members', was extremely dangerous. As a bomb tech, he would defuse explosive devices, inspect suspect packages, and occasionally rig doorways and entry points with improvised explosive devices (IEDs) so the others in the group could gain entry to a criminal's property. He also raided houses, staked out drug crops, carried out witness-protection tasks, conducted reconnaissance missions, enacted mobile intercepts, confronted and returned fire with armed offenders, arrested some of the state's most violent criminals and, most importantly, saved many, many lives.

I've always had a deep connection with Dad and grew up idolising him. He was, and still is, my hero. But I also admired Mum's strength and now have a better understanding of what she went through each time Dad went away.

Dad was in the army reserve and followed his four older brothers into the police force as soon as he was able. There were five O'Loughlin boys and three sisters – all the brothers joined the force in the order of Barry, Robert, Neil, Geoffrey and Dad (Doug). Dad was the youngest and the last to join, and the last to leave. His highly distinguished and decorated career spanned more than forty-seven years. Robert and Neil were also in the SOG and oversaw it as officers in charge during its formative years in the early- to mid-eighties.

The O'Loughlin name is one of the most famous in Victoria Police history, largely due to the influence Dad and his brothers had on the organisation. Neil climbed to the rank of deputy commissioner under Neil Comrie and retired soon after Christine Nixon took charge in 2001. Robert rose to the rank of superintendent, as did Geoffrey, while Barry made it to detective sergeant before he died in a tragic car accident in 1972. After he left the SOG, Dad was a crime superintendent and finished as a detective superintendent at the Forensic Services Department.

Although the five brothers are now out of the job and have officially retired, the O'Loughlin dynasty continues. At one stage, the family had about thirteen active members in the force, including my brother Ben. Five still remain to this day.

After Dad finished his time as a tactical operator in the SOG, he climbed the ranks and later became the officer in charge of the unit as its inspector in 1987 and then chief inspector in 1990. In control, his role was to manage the group and formulate its strategies and action plans during training and real-life operations. In layman's terms, the buck stopped fairly and squarely with him if anything went wrong.

While being the son of an SOG member and boss had some negative elements, there was also a significant upside that I was able to take advantage of later in life. I used to take every opportunity to go into work with Dad. If I didn't have school, I'd be up with him at 6.00 am scoffing Weet-Bix in the kitchen while Ben and Mum were still sleeping. We'd head to the city via the Eastern Freeway and Dad would always stop at the same newsagency on Rathdowne Street to collect the daily newspaper. The SOG office intrigued me and I looked up to all the men like other kids would look up to a star footballer or cricketer. The Soggies were my Gary Abletts, Wayne Careys, Michael Jordans, Pat Cashes, Allan Borders and Dennis Lillies. I remember going to a family friends' barbecue once and Hawthorn football champion Robert DiPierdomenico was there. Everyone was making such a fuss and I thought the kids should have been trying to get my dad's autograph, not his.

I always thought I'd join the police force and during my brother's twenty-first birthday speech I told him, 'One day who knows, we could be zipping up black jumpsuits together.' At the time, I thought it was a possibility, but I ended up going down a different path. Everyone expected me to join the police force and for that reason, I wanted to do something else. I didn't want to do what was expected, I wanted to challenge myself and follow my other passion for writing and storytelling.

My connection to all things police and the SOG didn't end there, however. My ambition to become a writer led me to journalism and an eventual job on television with the Seven Network. Working in the newsroom I covered endless crime stories while on police rounds. I was shot with a taser twice (voluntarily), was the first reporter on the scene when underworld figure Andrew 'Benji' Veniamin was killed by Mick Gatto in Carlton, covered the murder of Jason Moran in Essendon, interviewed drug boss Carl Williams on a few occasions, reported on high profile cases including the Matthew Wales King 'society murders', the murder of Maria Korp – the woman left to die in the boot of a car by Tania Herman – had dealings with John Sharpe, the man who killed his wife and daughter with a spear gun in Mornington, and was at the Chaouk family home in Brooklyn when young Mohamed was shot by an SOG officer after wielding a samurai sword. I also had a surreal experience when I came in direct contact with Dad during a twenty-four-hour hostage-siege in Craigieburn in 2004. He was the officer in charge of the scene, and if you were wondering: yes, he looked after me and I had the inside word the entire time.

So it was emotional at stages but, reflecting on my upbringing, I wouldn't have wanted it any other way. I learnt a lot through Dad and the SOG, including the importance of discipline, teamwork and respect.

To this day, some of Dad's closest mates are ex-SOG officers, and most would never have considered speaking publicly about their experiences with the group. When Dad would return home after work, I'd always ask him what he'd been doing, but all he'd ever tell me was 'just paperwork'.

Now, because of my family's history and the bond the men have with Dad, former members have allowed me into the inner sanctum of the SOG – a place that has always been considered a 'no go' zone. They've finally broken the group's strict code of silence and have given me rare, first-hand accounts of what happened during some of the state's most violent crimes, dangerous sieges and fatal shootings from the late 70s to the 21st century.

In these pages, I have kept my interventions to a minimum, providing background information, introductions and factual details wherever required. The rest is directly in the SOG members' own words, to give you the best possible insight into the dangers of their 'workplace', and the training, attitudes and actions that enable them not only to succeed but also to stay alive. To preserve their anonymity, I have had to change some of their characteristics and code names, but their perspectives and words remain all their own.

While researching and writing this book, I have finally been able to fully comprehend what Dad and his men went through when they had to leave their homes and families on all those occasions. Now, I have realised that, deep down, Dad was probably just as nervous as Mum was.

1

BETRAYAL (PART I)

A false witness will not go unpunished, and he who breathes out lies will not escape.

Proverbs 19:5

Shamus was distracted. His tail was down and it seemed he hadn't been able to pick up any trace of the two prison escapees or their female accomplice who had all gone to ground after sparking a massive, statewide police pursuit and ensuing manhunt. It seemed the veteran police dog had lost interest in continuing the search for the trio. 'It's just like Nam, isn't it?' Papa whispered jokingly to his colleagues, Mouse and Rogue. He was referring to the dense bushland they were surrounded by, which he imagined looked like a tropical jungle in Vietnam. Mouse, ten years younger than Papa and below him by a couple of ranks, just gave a smirk and a quick shake of his head, knowing neither of them had ever been there. Rogue ignored the conversation and continued to scan the area with his self-loading rifle (SLR) raised in a firing position, his index finger placed delicately on the trigger. They were all expecting the unexpected, just like they were trained to.

Despite being in country Victoria, the landscape did resemble that of a tropical jungle, but it was anything but warm and humid. Shivering, Rogue waded through the icy cold waters of the Goulburn River. Its chilly currents descended straight from the state's snowy alpine region and presented a challenge for the men and the dog handler, Travis Blackman, to traverse.

Shamus in particular found the going incredibly tough. Perhaps the only sniffer dog in the police force that hated water, he point blank refused to get in the river. Rogue – not a dog person by any stretch of the imagination – was forced to carry him for about fifteen metres to the riverbank on the other side. Already significantly weighed down with his heavy, ceramic-plated ballistic vest, array of weapons and equipment, Rogue's task became even more challenging when Shamus began to panic as they entered the water. He immediately started to thrash about in an effort to break free of Rogue's grasp.

ROGUE: The water was deep, up to my chest and just below my chin. I was holding Shamus out in front of me at arm's length and he arced up a fair bit. He was shittin' himself more so than trying to bite me or anything. But what kind of police dog can't swim? It wasn't right. The whole situation just wasn't right. Mouse was helping Blackman get across and Papa was carrying my SLR, as well as his own gear and weapons. We all had our hands full.

—

Struggling to contain the distressed German shepherd, Rogue eventually set him down on a small beach, about ten metres wide and twenty metres long, made of rocks and pebbles that had built up on the shore of the river. Blackman took back control of the leash while Rogue drew a deep breath and reassessed their approach. He knew it wasn't an ideal place to stop as there was little cover, but he had no choice. If the armed bandits were watching their search party from beyond the tree line, they'd be sitting ducks.

ROGUE: We were getting nothing from the dog, Shamus, at all. We were still searching the area and had our weapons up and in the ready position, but we'd become way more relaxed because it appeared we'd missed them. The lead we were given had gone as ice-cold as the river we'd just waded through.

—

The SOG had been deployed to the area after a historic hotel at Gaffneys Creek, a mining town between Jamieson and Woods Point, was burnt to the ground. Sightings of the violent escapees in the locality came in quick and fast. Nothing, though, was as solid as a report the SOG received via local police from a pair of fly-fishermen who had been angling at a site called Picnic Point – about twenty-five kilometres from Jamieson. The duo came across a four-wheel-drive Mitsubishi Pajero that had been parked conspicuously off the main road and was camouflaged with branches and thick foliage. It was well hidden and barely visible from just a few metres away. It matched the description of one of the getaway cars the prisoners used when they busted out of the Melbourne Remand Centre a few days earlier. One of the fishermen marked the exact location of the vehicle by resetting the trip meter in his car and driving to the local police station.

With the fire at the hotel under investigation and rumours spreading of sightings of the escapees, the mainstream media started to converge on the police's command post at the Jamieson Police Station. So significant was the story that several media helicopters had flown in and landed next to the police helicopter, also known as the airwing, on a vacant property next door packed with news journalists and cameramen.

ROGUE: A second team of about four SOG guys took off in the chopper for an aerial search to the north, and the rest of us were just sittin' around at the command post on standby. Next thing, Kek came over to me and whispered, 'Hey, mate, don't show any reaction when I tell you this, but we think we've got something on the escapees.' With the media watching us like hawks, Kek didn't want to draw any unnecessary attention; otherwise they'd try and follow us and could jeopardise the entire operation. Kek told me that a car had been found in the bush. It was frustrating because we'd been out to that location in Picnic Point only the night before and searched right along the river but found nothing. As far as we could work out later on, we'd searched up to about twenty metres of where the car was. So the escapees would have heard us, if they were there then.

—

Rogue, Kek, Papa and Mouse formed the SOG's Ground Response Unit and attempted to slip away discreetly without raising any suspicion from the media, but it wasn't easy. They split up and took two separate cars out to Picnic Point, but despite their best attempts they were still followed from above.

MOUSE: All the media had caught on and saw us leave. They followed us in their choppers. Knowing the op could have been blown, we pulled over to the side of the road and Kek got on the radio and spoke to someone about getting an air-exclusion zone set up to stop the media from coming any further. Minutes later, the choppers all disappeared. It happened very quickly. One minute they were up there hovering above us, the next minute they'd all pissed off.

—

Now in the clear and unhindered by the media, the SOG stopped on the main road and made their way down to Picnic Point by foot, where the suspect Pajero had been sighted.

ROGUE: We walked down there all stealth-like, looked around again and had Shamus the police dog take a good sniff about but there was nothing new to act on. It was a fairly big opening off the main track. The main road was just made of dirt and ran down to the left into the river. We found the car and then confirmed that it was the Mitsubishi Pajero that had been stolen by the fugitives. However, we couldn't find them. It looked like they'd gone.

MOUSE: We did a quick search around the car and found a heap of bloodied bandages and toilet paper. We then searched upstream and found even more bandages, but then the trail just petered out so we decided to double back. We got back to the Pajero and found another track that undulated along the riverbank. We had to go into deep water and duck under a big fallen branch in order to get onto a pebbly beach. That's when Rogue had to carry Shamus into the water.

—

With their lines of communication now down due to water-damaged radios and a weak signal, Papa decided to head back to the main road to try to re-establish a connection with the other SOG members who were off searching other areas in the heli-copter. But soon after Papa left the company of Rogue, Mouse, Blackman and Shamus, the situation changed dramatically for the worse.

Shamus suddenly became animated. Rogue and Mouse had worked with sniffer dogs long enough to know that when they pointed their noses to the air, the scent was fresh, and when they sniffed the ground, it was old. This was definitely a recent scent, and Shamus became increasingly enthusiastic.

ROGUE: Suddenly, Shamus started sniffing the air really excitedly. He smelt something suss [suspect]. Blackman looked over and gave me a nod and just mouthed the word 'Yep', indicating that Shamus was definitely on to something fresh.

MOUSE: Blackman pulled Shamus back and turned to me and said, 'They're right in front of us!' He said, 'They could be as close as twenty to twenty-five metres away.' I immediately took my gun off safety and I dropped to a crouched position because we were so exposed.

—

Following Mouse's lead, Rogue also crouched down and gestured for his colleague to cover to the north of the river while he pointed his weapon to the south. Rogue pushed Blackman down to the ground and instructed him to make Shamus lie low next to him. The tension was high.

ROGUE: I started shittin' myself and just felt like something really bad was about to happen at any moment. The adrenaline started pumping through my body but I kicked into training mode and calmed myself down almost instantaneously. Being all wound up inside in a situation like that doesn't help anyone. You need to be cool, calm and collected because when shit goes down, people will look to you to be the one in control and to be the person who makes all the right decisions. That's what we were trained to do and that's what we were paid to do.

—

Deep in the bushes and well concealed directly in front of the SOG's position, one of the escapees, Archie Butterly, lay in wait with his rifle pointed directly at Mouse's head. The sight of the

SOG, dressed in black and heavily armed, would no doubt have sent shivers up his spine. But it may have been Shamus that scared him the most, as Butterly had had some bad experiences with police dogs in the past. In Western Australia, he was chased by a dog and hid up in a tree with a firearm because he was so afraid.

ROGUE: I reckon as soon as he saw Shamus within about fifteen or twenty metres in front of him, he just shit himself really badly and thought, 'This dog's gonna get me!' He would have been watching us closely, and when Shamus picked up his scent, he would have been like, 'Ohhh fuck! He's sniffing around . . . I'm fucked. He's on to me!'

—

Butterly's finger hovered over the trigger as he kept his aim on Mouse.

ROGUE: Because my radio was fucked, I had to stand up briefly, take the earpiece out of my ear so I could try to talk directly into the receiver. I'd only managed to get out the words, 'Papa, it's Rogue, come in. The dog's just picked something up,' when the first shots rang out.

Six days earlier, Butterly, a notorious armed robber and violent criminal, had teamed up with fellow inmate Peter Gibb and his prison guard lover Heather Parker to hatch a bold bid for freedom. The pair was being detained at the Melbourne Remand Centre on Spencer Street, right on the fringe of Melbourne's CBD. Gibb, also a career criminal and armed robber, had just been handed a heavy sentence but had lodged an appeal and was waiting for a date for his next hearing. But patience obviously wasn't one of his strong suits. The duo used explosives, allegedly smuggled into the facility by Parker, to blast their way out of a second-storey window in the building. They climbed down a rope made of tied-together bedsheets to the ground below – it was just like a scene out of a Hollywood blockbuster. This escape didn't entirely go to script, however. Butterly fell from the rope and landed heavily, injuring his leg on impact. He was forced to limp to the getaway car, possibly another of Parker's generous gifts, and they sped off. But they had a few more obstacles to overcome before they were completely free.

Their Ford Falcon broke just about every road rule in the book and carved a path of destruction through the busy city streets. After two crashes, it eventually came to a complete halt. Unperturbed, the assailants then stole a motorcycle at gunpoint and continued on their way. Pursued by an off-duty police officer in a taxi, the pair crashed again and attempted to steal another motorbike as a police divisional van arrived to try to stop them. One of the police officers got close enough to strike Gibb's arm with a baton and broke it, but the officer was subsequently shot in the shoulder and the lung. Gibb then stole the officer's revolver, held it to his head and told the other police officer who was on the scene to 'back off!' or else he'd have to watch his colleague get shot and killed with his own gun. The escapees took the police van and coincidentally met up with Parker, before jumping into the second getaway car, a Mitsubishi Pajero, and heading to the high country. It was the beginning of the end for the trio, and little did he know at the time, but one of the outlaws was about to face the ultimate betrayal that would cost him his life.

The first shot that Butterly fired at the SOG came from the bushes to their north – the direction Mouse was facing. The bullet sizzled past Mouse's head, missing him by a matter of millimetres, continued over the top of Blackman and Shamus and brushed the back of Rogue's leg.

MOUSE: I felt a couple of rounds fly past my head. You know, just a big 'WHOOSH'. When a round goes past you in close proximity like that, you feel a sonic whoosh go past – it's hard to describe. I knew the rounds were extremely close to hitting me, though. That's one thing I do remember very clearly, the sound and the feeling of those rounds going past my head. All I can say is the shooter wasn't expecting to miss me. He had my head in his sights and there's no doubt he wanted to take me out and kill me.

ROGUE: I couldn't see the shooter or shooters, but they could see us, obviously. I presume he was trying to shoot Mouse, because Mouse was the closest person to his position. But he missed Mouse and hit me. It was just skedaddle and I hit the deck like a ton of bricks. It felt like getting a big corky [corked muscle]. Like when you're playing footy and someone cannons into your leg muscle. It was like someone hit me in the leg from behind with a baseball bat.

–

Rogue was down for only a matter of seconds and managed to get back to his feet quickly. His first reaction was to shove Blackman towards the bank of the river and into a large blackberry bush for cover.

ROGUE: He was pretty upset, Trav. He was doing it pretty hard. All he had was a little .38 revolver and Shamus was yelping, barking and howling like crazy. I can remember yelling at Blackman, 'Mate! Get Shamus in front of you! Fuckin' get him in front of ya!' Blackman kept shouting, 'Where are the bullets coming from? Where are they coming from?' I said, 'I don't fucken know!' I could just hear the blackberry branches breaking off all around us. They were being sliced to bits by all the bullets.

We were climbing through the thorns and prickles headfirst, just trying to get to a safe spot, but they had us pinned down. At that stage, I was thinking, 'We're absolutely fucked here,' because I had no idea where this bloody shooter or shooters were. The blackberry bush was so thick, I couldn't even move my hands without them being torn up by the razor-sharp prickles and thorns. We were covered in ten-foot-high blackberries and there was no way out, except the way we came in, and that wasn't an option so we just kept burrowing in for safety. I couldn't see Mouse. I had totally forgotten that I'd been shot in the leg, and all I was focused on doing was saving Trav and Shamus.

WHOOSH! WHOOSH! WHOOSH! WHOOSH! WHOOSH! The bullets were flying around us everywhere. We were absolutely pinned down and in real trouble. It was so intense and I didn't think we'd make it out alive. I remember thinking, 'Fuck! What have I done here?' I thought I may have stuffed up and killed us all by deciding to go into the bushes for cover. We'd been trained to 'Run, Dive and Crawl' whenever we came under fire, so that was my first instinct, but I started doubting myself when it appeared we were going to be trapped and killed like ducks in a barrel.

—

Rogue had no sight of Mouse but could hear that he was returning fire.

ROGUE: Everything was being done within a twenty-to-thirty-metre radius. It was a fucking horrendous situation to be in. Thank God Mouse was laying down some cover fire and putting up some resistance. Had it not been for him doing that, we all would have been absolutely rooted.

—

Upon hearing the cracking sounds of gunfire break out through the forest, Papa had doubled back. He received a radio call from Rogue with his location and eventually found his way back to him and tried to get a handle on the situation.

'Where are the shots coming from?' he asked.

'I'm fucked if I know!' replied Rogue. 'This is shithouse!'

'So are you all right? Are you all good?'

'Yep, I'm all good . . . I think.'

—

In all the chaos, and with adrenaline pumping through his veins, Rogue had completely forgotten that he'd taken a bullet in the back of the leg. He looked down and saw a rip in his black pants and blood on his leg. 'Oh fuck!' he barked. 'Hang on a sec, Papa . . . I think I've been shot!'

—

The shooting had ceased. Everything was quiet except for the sound of running water cascading over nearby rocks and down the river. A thin veil of gun smoke lingered in the air and slowly disappeared into the sky. The reprieve allowed Rogue to take stock and while he was naturally worried about his wounded leg, he was far more concerned for the welfare of Mouse.

ROGUE: I was relieved to see Papa and gave him a quick rundown on what was happening: 'I don't know where the

shots are coming from, mate, and Mouse is not answering his radio. I don't know where he is, Papa; I can't find him! I can't see him! I don't know where he is!' I feared Mouse had copped it and could have been dead.

2

GENESIS

God saw all that he had made, and it was very good.

Genesis 1:31

Former Victoria Police chief commissioner Sinclair Imrie 'Mick' Miller shuffled down the hallway of his home, towards his living room. Splendidly dressed in beige trousers and a spotlessly clean and immaculately pressed blue business shirt, it appeared as though he'd stepped straight off the golf course. His shoes were freshly polished and his hair was neatly combed to the side, without a strand out of place. His house, too, was super tidy – like a museum.

On his way through the lounge room, he stopped abruptly and lifted his walking stick. 'What do we have here?' he said, squinting at a tiny black spider on the hallway wall. He attempted to end the intruder's life with the rubber stop on the bottom of his cane. 'Take that!' he said with his first thrust of the stick. A worthy opponent, the arachnid avoided being hit and scampered across the wall. Miller had another go at the nifty little creature. 'Think you're getting away, do you?' he taunted, poking at it once more with his aid. Again, though, his aim was a little off and the spider was able to drop to the floor and seek refuge in a small gap between the carpet and the skirting boards. Refusing to concede defeat, Miller tried to jam the sole of his shoe into the crack where the spider had curled up. Pressing down firmly, he proclaimed, 'Gotcha!' feeling the familiar satisfaction of victory. Miller continued to the kitchen and flicked on the kettle, not knowing that the spider had, in fact, survived the encounter.

Anyone aware of Miller's reputation as a policeman would agree that the spider had joined a select few on earth to have somehow outsmarted the extremely popular and well-regarded top cop. Miller was a man who never took 'No' for an answer. According to those who worked under him during his decade-long stint at the helm of the Victoria Police Force, he demanded perfection and refused to accept failure. He was, however, always fair and courteous and remains one of the most revered figures to have ever worn a police badge.

As chief commissioner from 1977 till 1987, Miller guided the force through some of the state's most turbulent times. He now describes the inspired changes he made to the crime-fighting organisation as 'evolutionary' not 'revolutionary', though many of his subordinates disagree. Task force policing, the introduction of an airwing and the critical development of the SOG were just some of his many forward-thinking initiatives. After some time, officers affectionately labelled him 'God', because he had such a firm grasp on all areas of the police force, an overarching authority, and widespread adoration and respect.

When Miller took charge of the Victoria Police Force, the world was changing rapidly. The biggest risk to public safety was no longer just the regular, lowly criminals and thugs causing trouble on the streets; it was fast becoming terrorism. Violent acts from insurgents all around the globe were increasing, and the threat of an attack loomed large over Australia. As Miller recalled during my visit to his house, 'Overseas police forces and governments were getting awfully twitchy about terrorism and then we had the bombing in Sydney, and that was a peculiar situation.'

One October afternoon in 1977, Miller was summoned to the office of Victoria's chief secretary, Pat Dickie, in the old Treasury building in Melbourne's CBD. Unaware of the reason for the unscheduled meeting, Miller subsequently regarded it as a defining moment in his distinguished career. On that October afternoon, he said, he made a bold move. 'It's impossible to say what motivated Minister Dickie to ask me without warning, "Chief Commissioner Miller, how prepared are we to cope with a terrorist attack?" It was a pretty blunt question,' Miller recalled. 'I'd been chief commissioner for only a few months and did a double take. However, I had learnt to think quickly on my feet because various ministers tended to ask questions of me as if they were interrogators. Dickie in particular rather spoke down to me, and I thought, "Wow! How am I going to get around this?" I eventually responded, "It's funny you should ask me that, Minister, because I've been considering approaching you about the establishment of a counter-terrorist capability within the Victoria Police Force."'

The truth, of course, was much different. Miller had no such plans and his brain was now working overtime in an effort to appear adequately prepared and in control of the situation.

'Good. Tell me exactly what you have in mind,' the minister probed, suspecting Miller was bluffing.

'Well, of course my idea is all subject to the availability of essential funding, Minister,' Miller stated, slamming the ball directly back into Dickie's court.

Miller knew that any initiatives involving additional personnel or resources in government-run organisations such as the Victoria Police were always dependent on the state's budget. Innovations or additions usually needed to be planned well in advance, with the funding approved and tagged, and then set aside months prior to a roll-out. 'I knew the only option was to get access to what was known as a special Treasury allocation,' Miller explained. 'So I said to Dickie, "What I have in mind is the formation of a permanent counter-terrorism group under the direction of a particular officer."'

Harry Norton immediately sprung to Miller's mind. A Royal Marine commando in the Second World War, Harold Vernon 'Chippy' Norton was the perfect candidate to head up such an elite and specialised outfit. 'Norton was so gung-ho, when he walked into a room the paper clips stood up!' Miller joked. 'He was an absolute disciplinarian, and at the time he was running my Independent Patrol Group. He was definitely the right man for the counter-terrorism job, that's for sure,' Miller said, adopting the same level of confidence he used back in Dickie's office decades ago.

Miller's quick thinking captured Dickie's interest, but the curious minister wanted more details. The chief commissioner elaborated somewhat haphazardly to Dickie, 'Norton will need a sub-charge or deputy who would be an inspector, and they would need a senior sergeant who would run the unit, and that man would be in direct contact with the men doing the job on the front line. They would also need about three groups, each commanded by a sergeant, and each would be composed of constables and senior constables. I think you'll find that's a total of about fifteen personnel initially, Minister. These men will need to be specially accommodated with high security because they will have access to heavy weapons and only the best equipment. So that's in addition, and the weapons would have to be military-type weapons, and a vast range of them too, I might add.'

As Miller continued to reel off items on his seemingly endless list of requirements, Dickie began to do the maths and realised just how expensive this start-up group could become for the state government. He asked Miller if he could consult the premier before things got out of hand. 'I told him, "Not until I'm abso-lutely guaranteed the funding, because I'll have to take those men from somewhere else, where they're desperately needed,"' Miller stated.

Miller had well and truly taken the upper hand and wasn't about to let the opportunity to push the government into a corner pass him by. This was his chance to give the community a resource that would protect it from a type of evil previously not known. 'I was trying to envision what might happen if this new group was engaged or activated. I said to Dickie, "We would need to arrange a training with the Special Air Service [SAS] Regiment and fortu-nately Harry Norton has counterparts in the Australian Army, so that won't be a problem for us."'

On a roll, Miller decided the time was right to broach a more sensitive topic – wages. 'I paused for a minute and said to Dickie, "No doubt, there would also have to be some special allowances considered for the men," and the minister just looked at me and smiled. He then asked again, "Now can I tell the premier?" and I replied, "Yes. Yes, you can, Minister."'

Remarkably, Miller had taken the first steps to establishing the country's first special weapons and tactics (SWAT) group without any prior planning, strategy or preparation. But he had little time to celebrate his victory. 'So, when can you start?' Dickie asked him.

'If you give me the all clear, I can start establishing the nucleus this afternoon,' Miller responded matter-of-factly.

Upon returning to his office, Miller immediately summoned Harry Norton. 'He was a character with a military mind and, being an ex-serviceman myself, I could always understand where Harry was coming from, and he always understood where I was coming from. We saw eye to eye.'

Norton was steeped in military tradition and heavily influ-enced by the discipline of many years of service with the armed forces. He entered Miller's office, saluted and barked, 'Sar!' This was actually 'Sir' but was said with a typical British Army inflection to acknowledge a superior.

'Congratulations, Mr Norton,' Miller announced. 'You've just been appointed the officer in charge of the Victoria Police's new Counter-Terrorist Squad [CTS].'

'Sar!' Norton roared, without asking what the CTS actually was, who was in it or where it was to be established.

'You will establish this group, beginning this afternoon,' Miller then ordered. 'So, out you go; don't waste your time here. Find a suitable premises for your headquarters, some adequate vehicles and interim equipment until I authorise the purchases of more permanent resources. Any problems, you let me know. I'll be in touch. You are dismissed.'

'Sar!' Norton responded as he performed an about-face and marched out of Miller's office.

'In retrospect, one could think it was all like something out of the TV show *Yes Minister*,' Miller said, laughing. 'My future was in Norton's hands and I thought, "He'd better get it right."'

Only a few hours old, the CTS already had a hard taskmaster in charge, the promise of adequate government funding and the backing of the premier and chief commissioner. Miller then put some protocols in place to ensure the group could only be activated with the authority of an assistant commissioner. But there were some more alterations made on the hop as Miller and Norton continued the speedy roll-out of the crack unit. The following weekend, Miller was tending his garden and had another brainwave. 'It occurred to me these CTS fellows would need to have special clothing, uniforms and, of course, bulletproof vests,' he said.

Miller also changed the name of the squad, fearing the word 'Terrorist' could upset some members of the public. 'I worried they'd leap out of their vehicles and declare, "We're from the Counter-Terrorist Squad!" and some old lady would have a heart attack on the street! I didn't want to face that situation. No, no, no! I didn't need that on my conscience. I rang Harry and told him, "There's just one change. You're no longer or never will be known as the Counter-Terrorist Squad. You'll now be known as the Special Operations Group or SOG."'

Soon after the title change, the group was given a fitting nickname. As word spread around the Victoria Police Force, a new take on the acronym 'SOG' developed. 'Do you know what they're calling us now?' Norton asked Miller, referring to the force's general police officers. 'They're calling us the Sons of God!'

Deep down, Miller was flattered, knowing he was the reason for the 'God' label, but he deflected it. 'That name is appropriate,' he told Norton.

'How so, sar?' Norton asked.

'Think of your bible, Harry. Matthew 5:9 specifically. The verse reads, "Blessed are the peacemakers, for they shall be called the sons of God."' Miller went on to explain to me that, police have always had the responsibility for the preservation of the peace, protection of life and property, and the prevention of crime. Through all of those various issues and responsibilities, the community expects its police force to act in support of them at all times.

Before the SOG, it was the general police officer who always had to respond to any breach of the peace, however serious or dangerous. From armed robberies and domestic violence issues to mentally unstable offenders who may have barricaded themselves inside a house, making all kind of threats, the often ill-equipped, inexperienced and underprepared police had to answer the community's call for help. As a result, they constantly put themselves and the public at greater risk by intervening. Now, in addition to tackling terrorist threats, the SOG had the capacity to deal with hard-core criminal activities that surpassed the training of a general police officer.

Reflecting on his time on the front lines, Miller told me, 'There were occasions where pot shots would be taken at you from an offender within a premises. We learnt to do a drive-by of the suspect property for a look, on the basis that an eyeful is always better than an ear full! If you were in uniform, you'd have to sneak up to avoid getting your head blown off. It was all trial and error because we didn't have the necessary training that was required. It was asking an awful lot of the untrained and inexperienced officers. When one looks back on fifty years of experience and knowledge, things had to change. As a matter of progress and evolution, the Special Operations Group had to be formed.'

Miller's decision to create the SOG was an inspired one. Only months later, Australia was rocked by a terrorist attack. In 1978, an explosive device was detonated in a rubbish bin outside the Hilton Hotel in Sydney – the venue for an upcoming Commonwealth Heads of Government Regional Meeting. The blast killed two garbage-collection workers, Alec Carter and William Favell, as well as a police officer who was guarding the entrance to the lobby, Paul Birmistriw. Eleven others were injured, resulting in then prime minister Malcolm Fraser calling in the Australian Army to beef up security for the international event. The ripple effect of the bombing was felt throughout the country, and state leaders outside of Victoria were forced to establish their own counter-terrorism capabilities.

Like a proud father, Miller glowed when he talked about the SOG. 'Oh, there's absolute pride. Just to think that from that humble beginning, a professional group emerged that the people of Victoria and the Victoria Police Force can justifiably be proud of,' he said. 'They're some of the most gallant, best-trained, well-equipped and highest-performing members of the force that have ever been created, and I am always so proud of being associated with their origins.'

3

RESURRECTION

Truly, truly, I say to you, an hour is coming, and now is, when the dead will hear the voice of the Son of God, and those who hear will live.

John 5:24–5

Harry Norton stood at the top of the driveway of the offender's house and watched on proudly as his men kicked in the door and charged inside. With nerves of steel, gained from years of service as a British Marine, the SOG's chief inspector (and later superintendent) would have been well within range of a stray bullet from the crook inside but seemed more focused on puffing on his tobacco-packed pipe than his own mortality. Think Winston Churchill on the rooftops in England during German bombing raids in the Second World War – that was the way he carried himself at sieges, according to those who served under him in the early eighties. 'He would often be standing, rather stoically, right at the front gate, only a matter of metres away from the first man in during a raid,' my dad, Doug O'Loughlin, explained. 'It was actually ridiculous and quite unnecessary, to be honest. He put himself in harm's way for no reason whatsoever.' As was the case back then, it was Norton's way or the highway, and no

subordinate dared challenge the choices or decisions he made. But, as time went on, Norton's stranglehold over the SOG began to loosen.

Recognising that the SOG had to move with the times, Chief Commissioner Mick Miller had heard about a young Australian, Terry Drew, who was working with the Canadian Police in the south-western region of Ontario as a member of a Tactics and Rescue Unit (TRU). A sniper, Drew was facing growing pressure from his wife to return home to Melbourne with their two young children, to be closer to her side of the family. Miller caught wind of Drew's situation and saw an opportunity to advance the SOG's cause and abilities. 'Miller heard that I had skills and services that were superior to those within the Special Operations Group at the time,' Drew said candidly. 'Back then, the SOG was very, very military-minded under old "Chippy" Norton.'

Upon his return to Australia in 1979 for a brief visit, Drew agreed to attend a personal meeting with Miller. The chief commissioner explained that there was a big move within Victoria Police to 'really lift the level of training' for what was then the fledgling SOG. Drew said Miller gave him an outline of the current state of play and in doing so hinted that Norton's time in charge of the group was nearly up, because he was 'very strong and set in his ways'. 'He told me that Norton had done an outstanding job with the SOG after taking on the enormous responsibility of helping to create it and that he was driven by the love for the cause and the future need for the group. However, it was also made clear to me that Norton could be "quite difficult to deal with" and that "he would probably resist change, especially large-scale, quick change". Miller was particularly interested in talking to me about my future plans and whether there was anything I could offer Victoria Police upon my eventual return. His view was virtually, "We need to find someone with the ability to take the SOG from where it is today to a much higher, worldly, tactical policing standard."'

Confident in his ability and experience, Drew knew immediately that he could be the perfect man for the job.

When he was nineteen, Drew had served in Vietnam for thirteen months as a tank commander with the 1st Armoured Regiment in the Australian Army and had seen 'plenty of action'. After the war, he joined Victoria Police but only briefly, before heading to Canada for a life-changing experience. 'I met an American-born Canadian who was with the US Marines,' Drew explained. 'Before the war, he was with the Ontario Provincial Police in Canada. We became good friends and kept in touch. He invited me over and guaranteed me a job with the Nepean Township Police in Ottawa.' Married to Lorraine and with two very young children, Drew and his family took a leap of faith. 'Off we went on a bit of a wing and a prayer, to be totally honest,' Drew declared. 'Because it was a British-Commonwealth country, I'm proud to say that the Canadians embraced me like one of their own. I had things done for me that others weren't afforded.'

During his eight years in Canada, the majority spent in the TRU, Drew gained a tremendous wealth of knowledge and expertise. 'Canada was fortunate because it sits next to the United States – a world-leading power in tactical policing,' Drew said. 'So, while in the TRU, we were getting direct assistance and input from the Americans, with some cross training from the FBI with hostage rescue and so forth.'

During their one-on-one meeting in Melbourne, Miller had all but swayed Drew to return as a training sergeant, in a brevet position within the SOG. 'I saw a great man in Mick Miller,' Drew said. 'I saw him as a man of great stature, respect and wisdom. He was a really good man then, and I still feel that way about him today. He was by far the best chief commissioner

Victoria Police has ever had. He was someone I wanted to work for.'

Although a virtual sergeant in Canada, Drew had to start from scratch and get back up to speed with Victorian law at the police academy upon his return home, but he admits to being given a 'golden ride' throughout the training course. 'They were very good to me and allowed me to go home at night to see Lorraine and my young kids,' Drew said. 'The superintendent there, Derek Bateman, would call me to his office and check on me regularly, making sure I was happy and comfortable. They were all brilliant.'

In 1981, Drew joined twenty or so other aspirants in just the SOG's sixth intake. Ironically, when Drew enrolled in the TRU in Canada, the unit was being significantly enhanced due to an impending world event and the same occurred upon his entry to the SOG in Victoria. 'In 1976, we had to prepare for the Montreal Olympics, which came after the terrorist incident in Munich at the 1972 games. It was just "Go! Go! Go!"' he recalled. 'Then in Melbourne when I joined the SOG, we had to prepare for CHOGM [Commonwealth Heads of Government Meeting], and that created a real need to bolster our resources rather substantially.'

Despite his knowledge and vast experience, Drew's introduction to the elite group didn't go all that smoothly, as some noses were put out of joint. 'There was a lot of resentment towards me initially,' he admitted. 'Some were saying, "Who is this wanker, coming in here and talking all this Canadian bullshit?"'

Times were changing rapidly, and so too was the core function of the SOG. Doug O'Loughlin remembers a group divided. 'There was a new breed of SOG member coming in and we were demanding change,' he said. 'Eventually, we became larger in number than those resisting change, and we started to influence what was happening within the group. We could no longer be ignored. We were more willing to learn and had been learning about best practices from all around the world, and we wanted to be seen as best practice.'

Himself part of the sixth intake, O'Loughlin formed a strong bond with Drew and echoed the calls for improvements to training, operating procedures and resources. 'During our intake, one of the instructors kept referring to criminals as "the enemy",' O'Loughlin said. 'I remember looking at a fellow inductee, John Sheahan, and saying, "I thought everyone was supposed to be a suspect – isn't it innocent until proven guilty?"'

'Doug was in my corner straight away, along with Sheahan, Bob Broadhurst, Geoff Nash, Wayne Harris, Chris Harris and several others,' Drew declared. 'But the relationship Doug and I formed in particular proved to be most significant.'

While O'Loughlin's oldest brother, Robert, briefly took charge of the SOG from 1980 to 1982, it wasn't until his third-oldest sibling, Neil, replaced Robert at the helm of the group that the improvements started to ramp up. 'Most of those resisting change were ex-army and had that real strong mentality and thought that because it worked in the army, it should be applied to the SOG,' Drew said. 'They saw the SOG's work in the community as an operation in a "street jungle" or "domestic crime jungle". They simply hadn't seen the new, North American way of doing things and knew nothing about it. It was my view, and also that of Doug and then Neil, that we couldn't go onto the streets and yell, "There's the enemy!" There was a gradual, transitional change of thinking, created by the introduction of actual policemen into the training process as opposed to only ex-army types.'

As an inspector, Neil O'Loughlin remains the highest-ranking officer to have ever completed the SOG's brutal training course.

It wasn't a requirement, as he had already been awarded the job as the inspector in the group in 1983, but it came as a direct order from Superintendent Harry Norton as a form of payback. Months earlier, Neil had upset the apple cart after trumping Norton's preferred candidate for the inspector role by lodging an appeal after he was unfairly overlooked. Norton's choice was junior in both rank and experience and was subsequently stripped of the position after a protest that went to the Appeals Board. 'The fact he didn't pick me, and was told to pick me, coupled with the "O'Loughlin" factor, put a big target on my back,' Neil said.

On leave at the time, Neil received a message from Norton instructing him to complete the next intake course if he wanted the job. Not one to argue with an order from someone more senior, Neil agreed but began to panic when he discovered he had just seven days to prepare and get fit. 'I've got no doubt it was just to punish me. Norton was trying to send me a message saying, "If you're going to be a smartarse and appeal against my preferred candidate, then cop this!" I went for a few seven-kilometre runs and thought that would be a good base to work from but, little did I know, the very first run on the course was fifteen kilometres long. It nearly killed me.'

Despite being underprepared, Neil passed with flying colours, but he had another challenge to overcome before winning Norton over. With his brother Robert having been in the group recently as inspector and youngest brother Doug a current tactical member, Neil had to convince the stubborn Norton that three O'Loughlins wouldn't be a crowd. 'He was understandably worried about an O'Loughlin influence but I simply told him that I wasn't "my brothers' keeper" and was "my own man".'

With five brothers having joined the force, the O'Loughlin name was well known and regarded. When the second eldest of the five, Barry, joined the force in 1957, his four male siblings (Robert, Neil, Geoffrey and Douglas) all followed him over the course of the next eleven years. The O'Loughlin brothers' reputation as being 'tough but fair' cops was first carved out on the rough streets of Preston – a suburb that all but Robert worked in. 'Preston was a bloody tough area to be a policeman in those days,' Neil recalled. 'Some of the state's most violent and notorious criminals, like the Kanes, lived in the area. There were all sorts of violent crimes being committed, especially armed robberies of TAB outlets and banks, because they were seen as soft targets. There were no security cameras then and the tellers were just open counters with little or no protection.'

A member of the Preston Consorters (a unit designed to stop known criminals from consorting with each other) and later the Armed Robbery Squad (ARS), Barry was an 'old-school cop' and 'as tough as they come', according to Neil. 'He was known for never, ever taking a backwards step,' Neil said proudly. 'He locked up some nasty crooks in his time and was well known, and feared, among criminal circles in the days when things were done very differently. One story goes that he and another detective knocked on the door of a suspect's house and the bloke's mother answered. They politely asked if they could "come in and take a look around" but she snapped back, "Do you have a warrant?" Instead of following proper procedure and getting one, Barry puffed his chest out a bit and said, "Listen, lady, you don't really want to make us go and get a warrant, do you?" With that response, the door was thrown open and they were welcomed inside. They used intimidation and the crooks respected it and, more often than not, responded in an obliging fashion.'

Barry paved the way for his younger brothers, and even his nephews. 'When Geoff, Doug and I all worked out of the Preston Police Station at the same time,' said Neil, 'I knocked on a crook's door and a young boy answered and yelled, "Mum! Officer

O'Loughlin is here!" I heard her yell back from the rear of the house, "Which fucken one?"'

Despite Barry's untimely death after a car accident in 1972, the O'Loughlin name endured in the force for decades. 'Even some notorious criminals turned up to Barry's funeral,' Doug recalled. 'For two reasons: one, to see if it was the Barry O'Loughlin they all feared; and two, to make sure he was actually dead.'

When Geoff's son Shane joined the police force, he too served in the Preston area, and he arrested a crook his father and uncles used to lock up frequently back in their day on patrol. 'When Shane identified himself as "Officer O'Loughlin" and asked the old crook why he had pulled a knife on a citizen, the bloke, who was as high as a kite on marijuana, nearly fainted and said, "Are you the Phantom or something? Is this the O'Loughlin ghost that walks and never dies?"' Neil said, laughing.

Not long after completing the SOG intake course, Neil had another victory when Norton was moved on. It enabled him to make some long overdue changes. 'I don't think some of the SOG members particularly liked me,' he confessed. 'I was very hard on them, but it was all for the good of the group, as far as I was concerned. They considered a lot of what I had them do as petty, unnecessary and over-policed. But when I started making them wash and vacuum the cars, the shit really hit the fan!' he said with a smirk.

Neil's motivation to reform and revamp the SOG stemmed from one particular incident he observed from outside the group. On the scene of a fatal shooting in the CBD, he watched as the SOG arrived long after the gunman had fled on foot. 'They were late because they had to go and get changed and "kit up". Uniformed police who had been there for some time sniggered and yelled out "Hut! Hut! Hut!" and "Better late than never!" as the SOG ran past,' Neil recalled. 'They were taking the piss out of them, and it really made a mockery of the group and undermined everything it was supposed to stand for. I always had it in my mind as something that just wasn't right, and with Norton out of the way I had a chance to do something about it.'

To cut down response times and give the SOG an identity, Neil transitioned the group into jet-black, fire-retardant jumpsuits, high-cut black boots and tight-fitting black baseball caps. 'I had a desire to stop them from being ridiculed and make them elite, well respected and viewed as a valued and necessary resource of the police force. We couldn't have them running around in the grey tank suits that Norton acquired from the military. We had to educate the public and get them used to the fact that the SOG was in operation. I also made them carry their guns in public too. It was all about conditioning the people on the streets and making them realise that this new, elite group was there to serve and protect them.'

While the 'daggy' grey overalls were familiar to Terry Drew, he wasn't sad to see them go either. 'I wore that exact tank suit in Vietnam,' he said. 'I was shocked to see the SOG wearing it when I returned from Canada.'

For his part, Mick Miller pointed out that the original grey outfit wasn't what he originally had in mind for the group but also revealed that he wasn't sold on its replacement. In contrast to Neil O'Loughlin, Miller was worried about the public's reaction to a bunch of heavily armed 'ninjas' walking the city streets. 'I was opposed to them wearing this new, menacing black uniform when they were going to buy lunch and said, "Hey, if you want to go outside and buy your lunch, do so in your own clothes or put on your normal police uniform." But it was also for security reasons. We didn't want to advertise who they were and what they were in case of reprisals in the event of them being in a shooting situation and killing somebody. Their identities needed to be protected.'

Miller eventually conceded and the black uniform quickly became highly sought after and elusive. Becoming a Soggie meant passing one of the most gruelling mental and physical tests of any paramilitary unit anywhere in the world. Before long, the black cap was as revered as the Australian cricket team's famous baggy green cap.

Getting the new uniform over the line was one thing, but busting up certain cliques that had formed within the SOG proved to be a much harder task. Neil's constant demands earned him more than his fair share of nicknames. 'I wanted to know what was happening all the time,' he said unapologetically. 'If a splinter group was about to go off for some PT [personal training], for example, I'd stop them and make sure the whole group went, as a team. It resulted in some of the men calling me "singlet", because I was "all over them", and "sheepdog", because I was always seen to be "rounding the men up".'

Neil wasn't alone in wanting change, however, and he found many allies within the group. 'It was also about putting some of them back in their box a bit too,' Neil admitted openly. 'At some stage in those early days of me arriving, I saw that elements of the group thought they were the bee's knees. The problem with that was no one else saw them that way, and they hadn't yet gained the respect of detectives or uniformed officers. They were always professional when it came to doing a job and there was never any recklessness; they just needed some tidying up around the edges.'

It wasn't until the SOG started doing the occasional raid for the ARS that the wheel began to turn. Before the SOG came along, ARS detectives had always been the tough guys of the police force and never asked anyone to do their dirty work. They liked to break down their own doors and arrest their own crooks, and had been doing so for years. It used to be that crooks would rarely stand up to police of the ARS variety, but a new wave of criminal – more brash, with better weapons and sometimes explosives – started to emerge at around the same time terrorism reared its ugly head. Slowly but surely, the detectives began to look for specialist support and became more willing to let the SOG step in to make risky and dangerous arrests. Also helping the SOG's cause was the fact that several of its members, including the O'Loughlin brothers, had been in the ARS and were mates with many of the detectives. 'We gradually convinced them to lean on the SOG when their jobs started getting a bit too heavy or too dangerous for them to carry out themselves,' Neil said.

It wasn't long before the ARS and other squads realised how good the SOG actually was. 'I remember one senior investigator came to see me after a raid in which he'd used the SOG and he said, "They were so quick! They went into the house and had the crooks cuffed and arrested within seconds. They devastated the crooks!"' Neil revealed. 'The SOG scared the living daylights out of the crooks because they'd seen nothing like it before. It left them vulnerable to questioning because they were in shock and would sometimes cough up all they knew. Just imagine sitting in the safety of your own home, minding your own business and watching television or whatever, then all of a sudden the door bursts open and the windows are smashed in and, in the blink of an eye, you've been thrown to the ground with your hands tied and arrested – all in the space of ten or so seconds. It would be terrifying. There was one story that when they raided a house in Richmond, a caged budgie dropped off its perch and died from the shock of the SOG swarming in.'

Also to the detectives' advantage was that the crooks would direct any grievances they might have at the SOG, allowing them to come in after the arrest and play 'good cop' for a change. This helped them to build up a rapport and elicit confessions or acquire informants.

Not long after the bombing of the Hilton in Sydney, the Australian Federal Government created the Standing Advisory Committee on Commonwealth and State Co-Operation for Protection Against Violence (SAC-PAV). It recommended that all states and territories maintain specialist police units for counter-terrorism and hostage rescue, like the SOG, and it standardised all training techniques and equipment for them. 'SAC-PAV saw the obvious needs for tactical policing across the whole country,' Drew commented. 'They made a lot of money available.'

Doug O'Loughlin was on a federal-level advisory committee as a tactical advisor and was tasked with making recommendations to SAC-PAV for various improvements and equipment. 'The situation was that if Victoria wanted and was subsequently approved to have new Heckler & Koch sub-machine guns, then all the tactical police units around Australia got them too,' O'Loughlin explained. 'If we needed some night-vision gear, it would be purchased and distributed to all. The AFP [Australian Federal Police] played a big part in what we'd get, but all the states also had a decent amount of say into what various equipment was required.'

With a CHOGM to be held in Melbourne in 1981, SAC-PAV recommended an increase in the number of SOG members, and the chief commissioner approved the addition of new men, taking the number in the group from twenty-three to thirty-five. The unit was also issued with five Uzi sub-machine guns.

Slowly but surely, the SOG was beginning to catch up with the rest of the world. 'When I arrived, they were still using revolvers, and should have had semi-automatic pistols,' Drew described. 'The sniper's rifles were as outdated as you could get. They were basically just cheap, nasty hunting guns.'

'Early on,' said Doug O'Loughlin, 'it was a case of "This is what you've got, so that's what you work with". We didn't really know any better until our people travelled overseas, or people like

Terry came into the group and introduced us to best practices from around the world. Yes, change would have been inevitable, but Terry, no doubt, helped speed up that learning process and evolution.'

As the SOG's caches of equipment and weapons expanded at an unprecedented rate, the group's mode of transport also had to be reconsidered, according to Doug O'Loughlin. 'We were driving marked V8 Ford Falcon station wagons that were, in hindsight, terribly unsafe given the loads we were carrying around,' he said. 'I took one over a weighbridge with four men and all our equipment on board, and it was deemed far too heavy for its braking system. Because of the safety concerns, we were able to upgrade to four-wheel drives.'

For the SOG, it was the beginning of a new era.

4

TO HELL AND BACK

And let us not grow weary of doing good, for in due season
we will reap, if we do not give up.

Galatians 6:9

Tango was in pain. He could see the other men in the distance, but the gap between them was getting bigger and bigger as they continued to run ahead of him along the seemingly endless dirt track, unaware he was struggling and had been left way behind. There was no way he could stay with them, and that meant he would be targeted. The phrase 'Failure is not an option' was bouncing around inside his head as he'd heard it more than a hundred times over the past few weeks. He pushed on.

Wearing a blue boiler suit and armed with a .357 Magnum and a shotgun, Tango took a small sip of water from the tiny canteen that was hooked onto his belt. He knew there wasn't enough in there to hydrate him through to the end, but that was the point. The scorching sun made his back and neck burn, and the metal pins on his belt slid back and forth across the width of his lower back, tearing at his skin with every stride he took. He tried to think about nothing and drift off into a trance, but the pain he was suffering all over snapped him back to reality and forced him to endure. The heat was suffocating. His GP boots weren't made for running and offered no shock absorption, so the vibration from every step reverberated through the bones in his legs and jarred his joints. His socks were saturated with sweat, and his feet began to blister and bleed. He knew if he stopped he would collapse and wouldn't be able to get back up. He needed to maintain what semblance of rhythm he had, and push through.

This was the notorious SOG intake course, and Tango was beginning to understand why it had such a horrendous reputation.

TANGO: During a training reconnaissance exercise, I stepped into a pothole and twisted my ankle really badly. A week later, we had to do a twenty-kilometre run carrying kit. I didn't know my ankle was broken at the time; I just thought it was a bad sprain. I kept it to myself, because I knew if I couldn't complete all the components of the course, I'd be booted off. A few weeks prior to my injury, one of the other applicants slid on some gravel and cut his leg on a car's numberplate and was let go. He was super fit and had all the necessary attributes for the SOG, but it didn't matter to the instructors. So that's why I didn't seek any treatment for my ankle.

It puffed up very badly and I had to strap it myself. It was brutal and by far the hardest thing I'd ever done. I had run a few marathons and knew that I could put myself through pain, but this was a much different pain. I just kept telling myself, 'The harder it gets, the stronger you get.' I knew that was the type of person they were looking for. Much later on, I went and had my ankle looked at, and a piece of bone had snapped off inside the joint.

—

Tango didn't take anything lying down. Somewhere in his childhood, he had developed a sizeable chip on his shoulder, and it served him well later in life. He had tried to join the police force immediately after high school but was knocked back due to height restrictions – he was deemed too tall. When that archaic selection protocol was phased out, he quit his trade, reapplied and got straight in.

TANGO: I didn't know anything about the SOG initially, but because I was very much into fitness, a colleague told me I should apply for the group because they did lots of running and exercise. It was the fitness angle that got me interested. Then, once I started the SOG intake course, I realised that the instructors were trying to get rid of me the entire time. That just made me want to stay and stick it up them: 'Hey, you ain't gonna get rid of me!' That was the game – they were trying to get rid of me, and I was trying to get through the course.

I suppose I started to enjoy it when I realised what they were trying to do. It was a competition between the instructors to see who could get rid of the most people. That was the mentality – to get the best of the best and also separate the men from the boys. Everything with the SOG is a challenge, and you have to be successful at the end of that challenge because there's no one to come after us on a job. Failure is never an option for the SOG.

–

A police cadet at 16, Oscar joined the army as part of the Citizen Military Forces (CMF) and qualified as a marksman rifleman. He joined the artillery division in Richmond, also known as the '9-mile snipers'. After several years as a detective in the police force, he later tried out for a sniper position but missed out. He was placed on the reserve list and then found out about the SOG through his older sibling.

OSCAR: My brother knew about the SOG and urged me to think about applying. After listening to his reasons and explanation of the group, the SOG was something different and it interested me. I had been in uniform, I had also been a detective in the CIB [Criminal Investigations Bureau], was a member of the Armed Robbery Squad and had done a lot of raids, so I felt I was suited to it.

—

Rogue was from a large family. One of ten children, he'd grown up with extremely generous parents who were always willing to help others. Their values and attitudes rubbed off on him, and formed part of the reason why he wanted to join the SOG.

ROGUE: I've always liked helping people, and that's what appealed to me the most about the group. I heard about the Special Operations Group when I was a teenager and just wanted to join the police force specifically to get in. After joining the force, I applied and got into the group three years later. I was one of ten kids and I was never competitive, which was strange. At school, I was a good swimmer and runner and could beat anyone but just wouldn't do it when the time came. We had no money growing up in west Heidelberg, and I just remember my mum and dad being so caring and giving – they always looked after everyone before themselves. In the SOG, the shooting side of things and the guns – I had no interest in any of that, to be honest. In siege situations when people are being held hostage, I love the fact that we are the ones saying, 'Hang tight, we're coming to get you.' I love being the last resort and having everything come down to us. That was it for me.

—

Mouse had grown up in the country and spent his childhood on the family acreage camping out and hunting. He was comfortable being out in the wild and on his own, provided he had a rifle in his hands.

MOUSE: I was hunting from the age of about seven or eight. I was shooting regularly and spent a lot of time in the bush. I wanted to be a sniper because the shooting element came naturally for me and I like the bush work – looking for people and staking out drug crops is just me being 'home'. There's always been a righteous streak to me, even though I admit I used to be hard to control and mischievous. But I've always been someone who's tried to do the right thing. I saw the SOG as a group that did real work to right wrongs, and that's what interested me the most.

—

Dane's reasons for joining the SOG were similar to Tango's. He is a self-confessed 'mad trainer', who likes to run from Ferntree Gully to Oakleigh in his spare time. But despite his elite physical fitness, he still found the intake course incredibly tough.

DANE: There's nothing easy. You are exhausted, knackered and completely drained both physically and mentally. I was ninety kilograms with six per cent body fat when I started the course and I finished it at just over eighty kilograms. When I used to come home after a day of heavy PT, my wife would put me straight in the bathtub and fill a two-litre plastic container, half with ice cream and half with diced fruit. I'd just sit there and try and eat as much as I could to keep my calories up, and she'd keep coming in to make sure I hadn't fallen asleep. But I never thought about giving up. I'm stupid like that. If you want to get rid of me, you have to sack me.

As an instructor on a fair few courses, that's what I always looked for: someone who was resilient, who wouldn't give up or didn't know when to give up, and someone who just kept going no matter the circumstances. I saw guys who weren't super fit who passed. There was a thirty-six-year-old on my intake and he got through because he was so nuggety and determined. His attitude was, 'If you want to do these things to me, go ahead. I ain't gonna give up.' We hardly ever sacked anyone from a course; the ones who dropped out just gave up. We only ever sacked someone for a serious safety breach.

—

Unlike most, Bulldog didn't apply for the SOG per se, but was headhunted at a time when the group needed a senior sergeant. A seasoned police officer and experienced detective, he'd seen it all and knew that nothing in the SOG would surprise him.

BULLDOG: The first job I ever did as a senior constable in the homicide squad was on a Good Friday. Two young kids had been shot by their mother and I had to do the post-mortem. They were the same ages as my two youngest blokes at the time – about seven and three. Their mother had given them milk laced with sleeping pills right before she shot them. She'd made one of them write on the wall in red lipstick, 'We love Mummy so much more than Daddy.' Then she put them into bed, gave them the drink and shot them both in the heart. And then she shot herself, but she didn't succeed in killing herself. After about an hour or so, because of the pain she was in, she called for an ambulance and she survived.

I found out later that she had separated from her husband and he had dropped the kids off on the Good Friday as part of their custody agreement. He was supposed to pick them up on the Sunday, but she shot them because she didn't want them to go back to him.

A lot of people say that people like me are 'hard' and 'callous' and that we have no feelings. It's not that at all. It's just being able to switch off, do your job and at the end of the day go home and have a normal life. I still think about that scene – every time I see little kids about that age. I can still picture it now, the little kids tucked tightly in bed.

There was no counselling back then. You just had to suck it up and deal with it whatever way possible. Maybe you'd go to the old Police Club and have half a dozen beers and then go home – that was the extent of the counselling session. In those days, we didn't know what we know now. There wasn't anyone encouraging you to talk about what you'd experienced or seen; it was more a matter of, 'Well, that's just a part of the job and is to be expected.' But in terms of being prepared for anything, that scene was as bad as you could get. It was a good start and determined whether I was cut out for the job, I suppose.

Another time when I was a detective, we got a call saying there was a body in a car, so they sent us up there to have a look. After the initial investigation, we determined that it was a suicide. We had to wait for about four or five hours for the coroner's vehicle to turn up, which was just like the undertaker's, so instead of waiting I made the decision to drive the body back myself. I just threw the seatbelt on him to stop him from flopping around in the car and off we went. It was just the two of us in the car, travelling back from the bush in the middle of the night. It didn't faze me. He was stiff as a post by that stage and just sat there bolt upright. The radio was off; it was silent and a little bit eerie but I wasn't fussed – what was he going to do to me? He was dead. I could have kept him for the week to use the transit lanes on the freeway, I suppose.

So, given my background, I wasn't too concerned with anything in the SOG intake course. Yeah, it was tough, but I was a big boy and could look after myself.

—

For a long period of time, some elements of the SOG's intake course were as gruelling and torturous as an SAS intake or, to a much lesser extent, the French Foreign Legion. Applicants were pushed to their absolute limits and were broken down both physically and mentally.

After being in the Australian SAS for twelve years as a sergeant and emergency action commander of its counter-terrorism unit, Mack was convinced to join the SOG.

MACK: When I was in the army, I wanted to do something that was more specialised and higher up. I saw the SAS as a way to take a step forward and challenge myself and learn more skills in an elite environment. I wasn't from a military background or anything. I grew up in a country town and didn't want to stay on the family farm. There was nothing there for me and I just had to get away. The SAS involved a six-week selection course, and they have you 24/7 during it – there's no going home at the end of the day.

I was doing an exercise with the SOG one day out at Melbourne Airport and got approached by a couple of the guys to come across and join them. I was coming to the end of my time at the SAS and was looking for something new and equally challenging. It was the right fit for me.

—

In the initial few decades of the SOG, the first stage of joining the group was via a single selection day out at the police academy.

Close to a hundred police officers could turn up in the hope of one day receiving a coveted black cap. No matter the year, the level of training or the circumstances, every member of the SOG will claim that their intake was by far the toughest ever undertaken.

TANGO: My course started with seventy-two applicants. First up, we had a 3.2-kilometre time trial in Alphington, but, as I expected, it was far from an ordinary run. We had to wear a ballistic vest and carry a shotgun and revolver. We had to run down to the Yarra River, swim across to the other side, climb up the embankment on a fifty-metre rope, then do a kilometre circuit at the top, climb back down the rope, swim back across the river, then do a man carry for another hundred metres. When we completed that, they told us to do it again. When we finished it the second time, they told us to do it again. After the third time, we had to go to the oval and do a whole heap of push-ups, sit-ups and burpees.

You could pull out at any time; the choice was always yours and the instructors were always barking at you, trying to make you quit. Applicants were dropping like flies at one point. One guy went to hospital in an ambulance, suffering from hypothermia, as it just so happened to be the coldest day of that particular year.

That was just selection day – the course hadn't even started yet. Out of the seventy-two that started, thirty-one got through the physical and then faced a pretty intense selection panel. Of that thirty-one, only twenty-two were deemed mentally fit enough to start the SOG's notorious twelve-week intake course.

–

The next stage of selection was more unforgiving and had been set up to take applicants out of their comfort zones from the word 'go', and into a world where they'd constantly sit on the precipice of failure. No one was allowed to think they were going well or feel that they had impressed an instructor. The feedback from those running the course to an applicant, if any, was always negative.

TANGO: There's no friendship between the applicants and the instructors – it's just a fierce competition of both the body and the mind. You're trying to earn their respect the whole time and they're trying to make you feel like you have none; it's a constant battle. During the course, you don't have a life and you need a very supportive family. You train by day, and you have to do pointless research and write pointless essays at night. It was all designed purely to waste your time and keep your mind active so you'd feel fatigued physically and mentally. No one was rocking up the next day feeling fresh.

As the course progressed, you'd be out late at night or early in the morning doing reconnaissance on a house or building. Then you'd have to be up early in the morning and back training, running, learning tactics or weapons. And that went on for twelve weeks. Along the way, people were just dropping off and quitting left, right and centre. We did some height-orientated tasks like rock climbing and abseiling off buildings in the CBD, so those who were afraid of heights would just quit on the spot. The instructors would find your weakness and exploit it. Your uniform had to be clean and pressed for the next day and your boots polished. On the weekends, you'd be writing more reports, so while you'd get a break physically, mentally there was no letting up.

I certainly had one weak moment; I'm not going to lie. I had a squad mate who I went through the academy with doing the course with me and he was super fit. One day, he pulled out for some reason and it was a real kick in the guts for me. One of the instructors saw that I was a bit vulnerable as a result of his decision and tried to work on that and exploit it. He had me doubting myself for about half an hour and almost made me crack and give up. He was saying, 'You may as well follow your mate and quit. You've got no one left to support you now. You're all alone here. What are you doing this for anyway? This isn't for you. You're not what we're looking for. You're wasting your time.' No course was harder than the one I did.

MOUSE: It was tough. I mean it was really, really tough. I started at seventy-eight kilograms and three months later I was sixty-seven kilograms and wasting away. One of our instructors, Mack, had just come from the SAS and he ran a particularly tough course. Dare I say, there were none tougher than our one. They're all brutal but ours was out of the box. But I'm a sucker for punishment and actually did two intake courses, because I left the group for a few years to become a detective and when I came back I had to go through the selection process all over again. There were some concessions for me but it was still bloody hard. I can still hear one of the instructors constantly yelling the words, 'Switch on!' There are a lot of times in the group when you'd go from doing nothing to being involved in a life-or-death situation. We had to be able to flick that switch in an instant and be in full fight mode.

—

Those who excelled early in the course were targeted just as much as those perceived to be the weak links. As a civilian, Phantom was intrigued by the SOG after seeing one of the members dressed in black and carrying a gun on the city streets.

PHANTOM: He had the black cap on and just looked awesome. I asked him who he was and when told me that he was in counter-terrorism and explained what the SOG was all about, I pictured myself in that same outfit walking down that same street. I just wanted to do whatever it took to get in the group – there was something about it. I applied for the police force and got in a year later. When I graduated, the chief commissioner, Mick Miller, inspected our parade and asked each person what he or she wanted to do in the force. All the others were naming groups like the homicide squad, the dog squad, and when I told him I wanted to join the SOG, his face lit up like a Christmas tree.

I was brought up in a pretty tough environment and did martial arts for a very long time. I had my first dan and second dan black belt, and that was hard and intense, but it was nothing like some of the days on that intake course. We were loaded onto a bus and pulled up where the instructors were waiting for us. They were all standing there with their arms crossed. They looked fit, hard as nails and really pissed off. None of them were smiling and I had this immediate respect for them. The fact that they were already in the SOG meant they were legends in my mind. There was an aura about them.

Most of the guys were pretty nervous about what was ahead for us, but I was a bit cocky. I was as fit as a fiddle and I believed I would blitz the course. As soon as we jumped off that bus, we were in their hands, and we stood to attention like you would in the army. There were immediate rules we had to obey, like not being allowed to have your hands in your pockets at any stage. If you were caught, you'd have to do push-ups as punishment.

They made us run around an oval with shotguns. We had no idea how many laps we had to do or for how long; they just told us to keep running until they said stop. Me and a few of the other fitter blokes ran out in front of the rest of the group and started lapping people. We were having a giggle, thinking,

'How good is this?' I didn't know it at the time, but by doing that I'd put a massive target on my back. When we did the Yarra swim, I misunderstood the instructions and swam the width of the river underwater. No one had ever done that before and I nearly killed myself.

We did the three river circuits and I was putting on a brave face despite being spent. We were split into groups for a push-up and sit-up test and I noticed that the group I was in was made up of all the blokes that were out in front in all the exercises. We got absolutely hammered by the instructors and had to do way more than the other groups. They just kept us going and going until in the end we were just shuffling around on the ground, exhausted. The other groups were getting let off the hook and we were being punished for being too cocky. I was hurting inside, but I just didn't show it. In martial arts training, you never show your enemy that you are weak.

When we completed the day, we jumped back on the bus and one of the blokes in my group said, 'Mate, I don't know if I can do this. I think I'm going to pull the pin. This is fucked.' It didn't make things any easier when we were told that what we'd just endured was only a small taste of a standard morning on the twelve-week course.

—

The men who were selected to start the twelve-week course had a fortnight to recover and prepare for more punishment and testing. Having had an insight into the types of drills and exercises the SOG instructors were partial to, Phantom decided to train specifically in the lead-up.

PHANTOM: I knew the next part of the intake process was going to be like nothing I'd done before so I trained my guts out over that two-week period to get ready. Before that pre-selection day, I'd been training and doing the stock-standard chin-ups, weights, push-ups and runs, but I wasn't doing the more extreme stuff like swimming with clothes on, man carries or climbing. So I ramped things up, but at one point I took it a bit far. I had a .22 rifle at home so I put some overalls on and some heavy boots, grabbed the gun and ran around the streets near my house with it raised above my head. I copped some looks from the neighbours and just yelled out, 'It's okay. I'm training for the SOG!' I was that focused on my training that I didn't even consider what I was doing was inappropriate and probably illegal. I was lucky the SOG wasn't called out to deal with an armed man running around the streets! But I got away with it, somehow.

I also drove to Portsea and went for a swim and then ran up and down the sand dunes. I tried to fatigue myself as much as possible. Then I'd have a small break and do it all over again. It was like cramming for an exam.

—

Phantom's strict training regimen paid off. When the course started, he was able to lead the way.

PHANTOM: Some of the others were really struggling from the outset. You could easily tell who had prepared and who hadn't done much at all in the two weeks prior to the start of the course. One of the first things the instructors had us do was choose our 'pet bricks'. They took us to a pile of building rubble and we all had to select two bricks to keep with us for the entire course. We had to run with them, exercise with them and take care of them at all times. If you lost them or misplaced them, you'd be punished. Some of the blokes were picking bricks with lots of mortar on them, and we overheard an instructor say to another instructor, 'You'd think they'd figure out that the less mortar on them, the less heavy they'd be.' The next thing you know, all these blokes were chipping the mortar off their bricks to lighten them up.

The instructors were constantly in our ears, trying to break us: 'You're looking weak'; 'You're letting the team down'; 'Everyone is waiting for you to finish'; 'You should get on the bus now and save us all the energy and time'; 'C'mon, just get on that bus'. They went after the weak links or guys they just didn't like.

Guys were dropping out every day but a fair few dropped out during the gas exercise. They saturated a room with tear gas one day and sent us in, one by one, with a gasmask on [which was subsequently taken off]. Some guys just point blank refused to go in after seeing what it did to the first few guinea pigs, and as a result they quit the course on the spot. On my turn in the house, the instructors allowed me to get used to breathing in the mask, and, when I was comfortable, they pulled it off me and exposed me to the gas. The idea was to get us familiar with the effects of the gas in case we went on a job and someone ripped our mask off. It also allowed us to experience what an offender would be going through if we used gas on them.

Not wanting to be subjected to the gas, I closed my eyes and held my breath for as long as I could. Being fit, I thought I could hold on for a while, but that wasn't the point of the exercise and, as expected, the instructors had a solution for blokes like me. 'What's your name?' one of the instructors asked me. I refused to answer the first time. 'What's your name?' The request came with more gusto the second time, so I answered. 'Where do you live?' he asked next. I answered that one too but tried to speak without exhaling and then inhaling, but I couldn't hold on any longer. I gasped after I blurted out the name of my street and suburb and took in a huge amount of gas. My eyes stung and began to pour with tears. My lungs felt like they were being squeezed and my nose ran profusely with snot. It was horrible. Closer to the end of the course, there were only five of us left out of an initial group of about seventy because our course was the hardest out of all of them.

—

The instructors also used sleep deprivation to wear down the SOG aspirants.

PHANTOM: One time, they made us set up our tents on a hill so when you tried to lie down, you'd slide down the hill. I tied a tent rope to a tree and put it under my armpits to stop me from slipping, and just as I drifted off at about 2.00 am, I got raided. The instructors barged in with torches and started asking me questions and wanted to know where my bricks were.

MOUSE: In the tenth week, I really started to struggle when they began the sleep deprivation. There was one night there that they had us running stairs in full kit and with weapons – just up and down flights of stairs from the bottom floor to the twentieth floor at the top, over and over again. The gear is heavy and it hurts. They told us to stop on the fifth floor at one point, but I was delusional and just kept running up the stairs to the top. One of the instructors, Papa, chased after me and grabbed me and said, 'That's it! Stop!'

They never told you how long you'd be doing anything because they didn't want people to have the ability to set themselves a target and prepare for an exercise or challenge. It also mentally screwed with people and took them out of their comfort zones. If they said we are running stairs, but we're only going to the twentieth floor and back down again, then you could set yourself mentally and push through to the end more easily. When there's no end in sight, it's much, much tougher to get through.

DANE: There was always a fear factor because we never knew what was coming next. But that is the job in the SOG – you never know what is going to happen on any given day.

TANGO: It was all for a purpose. If you made it into the group, you might go away for seven days to sit off a drug crop. You could be fatigued, hungry, wet from the rain or dew, have leeches all over you and somehow you have to endure and just laugh about it. You can't let it get to you. It was important that the instructors knew you'd persist with whatever challenge they laid out for you, no matter how unreasonable it seemed or how exhausted you were. If the SOG can't do the job, no one else is going to.

OSCAR: We are the last resort, so there's no giving up, ever. That's what we drilled into the aspirants from the first instance and all throughout the course.

—

Haze was as fearless as any inductee, but despite a wealth of experience as a detective and years of front-line policing under his belt, he too found the course more testing than anything he'd ever experienced. His pet hate though was a notorious training component that became known as the Friday night 'Torture Track'.

HAZE: When the week's Monday to Friday training was coming to an end, there was always something extra to finish off the week. You'd look around the classroom and blokes would start sweating and dry retching after seeing the PT instructors suddenly appear outside of the classroom. It was part of the psychology of getting you in and out of your comfort zone. If you were doing an exam on tactics or weapons it was impossible to concentrate knowing that when you finished, you'd be absolutely fucking flogged on the PT track for three hours or more. The Friday night Torture Track was just the PT session farewell for the week. Some blokes didn't come back on the Monday following the Torture Track because they physically couldn't muster up the energy knowing there was every chance we would be flogged again to start the next week.

—

On one Friday night, Haze admits he had to use all his willpower and strength to avoid physically assaulting an instructor, such was his level frustration and exhaustion.

HAZE: They were trying to break me and they knew I was on the brink. I had my trusty pet bricks and had been PT training for about two-and-a-half hours. We had covered about ten kilometres in the session with all sorts of exercises and challenges thrown in. I was absolutely spent. It was the middle of summer and it was stinking hot. My heart was just about jumping out of my throat, my hands had blisters all over them and I was just fucked. The rest of the group had climbed up a grassy hill along the Darebin Creek but I just stood there in a trance as the instructor barked at me, 'C'mon Haze! Get up that fucking hill! That's all you have to do! Run up the hill with your bricks Haze! Otherwise just put your bricks down and go home. You can quit anytime Haze. It's okay . . . What do you want to do?'

Everything felt like it was in slow motion. I looked at the hill and saw the others trudging up it. I looked at the bricks in my swollen hands and looked down at my feet. I looked at the instructor. I looked to the sky. I looked at my bricks again. I looked at the instructor in the eye as he continued to bark orders at me and then I wondered if I had enough strength to smash one of the bricks into his face. I looked and I looked. Time stood still. Then something clicked and I trudged up that fucking hill. The rest of the team had done it, so I had to do it too. I desperately wanted to be in the SOG and on that particular day, I realised just how badly I wanted it.

—

Although Haze was behind the rest of the group and considered quitting, the only thing that mattered was he eventually summoned the energy and willpower to climb the hill.

HAZE: There wasn't any giving up on my part or throwing in the towel. It is all designed to test your character and we all got tested at some point.

—

Some argue that early SOG induction courses 'lacked science' and needed to be overhauled but in any case, it was an evolutionary process. The combination of a heavy military focus and uncompromising handling of inductees also sparked many claims of 'bastardisation' (deliberately mistreating and overtraining the recruits to toughen them up) but was ultimately viewed as a necessary evil when trying to select the best of the best.

OSCAR: There was perhaps a fair bit of inexperience in the actual training early on. The group relied on what the army had provided it in terms of drills and the way to conduct training courses.

DANE: You have to start from somewhere. I viewed the PT as not being very scientific initially. After I got in, I went off and got a sports science degree and was very much into thinking about making the PT component of the intake just as hard, but more designed for specific reasons and well planned out.

I had people on my intake course that popped their knees, and one guy popped his back. When you look back at the training they were doing, it was pretty clear why. You'd go for a twenty-kilometre run on a Monday, then on the Tuesday they'd have you doing two hours of duck walks and leg squats. There was no allowance for any recovery of the muscles in your legs, so no matter how tough you were, you'd be risking tendon damage and all sorts of other issues. It wasn't bastardisation; it was just a lack of actual knowledge. They did what they knew, so I'm not trying to be critical of anyone. If an instructor had a karate background or a gym background, that would shape the way he'd train everyone else and run the course. There was just no science behind it.

That science and knowledge eventually started to come in, and things improved. So PT never got any easier, but there was a program put in place to ensure it had a purpose. It became more structured so we didn't lose good people to silly, preventable injuries.

I had issues with shooting instructors making guys do push-ups or hanging them off a railing for thirty minutes for punishment, because in the training program we had them doing upper-body exercises the next day. I can remember doing some push-ups and upper-body work one day, then doing punching drills for two hours the next day. My shoulders and chest were ready to explode. It just ruined the on-flow and wasn't very professional. That's what was missing and that all evolved.

Nowadays, we do two weeks of selection, which is all PT and sleep deprivation, just to see who has that determination and resilience, but the actual intake course is more of an instructional thing. It's an adult learning environment. It is less about the physical stuff and more about the weapons and the tactics.

OSCAR: One of the instructors had them doing push-ups on their knuckles on gravel. That's the way he would train, so he expected everyone else to be able to do it. He would stand there and punch wooden boards and think, 'If I can do it, you can do it.' While I didn't agree with that particular approach, there were some things that people didn't like that I thought were necessary. What we're able to do without fail, however, and regardless of the training tactics and various versions of the intake course, is identify and recruit the most incredible men who are prepared to do whatever it takes to protect the community and arrest the worst, most violent offenders out there. Our men put their own lives at risk on a regular basis without the need for recognition or special treatment. The sacrifices they make are significant, but there are never any complaints.

MACK: There are lots of different personalities that come through. Some you can pick straight away and tell that there's going to be a clash with some of the members already in the group. They would have the wrong thought processes or would have the wrong reasons for wanting to join the group. I would often see what I refer to as 'pretty boys' try to come into the group – guys that have been in the gym doing all the weights but don't like to get their hands dirty. We would take them out of their comfort zone and make them do something they didn't want to do, and we knew they'd fold. If they got through, okay, we'd give them a fair go. But most of the time, when you applied that type of pressure on them – or 'bastardised' them, I suppose – you'd determine if they'd fit or not pretty quickly.

–

Uncompromising and tough, Odin was an experienced campaigner within the police force and saw some things he didn't like on early training courses.

ODIN: It was a 'one size fits all' approach, and we were losing really good people. The SOG had this image that encompassed walking around in tight T-shirts, riding motorbikes and showing off their muscles. A particular stereotype had been created. We lacked diversity, and, to be effective, we needed all shapes, sizes, personalities and skill sets. Instructors would run candidates into the ground and break them down with injuries and then say, 'This bloke can't cope; he's too soft.' There was no real compassion, and if the applicant didn't suit the group physically or wasn't to a particular instructor's liking, then they were somewhat ostracised and treated differently to get them off the course. The ironic thing was, some men got into the group and would instantly forget what they went through on the induction course and the treatment they endured, and would actively bastardise the next crop of hopefuls.

ROGUE: It was as hard as hard. It was horrible. I'd say there was a lot of bastardisation – they really beat the shit out of ya. There was boxing, wrestling – I broke my nose, broke a couple of fingers on the course, but I just had to front up the next day. We went for a run one morning and it lasted eight hours. We were in overalls and boots, so hardly running gear. It was just ridiculous. One guy's feet were that bloodied; there was just blood oozing out the side of his boots. His feet were rooted, but we did it – because we had to do it. Looking back on it, yeah, I'd say it was necessary.

Out of an initial group of more than a few hundred applicants, we got down to just four in our intake, and we weren't going to let each other down. We were just going to hang on no matter what. The four of us are still tight to this day, and we agree that our course was harder than any other.

DELTA: When you get woken up at 3.00 am and you're yanked out of bed and told to stand to, that's not bastardisation. I agree with that type of training because it's called mental toughening. That's getting in your head that when you go to bed at night, expect the unexpected – that's the code in a lot of tactical policing units. That's how it's got to be. There's no switch-off time in the Soggies. You could be put in a horrible situation at a moment's notice, and that horrible situation can go on for days, let alone for hours. You cannot say, 'Listen, boss. I'm a bit over this and I'd like to go home.' You've got to dig in, toughen up and stick it out. There may come a time when you have to take someone's life because they've chosen to have their life taken. You've got to be up for it, and if you're given the green light, you've got to be able to function at a high level. So those things we used to do to inductees were for a specific reason.

MACK: The harsh treatment is there to make sure that the people you're selecting in the high-pressure situations are going to be able to respond, even if they think things are a little over the top and unreasonable.

—

An experienced instructor on many intakes, Lima believes the punishing training helps SOG superiors learn everything they need to know before selecting new recruits.

LIMA: Am I brutal? I'm not sure. Am I hard? Definitely. We have to expose candidates to levels of discomfort and pain they never thought they were capable of enduring. We've had professional runners try to join, so why would we test their running ability? What's that going to teach us about their character, level of resilience and willingness to push on? 'Nothing' is the answer.

When you see someone in an exhausted state, where they're huffing and puffing and think they can't possibly do any more, it's amazing what a little bit of berating or external motivation can do. You'd often find that they could punch out another thirty push-ups. Some would break down and cry – like when you see a marathon runner collapse and break down after they cross the finish line; it's no different. It's not a reflection on them and doesn't suggest they're weak. They're all tough in their own way; these men are doing amazing things. To us, that man is at the point where we want him – the breaking point. From there, we can see if he's willing to go further and push through.

I don't care if a man cries for three hours, so long as he keeps going. I remember holding a bloke's legs while he was doing sit-ups one year – he must have done a thousand sit-ups that day. I was inches away from his face and he had started to cry but kept going. He'd do a sit-up, and when he reached the top he'd say to me, 'You're a cunt!' He'd do another one and repeat it, 'You're a cunt!' He earned a lot of respect that day.

—

After three months of pain and punishment, those lucky enough to have survived and completed the intake course were afforded the ultimate reward.

PHANTOM: We had a special parade where we were given our black caps – that was the best. Our family was allowed to come along and it was a really special moment for me. I thought back to the time that I stopped that SOG member in the city street, and I realised that I'd accomplished my dream to be what he was. To go through all that training and selection, to endure all that pain and come out of it a better person: it was an achievement all right. Besides getting married and having children, it's the best thing I've ever done.

LIMA: The ones who are left standing after that three-month course are the ones who can stand proud and can look you in the eyes and say, 'I'm still here. You tried to get rid of me and I beat you!' To that, we say, 'Well done, brother. Welcome aboard.'

—

But making it into the group was just the beginning. Transitioning into the SOG was a challenge in itself for the new kids on the block.

DANE: The time you can actually tell if a bloke is the right fit for the group or not is about six to eight months after their intake course. That's when their poker face or course-head comes off and their real identity is revealed. They can maintain a 'Yes, sir! No, sir! Three bags full, sir!' charade during the intake course and for a short while after it, but that first six or eight months – when they've actually passed and they're in their blacks and they're around the other guys – that's when you can actually tell if they're there for the right reasons or the wrong reasons. The wrong reasons being the three Bs: 'blacks, babes and bucks'.

There's a bit of self-selection too. Some blokes come in and show telltale signs. For instance, they won't put their kit or gear away correctly or look after it well enough. They leave important or dangerous items like weapons and stuff unlocked, turn up to work late or get on the piss and start talking about all sorts of crap. All those types of things are picked up by the more senior members of the group, who will go, 'Hey! You don't do shit like that and get away with it in here, mate.' It's all in, or none. If that can't be sorted out, generally that person will realise the SOG isn't for him and he'll leave.

I remember this one guy who had only been in the group for about three months. He would take one of the cars out to run an errand, and when he'd come back it would stink of cigarette smoke. No one in the group smoked – it wasn't a hard and fast rule but more of an unspoken one. The reason being, if you were on a job in the back of a van or in a car for twelve hours with a bunch of guys, you couldn't have someone who would be starting to twitch or have an inability to concentrate and stay focused for more than a couple of hours because of addiction withdrawals. I mean we have to stay put for that long sometimes, just waiting for a crook to turn up or for something to happen, that we'd need to piss in bottles and endure some really uncomfortable and trying circumstances. We can't have someone saying, 'Jesus. I've got to get out and have a dart to calm me down.'

Anyway, with this guy, we let it go because he kept denying that he smoked. One day, I was in the garage and he pulled in and I said, 'Mate, be honest. Do you smoke or what?' and he goes, 'Nah . . . No. No. Not at all.' As he got out, he tried to drop his cigarette to hide it from me but it fell into the cuff of his pants and was burning away. I just looked at him and shook my head. When I spoke about it to some of the others, it turned out there was a whole heap of other stupid things this guy was doing that didn't fit the standards of the group. Not long after that cigarette incident, he dropped out. Obviously there was a big trust issue there because he was straight-out lying to me and his other teammates.

The SOG is a unique workplace compared with the rest of the police force, but it's not unique from other special forces.

You're basically selecting alpha males and sticking them all in the same sandpit together. In most organisations, you have diverse groups, but we're deliberately selecting alpha-male types, who all have a similar temperament and strength of character. It was usually the person who shouts the loudest gets to rule for a while, which meant there were minor clashes here and there. All in all, when it came down to doing the actual jobs and getting the work done, all that bullshit went out the window.

MOUSE: You certainly had to do your apprenticeship, and that's always been the case. You had to prove to the existing members that you were capable of being relied upon, and some blokes took more convincing than others. You just had to prove yourself. I'm not a big guy and I knew some of the guys looked at me and thought, 'He won't be able to do all the work,' but I absolutely could do all the work and set out to prove them wrong.

Everyone came in under a cloud. You were told on no uncertain terms, 'You're here on probation and you've got to stack up.' The first two years were hard. It's not that you felt unwanted; more that you felt out of place. It took a long time to cement your position in there. But when you've been in the group for a while, you realise how elite your colleagues are compared with the rest of the world. The professionalism of the group on jobs and training was incredible and very orderly. When we went on a job, you just knew what every single member of your team was going to do, and that comes back to trust.

MACK: In the heat of the moment when things turn all pear-shaped, we need to know that the new guy will respond accordingly. You don't ever want to have to look over your shoulder to see whether someone is behind you, backing you up.

We work because we automatically know that there is always someone right there with you if shit goes down.

TANGO: You're the new guy when you start, and despite having done the course, you're not trusted. Who knows how the new guy is going to react when something bad really does happen? It's over time that you get tested. When I got through, someone started a rumour that I had left the priesthood to join the SOG, just to stir some trouble. I was pretty quiet on the course, and because of that rumour guys were very unsure about me and the impact I'd have on the office culture. Some men were thinking, 'Are we even allowed to swear anymore?'

It was about two months later when I thought there was something going on and found out what was being said. So you very much start on the outside and have to work your way into the group. Even on jobs, you have to do your time before you get to see any action. You start on the outside as a cut-off man, and then you might be selected to join a team. When you're on a team for an assault or raid, you'll be last in or fourth in line.

ROGUE: When you make it into the group and establish yourself as a worthy and reliable member, the bosses constantly remind you that you are good and have been selected for a reason. But we need that. We need to feel superior to any criminal element that we come up against. Our bosses are always telling us how good we are and how well trained we are. Going into a house to raid it, we have no fear because of that supreme confidence in each other and ourselves.

HAZE: I talk to my kids often about perseverance and resilience and the SOG intake course taught me a lot. If you can't run, you walk. If you can't walk, you crawl. If you can't crawl, then at the very least bat your eyelids and poke your tongue out. Make some movement but whatever you do, don't give up. For us to become Soggies, failure was not an option and the training course with all its flaws – selection, training, testing, bastardisation and sometimes downright cruelty ensured that those that completed it, were people that would never quit. Our motto at graduation was: 'Many Aspire, Few Succeed' . . . How true.

5

INFERNO

Whoever believes in the Son has eternal life; whoever does not obey the Son shall not see life, but the wrath of God remains on him.

John 3:36

In 1986, the Victorian minister for Police and Emergency Services, Race Matthews, suggested to Mick Miller that the SOG should be disbanded to save money. But Race's recommendation was never seriously considered after a car bomb was detonated outside the Russell Street police headquarters on Easter Thursday, 27 March. The violent blast killed twenty-one-year-old constable Angela Taylor and injured twenty-two others.

Oscar was on the phone at about 1.00 pm that day in the SOG's offices next to the Russell Street police complex when the windows started rattling violently.

OSCAR: All of a sudden there was this almighty WHOOMPF! Shockwaves from a large car bomb tore around the corner and cracked the street-facing windows in their wake. I dropped the phone and ran outside and saw a car out the front of the police complex on fire. I started yelling at people to get out of the area and started isolating the scene. It was chaotic and there was a lot of damage. It wasn't like anything I'd ever seen before.

—

One of the SOG's most experienced members, Delta was on his way back from a training exercise and saw the thick black smoke billowing into the air from the West Gate Bridge. When he arrived at the scene, the forensic examination and evidence collecting had begun.

DELTA: For the next six days, we crawled around on our hands and knees scouring the scene for any clues we could find as to who may have done it. Some of the debris was found two to three blocks away from the blast site. It was a huge and very powerful explosion. Detectives were piecing things together, and eventually they had a breakthrough in the case and we were called in to make some high-risk arrests.

—

Stan Taylor was suspect number one, and when he was arrested in Birchip, north-west of Melbourne near Wycheproof, he also implicated twenty-three-year-old Craig 'Slim' Minogue and his younger brother, twenty-year-old Rodney.

OSCAR: Taylor was all too quick and willing to spill the beans on where the others involved in the bombing were hiding out.

—

Craig Minogue had been groomed into a violent stand-over man by Taylor after they first met at a Mooroolbark youth club.

The trio honed their craft with violent robberies of country hotels and eventually moved on to banks. They loved to intimidate their victims and controlled them with fear and a fierce beating.

Taylor had a deep-seated hatred for the police, and the Minogues were at his beck and call. When the plan was hatched to bomb police headquarters, police detectives believe it was Taylor who stole the sixty sticks of gelignite from a mine and built the explosive device.

When Taylor told members of the SOG that the brothers were holed up in a motel in Swan Hill, they knew it was going to be a high-risk job and took no chances.

DELTA: Because of the danger these guys posed to us, there was real concern. Craig Minogue, in particular, had been involved in some pretty bloody heinous crimes that involved extreme violence and brutality. He was a nasty piece of work.

—

Two four-man SOG assault teams were flown to Swan Hill in helicopters. All the intelligence on the Minogues' hideout had been handed over when they arrived, so the men knew the layout of the room and what to expect when they hit the door. The motel was a standard two-storey, long, rectangular building that led away from the main road. The Minogues were staying about halfway along on the top level.

Just before 3.00 am, the manager of the motel was woken by the sound of the service bell on the reception counter. Bleary-eyed, he was startled to find two fully armed SOG members demanding his attention and cooperation. 'We need a room key and a cake of soap,' Delta told him.

The SOG entry teams lined up outside the motel door as Delta slid the cuts of a key to the Minogues' room into the cake of soap he'd obtained from the manager. The element of surprise was going to be crucial, as it was expected that the brothers would be well armed and possibly sleeping with firearms in their beds. By using the soap, Delta knew the key would slide silently into the lock without alerting the wanted men on the other side.

OSCAR: We knew they were in a twin-share with two single beds on the right as you entered. It was only a small room so we knew things could get pretty close and personal in there.

—

'Go! Go! Go! Police! Don't move! Get down! Hit the floor! Now! Move!' The room was suddenly illuminated by the lighting systems on the SOG's shotguns, and the Minogues were caught like 'deer in the headlights', according to Oscar.

OSCAR: They were still in bed, and Craig, my team's target, rolled off to the side of the bed. Before he could do anything, we were on top of him and had him pinned. It was that quick.

DELTA: Rodney Minogue tried to get his hands on a bag of guns that was only an arm's length away, but failed when we pounced on him. They were woken from their sleep and they were stunned and utterly shocked. They didn't get the opportunity to stand up and say, 'Jesus Christ, what the hell is going on here?' They were just ripped from their beds and thrown to the floor and strapped very rapidly.

—

Despite being under arrest, Craig Minogue started to resist when the SOG attempted to strap his hands. He was met with a heavy blow to the head, upon which he quickly submitted.

OSCAR: He started not to do as he was told. He hesitated and copped a whack for it from me. We can't let anyone hesitate when they've been given direct orders. If we allow them to hesitate or dictate terms, then we lose control of the situation and our safety is immediately at risk. We have to put them where we want them, and there can't be any question. We have to be extremely dominant with our actions when dealing with violent criminals, and we must always show them who the boss is. We couldn't give them an opportunity to rush at us, push us out of the way and get to that bag of guns.

—

The Minogues were handed over to detectives, who expressed their gratitude for the SOG's work.

DELTA: One of them said to me, 'Bloody hell, you guys did a job on them all right! Craig's physically shit himself. He's got a hard drop of shit in the back of his undies.' He shit himself. I'll never forget it. Here's this so-called, big, tough crime hero and he actually crapped himself. It would be traumatising being a criminal, especially a murderer that just killed a young policewoman in Angela Taylor, to be asleep and have a highly trained special weapons unit hit your room. It'd be the most fucking horrific thing to experience. I think I'd shit myself too if it happened to me.

—

Oscar recalled his brief encounter with a smile on his face.

OSCAR: Craig was a blubbering mess. He was crying and sobbing like a baby because he thought he was a dead man. He later told detectives that he thought the SOG was going to kill him for what had happened to Angela Taylor.

—

Taylor and Craig Minogue were both sentenced to life imprisonment, with the latter receiving a thirty-year non-parole period. Delta hopes he never gets out of prison. Craig Minogue though, was acquitted.

DELTA: In the old days, Craig would have been hanged for what he did. He should be left where he is to rot. Had the bomb been placed where they'd actually wanted it, inside the perimeter of the Russell Street building, they would have killed hundreds of police and other innocent people. The building would have just caved in. Structurally, they say that type of bomb would have brought down about three floors of the nine-floor building, because the more you confine an explosive, the more pressure and bigger the blast. It would have been one of the biggest mass killings in the world. It would have been fucking unbelievable.

OSCAR: It could have been so much worse had it not been Easter, notwithstanding the tragedy that occurred with Angela Taylor losing her life. But the fact of the matter was, we normally got paid on a Thursday, but because it was a public holiday with Good Friday the next day we got paid on the Wednesday instead. Most people would head out between twelve and one for lunch and cash their cheques at a pub or bank. So there would have usually been a lot more people swarming the street at that time when the bomb went off. Normally there's also a group of schoolchildren waiting to have an excursion inside. The car was parked right next to where their bus would have pulled up.

—

Former Victorian Premier John Cain said of the bombing, 'We've read about it and, I suppose, abhorred it in other parts of the world. We get violence in all shapes, in all sizes and all forms, but this sort of violence is new to us.'

His quotes were echoed by a senior detective at the time who stated:

Ten years ago, there was mutual respect between crims and police. You had your uniform, your firearm, your baton and handcuffs, your mouth, your brain and that was enough protection. The Russell Street bombing, and now Walsh Street [the Walsh Street police shootings of 1988], have changed that. There is no longer any respect for the uniform. There are people out there who hate all police officers, and every officer is now aware of that . . .

Now, rather than leave the weapon in their holster and be caught cold, they are drawing their firearms even when going on seemingly routine jobs . . . I am sad to say that, but it's happening. People are going to be asking why policemen are walking around with their guns out. A lot of youngsters going out on patrol are experiencing daily that tightening of the gut previously only felt on special raids. There is always the concern that operating under such stress could lead to accidents. Noises, such as the wind, could prompt officers to spin round with their gun drawn; it's a gut reaction . . .

Every job is taking much longer. We apologise to the public, but they will just have to wait . . . Take a report of a suspicious vehicle parked in a street. Before Walsh Street, it would be pull up, jump out, check the boot, see if it is stolen and off to the next job. Now they will drive up and down the street several times and possibly call for backup units before getting out of their car. Every officer wants to go home when they have finished their tour of duty.

In 1994, the Task Force Victor Review into Police Shootings would describe the mid-to-late eighties as a turning point in policing, due to the new threats the police were facing from armed and dangerous criminals:

> The randomness of the Russell Street bombing of 1986 emphasised the risk, and the aggregate level of apprehensiveness among police officers rose accordingly. At the same time, a number of violent persons were proving resistant to police efforts to control them, and several police officers and criminals were shot in the course of armed encounters. The violence continued over 1987, including the mass shootings at Hoddle and Queen Streets. Shooting incidents in fact remained at a relatively high rate throughout 1985–1988, the highest number occurring in 1988.

In this climate, the case for bolstering, rather than disbanding, the SOG practically made itself.

6

BLESSED ARE THE PEACEMAKERS

*They must turn away from evil and do good. They must seek
peace and pursue it.*

1 Peter 3:11

Five heavily armed SOG lined up at the back door of the small
weatherboard home. The rain continued to pour down as it had
for several days. Water beaded off their black jumpsuits and onto
the patio deck, pooling under their mud-caked boots.

With just one look at the back door, the SOG member at the
front of the queue knew from experience it was made of hollow
timber – one heavy hit and it would swing wide open. There was
no need for a battering ram; a swift swing of the sledgehammer
would do the trick and probably take it off its hinges. Tightly
bunched up and split into two groups of three men, the teams
were positioned on either side of the doorjamb, awaiting the
green light to make a surprise forced entry. At the front of the
property, a second team of SOG members clutched flash-bang
grenades, with their pointer fingers ready to make a sharp tug on
the pull rings.

Inside the home, a twenty-nine-year-old mentally disturbed
man sat in an armchair in the shadows of the blacked-out

lounge room with a rifle in his hands. Hours of attempted negotiations between him and police had proven fruitless, and Force Command had decided it was time to bring the already violent day to an end.

Earlier that morning, a relatively new SOG tactical operator, Rayden, was tending to his small garden in Melbourne's outer east. Although he was supposed to be off-duty, when his pager began to vibrate at 1.20 pm he felt a shot of excitement and then a dump of adrenaline rush through his body. A planned day of housework was about to become another item on his ever-growing 'to do' list. Rayden was on the SOG's Reserve Duty Team (RDT) – a backup unit on standby to cover for any members of the Active Duty Team (ADT) who weren't reachable or available for duty.

Rayden was given little detail via the message on his pager – it only instructed him to head to the office for an urgent siege situation. As was the case with every member of the SOG, Rayden was thrilled to get the call-up. There was nothing worse than missing out on a job, especially one that promised some high drama and potential action.

RAYDEN: It was one of those things . . . just part of the job. We always expected the unexpected and you were never really on a day off. You always had one eye on that pager, hoping it would come to life all of a sudden. On the way into headquarters, I got told there was a gunman in a house in Deer Park and he'd shot a woman and had laid siege and he may have hostages . . . I'm like, 'Yeah, okay, I'm on the way.'

—

Rayden headed to the Victoria Police's headquarters in the city to collect the logistics truck and equipment before joining the rest of the SOG crew at the scene.

RAYDEN: I always loved the part where we'd all arrive at the office and exchange information about the situation we were about to attend. Some blokes had to have as much information as possible, while others just needed the bare minimum. I always liked to know as much as possible and played out different scenarios in my head like an athlete would before a big game. It's how I focused and switched on, because in our profession one slip-up could be the difference between life and death.

—

As Rayden and the rest of the team made their way to the Deer Park house, more information began to slowly filter through over the police radio.

RAYDEN: All our various teams, on- or off-duty, have a range of specialists. There are snipers and marksmen, bomb technicians, tactical operators, training and research cells, waterborne operators, roping/rappelling experts, explosive breaching experts, hostage and rescue operations, armed offender operations and also special weapons instructors, just to name a few. They are all vital and unbelievably good at what they do – in fact, they are the best in the world. We are well equipped to handle anything that is thrown at us on any given day, and this job was no different.

Sixty-six-year-old retiree Mrs McGaw fell to the floor in the hallway next to her lounge room writhing in agony. Blood began to pour from the bullet wound in her stomach and she screamed in pain. Only moments before, she was enjoying a nap with her husband when their quiet afternoon was interrupted by the sound of breaking glass coming from the front of their home.

Standing at the door and using the butt of a rifle to smash through the window was psychiatric patient Anthony John White.

Before the McGaws could even question the man about his impromptu visit and what he was doing, he began clearing the glass out with the butt of his .22-calibre Browning long rifle. The couple retreated into the hallway as White started to climb through the window frame and into the lounge room. Mr McGaw slammed the door shut to the hallway and lay across it to stop the intruder in his tracks. White made several menacing threats and demanded the couple open up, but they refused and the consequences were almost fatal. White opened fire. An ear-piercing CRACK! rang out from the lounge room, and Mrs McGaw was thrust backwards into the wall and fell to the floor. White's bullet had shot through the wooden door and struck her in the lower abdomen. In a rage, White then pulled the door off its hinges and threatened to bash the McGaws' heads in with the butt of his rifle.

White stood over Mrs McGaw and told the couple to give him more ammunition before he turned the house upside down in search of some. He fired another shot through the bathroom window. The McGaws kept pleading for mercy, and, for whatever reason, White buckled and allowed Mr McGaw to carry his seriously wounded wife to safety. Bullets whizzed past them and disappeared into adjoining properties as they scampered to a neighbour's house and called the ambulance and police.

RAYDEN: This nutter was a hairdresser and was a diagnosed schizophrenic. He had driven to Deer Park from South Australia and was apparently looking for his girlfriend, who had moved back to Victoria, away from him. She'd cut ties with him and he couldn't handle it. Before he shot the old lady, he was seen in the streets around the house firing shots into the ground and seemingly looking for targets. He was walking on top of car roofs and had also threatened a couple of guys who were working on a car in their driveway. He also shot at them.

—

Residents in the quiet neighbourhood began to flood police with phone calls, reporting the sounds of gunshots. Before long, the wail of sirens filled the air, and dozens of police cars and a few ambulances arrived.

White barricaded himself inside the house and prepared to put up a fight. The first uniformed police on the scene had attempted to get the situation under control, but when four officers cautiously approached the home, they had to dive for cover when White opened fire through the smashed window in the front door. White was heard yelling out, 'If you move, I'll kill you,' and then in a complete change of tone he yelled, 'Kill me, please. Please don't leave me like this; kill me!' Realising they were way out of their depth, the uniformed police officers made a desperate plea for the SOG to be called in.

At the Western Hospital, Mrs McGaw was stabilised after emergency-room doctors removed the bullet from her stomach. When she was well enough to talk, the couple gave detectives as much information as they could about White. Among other things, they were able to tell police what type of firearm he was using and informed them it was fitted with a telescopic sight. Their information resulted in police creating a larger than normal perimeter around the home, and they evacuated residents within a 500-metre radius. But there was one property that couldn't be vacated because the people inside had special needs, so steps were taken to ensure their safety. A uniformed policeman was sent in to guard and protect them.

When Rayden arrived at the scene with the SOG logistics truck, he and the SOG began to kit up. New to the group and about to participate in one of his first raids, he had packed a new 'whiz-bang' shotgun belt that held thirty rounds of ammunition and sat diagonally across his chest. While he felt he more than looked the part, his colleagues were far from impressed, particularly Onyx.

RAYDEN: He was much more experienced than me and had been in the group for a few years by the time I started. He looked over, shook his head, and said, 'Get that off! You look like a fucking wanker! Where the hell did you get that?' Being the junior of the group, I quickly took it off but discreetly defied his orders and stuffed all the shotgun rounds into the top front pockets of my tactical vest. Looking back, it wasn't the smartest idea, because if I'd been shot in the chest, I would have gone off like a Roman candle!

By the time I added all the other gear – tear gas, stun grenades, a 9-mm pistol, knife, and shotgun – I felt invincible. A weaker bloke would just topple over or buckle at the knees carrying that much shit. Sometimes you're required to scale fences, chase down offenders, jump, dive and roll – all fully kitted up. It's not great for the back but I'd rather have it all on me than not have it at all. My opinion is that you can strap as much stuff to me as you want – if it's got the potential to save my life, I'll find a way to lug it around.

Going back a little while, one of our guys had to sprint several hundred metres with all his gear on, chasing after an offender. We'd raided a joint and the crook jumped out of a side window to avoid being arrested. The Soggie in pursuit was determined not to let him go and went after him on foot, but with so much gear on you'd think it was next to impossible for him to catch him, considering the crook had nothing weighing him down at all. However, you often hear of amazing acts of courage, bravery and sometimes miracles in our line of work, and as it turns out the Soggie got close enough to drag the crook down by the scruff of the neck and enact what we call a 'heavy arrest' – that is to say, he definitely knew he was in custody.

—

Sarge had been on his fair share of stake-outs. Before the SOG he was a member of the Major Crime Squad. A seasoned detective, he was looking for a promotion to sergeant when he noticed an advertisement in the police gazette calling for officers to apply for the SOG. During a certification shoot, he caught Doug O'Loughlin's eye because of his deadly accuracy. A few words of encouragement from O'Loughlin was all that was needed to convince Sarge that he should try out for the group. On the same night he sent in his application, he ran from the St Kilda Road police complex to his home in Tullamarine – some 21 kilometres. His training had begun and nothing was going to stop him from becoming one of the men in black. He was always up for a challenge, and this stake-out was just another one he was determined to overcome, especially being the senior ranking team leader.

As the afternoon wore on, the temperature continued to plummet and driving rain set in. Time was against the SOG.

SARGE: It was fucking freezing. Just freezing. It was about 2.00 pm but it was a really rainy, overcast and miserable grey Melbourne day. We were sitting out in the drizzling rain for hours and were soaked through. For some reason, we didn't have any wet-weather gear.

RAYDEN: There was only about half an hour of sunlight left in the day, and once it was dark the gunman's scope would be rendered useless. Our sights, on the other hand, are infra-red and would be unaffected. Night-time is when we do our best work, and under the cover of darkness we can close in on an offender without being seen or detected. It also gives us the opportunity to guarantee the safety of any people trapped in nearby houses.

The call was made to cut the power to the streetlights in order to provide a safer environment for those of us positioned around the property. The glow that was coming from them was enough to give White an idea of what was happening around him. But when we switched them off, he turned the porch light and floodlight out the back on. We eventually moved into an old chook shed over in the back corner of the backyard of the house . . . it was the only cover we could find from the wet and cold. It wasn't ideal but it was much better than sitting in the rain freezing our arses off.

—

With no option but to wait and secure the back of the property, Rayden and four others – Sarge, Onyx, Tango and Haze – huddled up and watched the back door and sides of the house closely in case White tried to get away. They also put plans in place to make sure White couldn't use the McGaws' car, which was parked in the driveway, as an escape vehicle.

RAYDEN: We didn't want to do the old car chase down the road. He was armed and could have come out all guns a-blazin' at us. As a general rule, we always tried to avoid shooting at fleeing vehicles because there was too much risk to public safety. If he did somehow escape in that car, we would have to try and get up alongside him and risk being shot at, while trying to disable the vehicle. The only way you can really do that is to ram it with one of our cars and push him off the road . . . It would've been messy and, again, the public could have been put in harm's way. So we put some contingencies in place to make sure he couldn't drive away, that being having another car there to block it in from behind.

—

Although uncomfortable and sopping wet, Haze wouldn't have traded his position in the chook shed in the backyard for the world. After years of being a divisional detective, he yearned for more excitement and action as a police officer. He'd become sick of all the paperwork his role required but, most of all, he'd grown tired of watching criminals continuously walk free from court after he'd arrested them. The opportunity to join the SOG was too good to refuse plus, as he pointed out to me, his partner at the time and now wife felt he'd look very handsome in black. A couple of years later as a SOG Tactical Operator, that was the furthest thing on his mind as he sought to resolve a siege, his teammates as a barricaded armed gunman waited for the police to make their next move.

—

Negotiators obtained the McGaws' home phone number and dialled it. White answered and demanded that his girlfriend be brought to the house immediately. He was yelling the entire time in a high-pitched voice. When he was asked to throw his gun out and surrender, he laughed and became abusive before slamming the phone down. In another conversation, he mentioned his family and was heard whispering, 'I didn't mean to do it, Mummy, really.' Negotiators concluded that it wasn't possible to hold any intelligent conversations with him due to his agitated condition. With no incoming calls coming anymore, White called his mother in South Australia and told her, 'I'm going to shoot them or they are going to shoot me.'

Negotiators decided to bombard White with one-way messages via a megaphone in an effort to tire him out. 'We understand you're upset,' one negotiator announced. 'We want you to come out the back door with your hands in the air, no gun, and I promise no harm will come to you. Everything will be okay and we can all go home. You have my word.'

RAYDEN: They were extremely reassuring words from the negotiator and I'm sure they meant every one, but when it's me taking an offender down, I ain't worried about handing out a few bumps and bruises to him – I'm more worried for the public's safety, the safety of my team members and my own personal safety. Hit 'em quick and hit 'em hard is normally the best philosophy.

—

While the initial information from the McGaws was that White was alone inside, after the brief phone call with her son, White's mother feared there could have been a hostage in there with him. That coincided with SOG members who started to hear strange noises coming from the interior.

SARGE: There were sounds of a woman's voice coming out of the house and she was pleading for help. We thought it may have been the television or radio at first, but we couldn't discount the possibility that he had a hostage. We had to question our intelligence despite the fact there was no evidence of any other female living there or being involved, other than the elderly female homeowner.

—

A call was made to the hospital where Mr and Mrs McGaw were recovering. They were asked if they'd seen anyone else, if they were sure the gunman was alone and whether there could've been anyone else in the house at the time of the shooting. The elderly couple told police that, to the best of their knowledge, he was alone.

SARGE: We were becoming increasingly confused as more and more strange noises came from inside the house. 'Are you guys hearing that?' I asked the others. It was a female-like voice going, 'Help! Help me!' It wasn't until the snipers were able to lay eyes on White that the confusion finally ended.

RAYDEN: They actually saw him yelling, 'Help me! Help me!' in a feminine voice. It was weird. They said he was also meowing like a cat. I just thought, 'We've got a fucking wacko here.' We're all looking at each other, thinking, 'Normal people don't do this sort of shit.'

—

The siege continued to drag on, and Sarge was growing impatient as the conditions worsened.

SARGE: I radioed the command post and told the inspector in charge, 'We've got to go in now!' We knew White wasn't going to come out or negotiate with us; he'd made that pretty clear. I was worried he'd be able to escape our cordon and start shooting more innocent people. We had the chance to grab him while he was right in front of us.

RAYDEN: The various options available to us on any siege are always conveyed to an assistant commissioner [A/C], who has to approve any course of action we might take. The A/C is not usually at the scene but he will always ask what the preferred option is from those of us on the front line. If the A/C doesn't like that option for whatever reason, he'll want another plan to be drawn up or tell us to keep trying to negotiate. If he agrees with our preferred course of action, he'll tell the chief inspector or inspector who is at the command post on site to 'proceed'.

All we knew with this fucker was that he had a rifle, that he'd shot someone already and he was letting bullets fly the whole time we were there. Rounds were popping off every now and then to let us know that he meant business, I reckon. The snipers had eyes on him, but they couldn't see him all the time – just when he got up and walked around the house. The A/C finally approved the raid. We planned to sucker-punch White to the front of the house because the back was all clear and it was by far the safest point of entry for us, because he had little visibility out that way.

—

Four of the five Sons entering through the back were armed with 9-mm SIG Sauer semi-automatic pistols and also pump-action shotguns. Two others at the front of the property were tasked with throwing distraction grenades to make White think they were all coming in to get him through the front door.

RAYDEN: We wanted him focused on the front of the house and to completely forget about the back. We wanted to compress him towards the lounge room, where he'd have nowhere to go. The only concern was that we didn't know exactly what type of gun he had or how much ammo he had. That's the thing: if someone hears a gunshot and says that's a .303- or that's a .308-calibre or something, it's absolute shite . . . I mean, you can tell if it's a .22

generally, but then there are .22 subsonics, supersonics, hornets and all this other stuff. Some of the guys who have been around guns their entire lives could pick them pretty well. Anything that starts with a .3 is bad. You know a .3-whatever is gonna kill you if it hits you. So we just hoped he didn't have one of those.

—

It was almost 5.00 pm when Sarge used hand signals to count down. 'THREE, TWO, ONE, GO! GO! GO!' When his last finger disappeared, Tango swung the sledgehammer at the door, just below the handle. The door flew open and Onyx pinged a distraction grenade into the kitchen, but instead of continuously exploding across the lino floor like it was designed to, it only made an underwhelming clanging sound as it came to rest completely intact beneath the kitchen bench. When Onyx had pulled the pin, it had snapped off and the lever hadn't been able to release, which prevented the detonator from igniting. So the SOG's planned surprise attack got off to a bad start, and unfortunately White now knew they were coming at him from all directions. The sound of the grenade hitting the floor had alerted him, and the lack of any explosion meant he could hear movement at the back door. He took cover behind a wall across from the kitchen towards the rear of the house.

HAZE: I was first through the laundry door and had a pistol-grip, short-barrel shotgun with an under-barrel lighting system. I was yelling, 'Police. Don't move!' I lit up the area immediately in front of me and the first thing I saw was the barrel of a firearm that just looked so big and was pointed right at me. It looked like a cannon. The gunman was standing in a shooting position and I heard an almighty *CRACK!* A shot had been fired right at me. So much for the element of surprise.

RAYDEN: As soon as we burst through the back door, I heard a gunshot, and then it was just full on and we were yelling, 'Police! Don't move! Police! Don't move!' The second I got inside, I saw a muzzle flash . . . everyone split and it was like, 'Fuck! Here we go! He's shooting at us! He's shooting at us!' I remember it was like the Red Sea just parting in front of me . . . everyone had to hug a wall. He was just unloading on us, and Onyx, who was in front of me, was firing back with his handgun. He was left-handed and on the right-hand side of the doorway, shooting back at him, while I was on the other side, which was good for me, being a right-hander.

—

Under fire, Haze went on the attack in order to defend himself and his team.

HAZE: White was in a doorway across the other side of the small kitchen. There was another doorway and opening just off the laundry leading into a kitchen. After he fired at me, I let two rounds go back at him with my shotgun as I moved forward. It was all in slow motion and like many others who have found themselves in life-or-death situations, the adrenaline dumps you experience make time and space feel compressed. I could see that I had shot White in the upper body and upper part of his arm. He seemed to reel backwards slightly. It was *BOOM! BOOM!* and then I felt it. At the exact stage that I fired back, my muddied boots skidded on the lino floor. It felt like I was floating for a second or two, but I wasn't floating. I was slipping. Despite all the best training we'd had to go heel to toe and keep your feet during an entry. I landed on my ass. If you can imagine going onto an ice rink in heavy GP [general purpose] boots while trying to make a tactical entry and dodge a bullet, that's what it was like. We are trained not to baulk when we're the first man in on a raid. You just have to get into the room and engage with the offender, but there's a difference between making a decision to stop and having no control of your body and slipping over, all in an unfamiliar place

SARGE: Haze was just *Voom!* Gone out of sight. In my mind, there was no doubt Haze had been shot. I remember seeing the gunman and firing in his direction. One of the others yelled, 'Man down! Man down! He's been hit! He's been hit!' I was just hoping my rounds were hitting White. As I moved forwards to advance into the kitchen, I slipped on the muddy floors and hit the deck.

—

Tango, Rayden and Onyx feared the worst when two of their teammates went down. Unaware they'd merely slipped because of the combination of mud and linoleum flooring, they incorrectly assumed White had shot them both. Understandably, the mood of those left standing changed. The level of violence of tactics always needed to be compared to the threat and the situation.

TANGO: It definitely made me a bit angry thinking that this bloke may have just killed two of our men right in front of us. But in those situations, you can't afford to think about the wounded. You can't afford to hesitate or stop if the threat is still there. White had to be dealt with first before we could tend to the welfare of Haze and Sarge.

RAYDEN: I just thought, 'Fuck! Bad luck, boys . . . we'll get to you both in a minute. There's a little bit going on right now. Just hold on!'

—

With Haze and Sarge out of action, the SOG pulled back slightly and took cover behind the walls in the laundry area. Tango and Rayden retreated through the rear door and tried to get a better vantage point on White.

TANGO: We went around the side of the property because the rest of the team seemed to be bogged down in front of us and had created a bottleneck. We looked through the kitchen window and could see the offender's gun and hand poking out from behind the wall. We blasted at him through the window, but a large fridge was in our way and it stopped most of our rounds from going through because the freezer was full of meat. Some of the rounds skipped off the front door, but our manoeuvre was largely ineffective, so we aborted.

RAYDEN: The move didn't work out so well, but Tango managed to kill the fridge, which was good. After a few seconds, we moved back inside because if the rest of the team advanced, there'd be a risk of some crossfire. The gunman kept unloading on us. He was sitting with his back to the wall, facing the front door. He was shooting over his shoulder and around the corner at us, and continually reloading and firing. I thought, 'Fuck you! Do you really want to hide behind a plaster wall?' We knew that wouldn't offer him much protection and that our rounds would easily get through, so we just kept punching bullets into the plaster.

HAZE: I had knocked White off his feet with my initial volley of shots and he was aiming at us from around the architrave. I stayed in a seated position from when I'd slipped over, and Sarge had got back to his feet and fired at White from above me. It's not like what you see in Hollywood when a baddie gets shot. When you shoot someone, they don't fly thirty feet backwards through the air, burst into flames and die and the good guys just roll on through. I fired three more shotgun rounds from my seated position at White in his semi-concealed position. Although he had taken hits from my initial volley and most likely shots from Sarge and Onyx, he was still a lethal threat to our entry team. We had to stay in the fight.

—

Also shooting at White was Onyx, and he was running out of ammo. He'd erred in taking only a few clips from the logistics van and was left red faced when he had to order Rayden to give him more.

RAYDEN: The same guy who called me a 'wanker' back at the truck for looking like Rambo with my new ammo belt had only gone into the house with a sidearm and three spare mags. Onyx had been going BANG! BANG! BANG! across the room at the gunman, then showed me an empty hand and his gun, which meant, 'I'm empty.' It brought about a funny scenario with me saying to him, 'Oh! Fucking Mr Smartarse here telling me that I wouldn't need all those shells, hey!' I let go a volley of gunfire at White, then looked back at Onyx and let him have another earful: 'Oh fuck, that's right . . . I won't need all these shells, hey?' I was like Pablo Escobar, up to my eyeballs with ammunition . . . I mean I had more shells than the Bismarck. Then Onyx cracked the shits and yelled, 'Just gimme some more fucking rounds!' I threw him my handgun, and that made him happy again.

HAZE: I had fired off all of my shotgun rounds and rather than reload from my seated position, I went straight into my

'Immediate Action' or what we call 'IA Drill' and grabbed my sidearm. I could still see White in the doorway across from me so I aimed my handgun at the wall and where I felt most of his body mass would be, as did the other guys. After another barrage of gunfire, White slumped very noticeably. There was a collective sense of relief and we knew it was time to try and move forward on his position and clear the rest of the house.

—

The shooting suddenly stopped and it was quiet. The house was full of smoke and there was the strong smell of cordite in the air. In that hair-raising few seconds, the members of the SOG had fired a total of thirty-six rounds at White.

SARGE: At one point, I remember standing there with no one around me. I was completely exposed in the kitchen area but I wasn't afraid. I was the aggressive one now, with a lot of support behind me. I had fired seven of the fifteen rounds in my handgun and had my finger on the trigger in case things suddenly started up again.

—

Bulldog waited patiently at the command post, about a hundred metres from the house out in Station Road. After spending the first part of his policing life as a hard-nosed detective, he was lured to the SOG as a sergeant at a time when the group required more experienced officers within its ranks.

BULLDOG: The guys had been given the green light to go in, and after a short period of time there was all this continuous gunfire coming from the house. My immediate reaction was concern for our guys in there. I just listened intently to the radio to receive word as to what was going on and whether everyone was safe. It's not a good feeling because you're pretty useless and can't do anything to help.

—

Inside, the group began to close in on White's position.

RAYDEN: Pardon the pun, but it was deadly quiet. He was either out of ammo, dead, or lying in wait for us, setting a trap. We advanced tactically and were very conscious that there could be danger lurking around every corner. We never took anything for granted. You just don't know. You don't just say, 'Oh, it's all gone quiet; let's go in there and see where he is and what he's up to.'

—

Rayden slung his shotgun to his side to free up his hands in case the gunman lunged at him and he needed to wrestle. He was the first to make it to the corner, where he spotted a rifle on the floor.

RAYDEN: I found White slumped with his back to the wall. He didn't look like a threat and he didn't have anything in his hands, so I dragged him away from the rifle while the others covered me. Then all of a sudden, he started resisting.

SARGE: We jumped on him. We struggled with him and he wouldn't give up. He just wouldn't stop. We gave him a couple of 'Don't be sillys' and then we switched the lights on and threw him onto his stomach and eventually strapped him [handcuffed him temporarily with plastic zip-ties].

HAZE: After we recognised he was down, there was a cautious pause before we moved further into the house to clear the rooms. As Sarge and Rayden took control of White, Onyx and I secured the rest of the house. White had trashed the house and created barriers and protective cover by placing doors and furniture in the central hallway and lounge area. He may have been clinically 'crazy' but he was clearly crafty and clever.

Some hard choices were made that night on whether we undertook a forced entry or continued to wait. The lives of the entry team and White's were in the hands of Police Command. We didn't have ballistic shields in those days. White was up for it and he tested us. We were up to being tested. It wasn't textbook, it wasn't pretty – not many jobs involving a lethal confrontation ever are. He tested us for sure, but we got the job done.

—

One of White's arms had almost been sliced off by Haze's first shot. Tango recalls seeing a bone protruding from his skin just below the elbow and hesitated when he had to grab hold of the busted limb to help make the arrest. When they rolled White back over, there was blood everywhere. Sarge radioed for the paramedics who were on standby out at the command post.

SARGE: We pulled up his shirt to check for wounds and he was like a colander. There were holes in him everywhere. So many holes, you wouldn't read about it. It was remarkable that he was still alive, let alone fighting with us.

—

The paramedics arrived on the scene and worked to save White, but his health rapidly deteriorated.

RAYDEN: The ambos were losing him and couldn't get a pulse. They were there with us within a minute of the shooting, and by that stage we had moved from the hall into the larger lounge room area and were standing back to give them room to work, because he wasn't a danger to anyone anymore. They asked if they could cut the straps off his hands, which was fine, and then they laid him out. I've never seen scissors work so quickly – they cut all his clothes off in an instant and pulled his trousers off. He was going white, like ghostly white. It was as if someone had poured a big can of tomato soup in his lap. It didn't look good for him.

The others had finished clearing the rest of the house to make sure there were no other bad guys. You never stop and go 'Oh jeez, that was a close one' and relax, because what if the bloke lying on the ground in the lounge room was actually a hostage made to look like the offender? A clever terrorist's tactic and a good criminal's tactic is to swap clothes with the hostages so the snipers shoot the hostages and not the bad guys. They give the hostages unloaded weapons, because we can't tell if a weapon is loaded or not. The only way you can tell is when someone shoots at you, but by then it's usually too late. It's the same with trying to determine how many rounds are in a gun – you can't. We could have been shot in the back by the actual gunman who could have been hiding in another room. Despite our intelligence, he could've had an accomplice.

BULLDOG: I came in after getting the 'all clear' from Sarge and saw White lying on the ground, covered in blood. I didn't have enough fingers on my hands to plug the amount of holes he had in him. I saw that all our guys seemed okay, so my immediate concern was for the gunman. Even though he'd shot at our guys, you still don't want him to die.

—

Among other wounds to his face, right arm, right upper arm, shoulder, pelvis, abdominal wall, lower abdominal wall, right hip and thigh region, left forearm, right knee and lower leg, White had taken a bullet in his femoral artery.

Attempts to save his life proved futile, and he died within minutes of the paramedics arriving. No single injury was identified as the fatal shot.

RAYDEN: He would have had about 120 bits of metal in him, I reckon. He must have been standing when we first shot back at him, and then he slumped down against the wall and fired at us. When one of the paramedics declared White had a bullet wound in his femoral artery, I didn't really know what that was at the time, but I soon learnt. I've since seen it in that movie *Black Hawk Down*, where there's a guy shot in the same area of the groin and another bloke sticks his finger in there to try and plug the hole, but he can't find the hole to stop the bleeding. Then he puts his whole hand up there and the bloke who's been shot is screaming because this bloke has his whole hand inside his groin, trying to grab it, the femoral artery, and clamp it off. It's not good to get shot there.

SARGE: All five of us fired that day, so every one of us could have been wholly and solely responsible for ending his life. With shotgun pellets, you can't determine who has shot them, because they can't be matched ballistically. The only way you can tell is if one person is using SGs [small game/grape, nine-pellet rounds] and the other is using SSGs [special small game/grape, smaller eighteen-pellet rounds]. No one knows which particular shot killed him anyway because there was such a massive loss of blood.

—

Immediately after White was declared dead, Sarge ordered the SOG to strip off to check for any gunshot wounds of their own.

SARGE: There was a fair chance one of us could have actually been shot and didn't know it. That's happened before, especially when you're wearing a vest. The adrenaline is pumping and so much is going on that you don't even realise you've been hit.

HAZE: It wasn't until that moment after all the shooting that I went into a bit of shock. I'd done my job and we'd cleared the house and we went into our 're-org' [re-organisation] protocol. I stood out the front and I was feeling for the hole in me from White's first shot. I was feeling my vest, saying, 'He shot me . . . He shot me. Can you see where he shot me? How could he have missed me?' I just remember being a little bit overwhelmed by it all. The adrenaline dump was dissipating and I couldn't work out why I hadn't been shot. He had lined me up from less than five metres away from a semi-concealed position and fired straight at me. There should have been a hole in my vest or worse, in my head. None of the team had been hit.

RAYDEN: I was on a high seeing that everyone was okay, none of us got shot or injured . . . beautiful. That's my high. I didn't want the guy to die, if you know what I mean? If we'd just winged him – injured him but not killed him – that would have been my preference. It was all over in less than a minute. Everything is brought into your focus and expanded, while time seems to slow to a standstill almost. The entire ordeal lasted somewhere between ten seconds to maybe a minute at most. It's always our desire to end these things peacefully. The best sieges are the ones I've turned up to and the negotiators get a resolution without needing us to act or go into the house at all.

—

The SOG had little sympathy for White after he was declared dead. While they all had to deal with the fact they'd shot and killed someone, on this particular job they experienced very similar emotions.

SARGE: He was like an insect to me. He'd been an unnecessary threat to us and others, and we terminated that threat to restore the peace. I wasn't perturbed by his death at all.

RAYDEN: We didn't cause his death; he did. I couldn't care less. I'd say to anyone who finds that a bit harsh: I didn't initiate it; he did. He should have thought about the consequences of his actions when he chose to engage us. He had ample opportunities and time to surrender. Don't forget, we are always the last resort – never the first. I didn't have any animosity towards him, or any feelings of sympathy for him. I couldn't even tell you what his face looked like. I'm not interested either, to be honest. I just remember his name because there used to be a car dealer with the same name who I'd bought a car from once. We always want a peaceful resolution, always, but reality says, 'Shit happens.'

Do I have nightmares, or did any of the shootings I was involved in keep me up at night? Not in a million years. They were his consequences because of his actions. It's the same as if I got shot and injured, or I became a paraplegic and was in a wheelchair as a result of being shot by him or someone else. That was my choice and my option to be there. At any time, I could have withdrawn, but you don't and I didn't. There's no use later on me pushing myself around in a wheelchair thinking, 'Ah, fuck. I should never have joined the SOG. I should never have done this or done that.' I could have stayed at home in the garden that day and wrapped myself in cotton wool . . . it's a choice. Everyone has a choice.

It's as black and white, cut and dry as that. He had the option to surrender, to peacefully come out and be processed . . . He chose not to go down that path and these are his consequences, not mine.

As for the number of shots we fired, well, it's not over until you're confident it's over. If someone shoots at me even once, I'll keep shooting back at them until their weapon is down. If they're still holding on to the weapon, I'll keep shooting them until I know that I've severed their spinal cord and they can't move anymore. That's what you have to do, so you do it. It really is a test of character because it's not everyone's cup of tea. Some guys who joined the SOG just said, 'Fuck that – I don't want to do this shit', and quit. That was their choice.

—

At the coroner's inquest into the shooting, an examination of the gunman's weapon offered a vital piece of evidence that vindicated the SOG's actions.

SARGE: There was a bullet from one of the 9-mm handguns lodged in his rifle scope. It was so disintegrated they couldn't tell what it was at first but forensic testing showed it had come from one of our guns. That corroborated our accounts that his weapon had been pointed directly at us during the shootout.

—

Because of the incredible circumstances relating to the lodged bullet, White's damaged rifle scope has become somewhat of a trophy and still hangs proudly on display at the SOG headquarters.

RAYDEN: People could ask, 'Who shot first?' Well, we don't shoot first unless we know that we're under threat. All I saw initially was that muzzle flash when I came in the back door and thought, 'Fuck! He is shooting at us!' With the distraction grenades going off at the front, it was hard to hear everything that was going on inside at the beginning. If there were no distraction grenades, then we would've heard all the shots coming our way and we would have known he was firing, but, as it was, I couldn't hear him shooting at us initially; I could only see the flashes. When the grenades stopped, then we could hear him firing, but the bullet in the scope was proof that he definitely was shooting at us and he definitely had the gun aimed at us.

—

Talk also spread that the gunman never fired a shot at the SOG, because investigators couldn't find any empty shells at the scene from White's .22 rifle. Those rumours were later quashed by another critical discovery.

SARGE: Five of my handgun rounds had hit him, but two were unaccounted for. It turned out, the missing casings from my gun, and some from the gunman's rifle, were embedded in the bottom of our boots, stuck in all the mud.

—

Despite the favourable evidence, the SOG was still put through the wringer by members of the homicide squad and the state coroner. Some felt that the level of scrutiny placed on them was unjust and over the top.

RAYDEN: The only thing that really pissed me off about that job was being investigated for supposedly using too much force. That's the thing that kept me up at night, nothing else. As I said to the A/C who initiated the investigation, 'You fucking sent us in there to arrest him and now you're saying we used too much force? This bloke shot an old lady who he'd never met and then shot at us. What were we meant to do?'

I couldn't believe they were coming at us with all this bullshit. We were trained never to retreat and to always advance. Were we supposed to run away while we were being shot at? Cut me an arse! This officer was of the belief we'd overstepped the mark and I'm thinking, 'Where are you getting off, mate?' He wants to chase every rabbit down every burrow, but he never spoke to us directly about it. Not once did he come to me and explain what was happening and why he wanted to investigate us. It was all done on the belief that we had done something wrong. I remember thinking at the time, 'Fuck it. I'm gonna resign and get out.'

At the SOG, we had the hardest job in the force but constantly copped it up the arse. There was very little support back then. When someone from Force Command orders you to go into a house occupied by a crazed gunman, you don't ask questions; you just do it. It's like being a player in footy. When the runner comes out and gives you an instruction, you don't say, 'Oh, hang on. Can you go back and ask the coach why he wants me to do that?' That's not part of what we do. Others formulate the tactics and we execute those tactics to the best of our ability. The sideline critics are always there, and in our line of work everything should be scrutinised, but sometimes they just don't get it, because they're not there or not educated in our area of expertise and can't understand how and why certain things happen. Some people aren't out on the ground playing the game because they're on the bench, where they belong. No one can appreciate what it feels like to have a gun pointed at them, until they have a gun pointed at them.

HAZE: We had to surrender all our tactical gear including our blacks and gloves so they could be formally examined for GSR [gunshot residue] and for swabs to be taken that night. As a former detective, I understood investigations, transparency and the need for the truth to be determined, however we were not really given much time in the immediate aftermath to debrief the job on a personal and professional level. We were in effect, treated like homicide suspects, with little recognition that we had just performed a lawful, forced entry under orders into an ambush situation in order to protect members of the community. The next morning, I was interviewed by homicide squad detectives back at the scene and had to do a video re-enactment. The blood on the floor hadn't even coagulated and there were bits of White's body and flesh on the floors and walls even though the scene had been processed overnight. You could still smell the cordite from the gunfire and here we were, walking through the scene expected to calmly respond to questions under a formal caution that we could face court. Everyone has a PhD in hindsight but thinking about that over the years since, it was a pretty ordinary way to be treated for doing our job.

There were many, including a number in Force Command, that wanted to know how we could have possibly fired thirty-six rounds during a house entry. There is an expectation that just like the movies, we all stick to the script and just wander into a life-threatening situation and do a double tap [two quick shots in the same spot] right between the crook's eyes and it's all over.

Before this job, I had won the best assaulter award on a police tactical assault group with the Australian SAS. I, like the rest of the team, was an accomplished close quarter battle operator and know things don't always run to script.

TANGO: If someone only squeezes one round off, to me, that says maybe there's not a real threat there to begin with. If you need to shoot, it will be a fast BANG! BANG! BANG! You've got to pull that trigger until the threat is gone. If you go BANG! and then wait, then you're not very well trained or you should be thinking, 'Should I be pulling that trigger again?' To shoot once just doesn't make sense to me.

If you've done the right thing, why should you be worried? Everyone is different and it's not for me to judge them, because I know some guys have had some close calls and have quit as a result – it affects everyone differently. But the criticism is just water off a duck's back to me. You weren't there and you don't know what it's like. If you hear the criticism, there's no use getting upset about it. The offender always dictates the way it's going; it's not as if we make the path. They've made the path by their actions and they're always given ample opportunity to end things peacefully.

—

An autopsy revealed that White had 139 pieces of shrapnel embedded in his body, which fed the hysteria regarding allegations of excessive force even further. Compounding the sense of tension in the court was the attendance of the gunman's foster parents. Being face to face with a deceased's family was always tough, but on this occasion Sarge was surprised by the treatment he received.

SARGE: I felt that society let that guy down; it wasn't our fault he was killed. Society put him in that position and we had to clean that mess up. When the inquest concluded, his foster mother walked over and hugged me. There was a bit of trepidation on my part. She knew all of our names, having been in court for so long, and said, 'I'm so sorry.' I was like, 'Jesus

Christ. What do I do here?' If she had abused us, it wouldn't have worried me. She was trying to say, 'Don't worry about us, we're all right. We're at peace with it.' It certainly surprised me to have someone come up and say 'Sorry' after you've just killed their son.

—

In handing down his finding into the shooting, state coroner Iain West said:

> In looking at whether the police response was in proportion to the threat that confronted them, it is necessary to consider not only the immediate threat, but the background circumstances. Prior to the entry occurring, the SOG entry team were aware of the deceased's propensity to violence or, at the very least, irrational behaviour. They knew he had menaced members of the public, firing shots prior to entering the Station Road premises, that shots had been fired at or in the general direction of police members after entering the premises, that Mrs McGaw had been shot and that remarks in the nature of threats to kill had been made on several occasions.
>
> Upon entering, I am satisfied the police were confronted by the deceased in a 'shooting stance', with his rifle at his shoulder and aimed in their direction immediately prior to a shot being fired. After an initial volley of return fire, I accept that the threat remained, with the deceased positioned behind the door architrave and his firearm pointed in the direction of SOG members. A second shot I am satisfied was fired by the deceased, resulting in a second volley of police fire.
>
> The response by police resulted in a large volume of shots fired. However, this must be viewed in light of the incident occurring over a matter of six to eight seconds, with a simultaneous

response to the threat by a number of SOG members. The fact that there were two volleys of return fire is consistent with a controlled and proportioned use of force. This, coupled with the fact that they had been fired upon by the deceased, satisfied me that they acted appropriately in their self-defence . . . no police member can be said to have contributed to the cause of death . . .

A few weeks after the shooting, when all the evidence had been collected and the crime scene was cleared, the SOG returned to the home. It looked like a war zone inside. There were bloodstains all over the floors, the architraves and cornices around the doors and ceiling had been blasted to smithereens, and sheets of plaster had been torn off the walls by numerous handgun rounds and shotgun pellets. Shards of glass had been scattered across the carpet in the living and lounge rooms, and mud had been traipsed through the entire house. There was only one thing left to do.

RAYDEN: It wasn't a Toorak mansion by any stretch of the imagination but it was a nice old home. It was clean and tidy . . . well, at first. But we went back there anyway to help clean it up and repair everything that had been damaged afterwards. If we didn't do it, no one else was going to. We didn't have to do it, but we chose to.

7

THE FUNNEL OF FIRE

Whoever says he is in the light and hates his brother is still in darkness.

1 John 2:9

If there's one place you never want to be as a member of the SOG, it's caught in the fatal funnel of fire. Assault-team members are drilled to get in and out of the funnel of fire as quickly as possible; otherwise, they risk being killed in a hail of bullets.

The term refers to a doorway or narrow entry point to a room or a house, where a police officer or soldier is most vulnerable to enemy gunfire. It is best illustrated as a cone-shaped path leading in both directions away from the entry of any given room. When a raid occurs, anyone expecting intruders will instinctively focus all their attention and firepower on the doorway, because other than a wall, roof or window breach, it's the only way of entering a room.

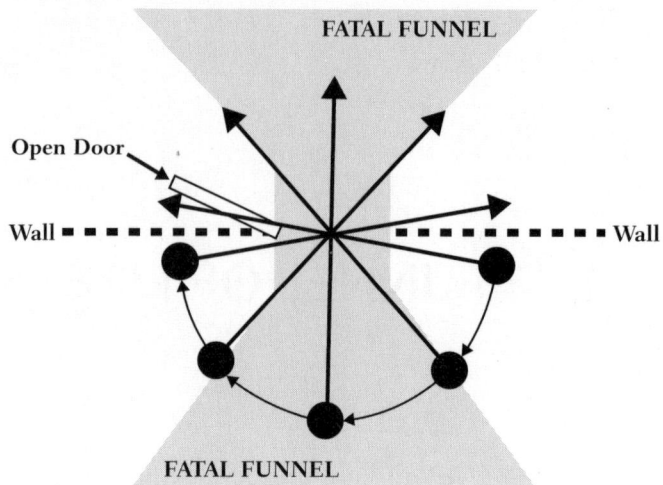

In tactical policing and the army, not respecting the fatal funnel of fire can be the difference between life and death.

DELTA: We do a lot of raids at night and in complete darkness, and our torches will be the only source of light. So when a door opens and the gunman sees all this light suddenly spilling into the room he is in, even the worst shot in the world in terms of accuracy only needs to aim and fire in the general direction of that incoming light and the chances are he'll strike anyone or anything in that lit-up zone.

OSCAR: When we enter a house, we have to focus on so many different areas, but all a gunman has to do is point at one door and fire at the fatal funnel when he sees any movement. So when we open that door, members will go high [stand], low [crouch], break left and break right to avoid being in the fatal funnel, or the light, for too long.

Thomas 'Tommy' Messinger awoke to the sounds of someone trying to break into his home just after 5.00 am. When he peered out of his bedroom window to investigate, he caught a glimpse of some movement at the front of his house. He armed himself with a .32 automatic pistol that he normally kept under his pillow, and a semi-automatic M1 carbine that was next to his bed. As he prepared to confront the intruders, his wife and eighteen-month-old daughter remained asleep. The twenty-six-year-old had reason to fear the worst, having made many enemies. Part of a small but heavily armed paramilitary group of about four men, the security guard was on the police force's radar.

—

As a former member of the Victoria Police Force's major crime squad, Viper was used to dealing with the state's top ten wanted criminals. On various jobs within the squad, he'd worked closely with the SOG and was so impressed and full of admiration for its members, he felt compelled to join the group. On this particular raid though, he was about to face a level of violence and resistance he'd never before encountered.

VIPER: Our intel was that Messinger and his crew were heavily influenced by neo-Nazi philosophies. Each member was always armed, with at least a handgun, and they were to be considered incredibly dangerous. They would boast that the police would 'never take them alive'.

—

Messinger and his group were suspected of several car thefts, a car bombing, assault, two factory bombings, possession of illegal firearms and a handful of armed robberies over a three-month period. Most concerning, however, was their reported desire to 'take down' the SOG.

Detectives had been watching the gang for some time and had observed them undertaking intensive physical exercise and training sessions on a country property with semi-automatic weapons. A man close to the crew advised detectives that the alleged ringleader, Phillip 'the Iceman' Wilson, recently claimed to have been visited by Adolf Hitler and was ordered by him to commit crimes and other 'jobs'. Wilson adopted the alias of Kurt Sepp Philippe Hessler and was a self-confessed 'gun freak' who 'liked to hear things go bang'. Because of his ability to build and willingness to use explosives, he was later suspected and ultimately cleared of having some involvement in the Russell Street bombing. It was also said that Wilson was a 'madman' who would 'shoot anyone who gets in his way, including police' and was 'capable of murder'. He was in possession of genuine Nazi daggers and often cut himself with them, such was his fanaticism.

A stand-over man in the making, and a 7-feet-plus-tall one at that, Wilson wanted his days of selling home-made brass knuckles for $70 a pop to be over. He also wanted 'a lot of money in short time' to start up a security company. His idea was to rob and bomb companies, then return several days later and offer them security and protection. But to begin, his gang needed the right tools. They targeted a historical society museum west of Bendigo and raided the building for its treasure trove of firearms. Using bolt-cutters to remove a window grille, they smashed the glass to gain entry to the building and stole the most modern weapons that were on display. Their haul included a Japanese sword, five pistols, fifteen revolvers and three sub-machine guns. Wilson put someone close to him, a tool-maker, to use producing silencers for all their new toys and had him working on a special gun that could penetrate armoured cars and ballistic vests, as well as fire tear gas.

Now well equipped, Wilson began taking private helicopter lessons and was planning to steal an aircraft to use for a 'big job'.

He also started experimenting with explosives that were given to him by a friend who had a licence for them. They first blew up a car, followed by two wreckers/spare parts yards. Each day, their confidence and daring grew.

Among the targets next identified by the group were a university that held large sums of cash on site, another museum with more machine guns and – finally an easy heist – a small regional bank that could yield them about $20,000.

The ARS formed a special task force codenamed 'SAS' to work exclusively on the job. When new information came to light that the suspects were in the process of obtaining a grenade launcher and had been monitoring the movements of the SOG, they decided to pounce.

VIPER: It was getting too dangerous, and the real fear was that members of the public were going to get injured or killed if we allowed these blokes to continue doing what they were doing.

–

Seven houses and properties belonging to the suspects were listed for simultaneous, early-morning raids by seven teams made up of SOG members and ARS detectives. One of those was Tommy Messinger's place.

Viper charged at Messinger's front door, using his body weight as a battering ram. The technique had worked for him just a week before, when he successfully broke down a door during another raid, but what he didn't know was that this door was a lot different.

VIPER: It was a much heavier door, and Messinger had put extra locks on it, so when I took a run to hit it, it didn't budge. So that first loud bang on the door, unfortunately, would have been the noise that woke Messinger up. Otherwise, he would have been sound asleep when we came in.

—

With the door still intact, one of the men, Alpha, took two swings with a sledgehammer, but, surprisingly, he was also unable to bust it open.

Positioned at the front of the single-storey, brick-veneer home, one of the SOG's cut-off-team members saw the curtains in the front bedroom move and knew the element of surprise was gone. 'Go! Go! Go!' he yelled to the SOG team at the front entrance. 'He's seen us!'

Viper took another run at the door, and this time it snapped in half. First in, he headed towards the main bedroom, which was just metres away on his right-hand side.

VIPER: It was pitch-black at that time. The torch system that was attached to my shotgun broke when I rammed the door, so I couldn't light up the room. I still have the vision of blackness, but also seeing these bright orange sparks suddenly appear from inside the room.

—

The 'sparks' were muzzle flashes from Messinger's .32 pistol. Viper had been shot twice, but he didn't know it at the time and didn't have time to check.

VIPER: I can recall feeling something, but I thought it was just pieces of wood splintering off the doorframe and hitting me. You see it in the movies that when people are shot they get knocked down from the force of the bullets. I was still standing, so I didn't think much of it at the time. I later discovered that the first bullet deflected off my two-way radio, which was strapped against my left armpit, and into my vest, over my heart, while the second shot sizzled past my chest and grazed my right arm.

—

Viper had intended to enter the bedroom leading with his right shoulder, but he was forced to spin out of the doorway when Messinger started firing. Now out of the 'fatal funnel of fire', he spun out of danger and sought cover down the hall.

VIPER: I was meant to go into that room; that was the plan. The first man in is not supposed to stop and is supposed to cop the rounds so the others following him could come in and take out the shooter. The door is only as wide as it is. It's a bit like the 'Spartan on the bridge' – one man can stop an entire army if he stands at that choke point and puts up a fight. But I couldn't go in straight away because the initial shots prevented me from doing so.

—

When Messinger realised Viper was still standing and was mobile, he grabbed his more powerful M1 rifle, which had two thirty-round magazines taped together end to end, and opened fire again.

VIPER: I fired at a forty-five-degree angle from the hallway to where I thought I'd last seen those sparks come from. But there were rounds coming back at me and I could tell by the sound and force of them that they were much bigger ones this time. I could feel them moving through the air as I was back-pedalling down the hallway, trying to get out of the line of fire.

As I took a step backwards, a round would hit the wall just in front of me, so I was getting out of the way just in time. It was a semi-automatic, so he just kept pulling the trigger and was just pumping bullets through the walls, guessing where I was. One round narrowly missed my head and passed through a plaster wall, wooden doorframe, brick wall, back fence and ended up lodging in the side of a boat that was sitting in a neighbour's yard.

If Messinger had used the M1 first, there's no way I would be here today. The .32 pistol is probably one of the weakest guns ever made, but the M1 certainly would have gone right through my vest and done some serious damage. I'm probably lucky he didn't hit me in the face with the .32, to be honest. It was just pure luck that he had the smaller gun and pure luck where it hit me.

—

Stranded in the hallway and under fire, Viper tried to reload his shotgun but it jammed, putting him in an even more precarious position.

VIPER: When I fired my first shot, I had automatically reloaded, but in the mayhem I did it without even knowing. So after my second shot, I thought I had to reload, not realising I still had a live round in the chamber.

—

Viper cycled the live round out of the gun in an effort to clear the mechanism and get his weapon working again.

VIPER: I remember thinking, 'I'm fucked here. He's coming to get me and there's nothing I can do about it.'

—

Messinger had moved forwards and into the doorway of the bedroom to get a better vantage point down the hallway on Viper, but it proved to be a deadly mistake – he too had stepped directly into the fatal funnel of fire.

Opposite Messinger's bedroom and slightly to the left, crouched behind a rubber plant that offered little cover, Kek took aim at the now exposed gunman.

VIPER: Kek had followed me into the house and broke to the left and into the lounge room. When all the shooting started, he dropped to one knee and then saw Messinger emerge as he was trying to poke his gun down the hallway, looking to finish me off with the M1. By putting himself in his own doorway, Messinger gave Kek a clear shot. The rest is history; Kek fired a single round and virtually blew his head clean off.

—

Kek's shot hit Messinger in the left eye, killing him instantly.

VIPER: Kek saved my life, because if he hadn't blown his head off, Messinger just would have come and found me in the hallway, and we would have continued the shootout. Given the weapon he had, he would have probably won, I'd say. Add to that the fact that he'd only fired about ten or so shots at me, and he had sixty rounds on him, whereas I only had a shotty.

—

Although Messinger was down, the rest of the house still had to be cleared, and Viper feared the main ringleader of the neo-Nazi pack, Phil Wilson, was in another room in accordance with the intelligence the SOG received during briefings from detectives.

Kek flicked the lights on in the lounge room and bedroom and ordered Viper to, 'Clear the rest of the house!'

VIPER: I moved back down the hallway and entered a bedroom at the rear of the house. As you can imagine, we were pretty wound up at that stage, having been shot at by Messinger. I detected movement on my left side and spun around and put my finger back on the trigger, ready to fire again. I looked down the barrel of my shotty, and stopped. Inside was an eighteen-month-old girl, and my heart sank as a wave of emotion swept over me. Fuck! I still, to this day, shudder at how close she could have been to being shot and killed in all the chaos. The poor thing would have been terrified. I picked her up in my left arm, with my shotty in my right, because I was still waiting for Wilson to appear at any moment, and I took her to her mum as the other boys cleared the house.

—

Wilson was arrested, without any resistance, at another location during a simultaneous raid.

VIPER: Talking about the shooting like that in a sequence, it sounds like it took minutes to happen, but it was far from it. It would have all been over in five to ten seconds at most. It was that quick. The shots were all over the top of each other. It was just CRACK! CRACK! Then BOOM! BOOM! BOOM! BOOM! BOOM! BOOM! BOOM! BOOM! BOOM! And then Kek's final shot, BOOM! And it was all over.

Looking back on it, our biggest concern was Phil Wilson. He was the leader and was meant to be the real 'bad one' of the lot, not Messinger. Messinger was just the B-man or second in charge, and wasn't meant to be the one who would fire up and

Meet 'God'. Former Chief Commissioner Mick Miller, now ninety-one, took over the force when terrorism first reared its ugly head in Australia. He started the Special Operations Group in 1977, dubbing its members the 'Sons of God'.

Simon O'Dwyer / Fairfax Syndication

Courtesy Victoria Police

Left & below: Being the son of a Son of God wasn't easy. My older brother Ben and I never knew when Dad was going to be called out. When Dad 'suited up' it was my signal to hang on to him and not let go!

Opposite top: Brothers in arms. At one stage there were thirteen O'Loughlins serving concurrently in the Victorian police. From left: Robert, Albert (Grandpa), Neil, Douglas (Dad), Geoffrey, Barry – the rest are my uncles.

Opposite bottom: Harold 'Chippy' Norton (front row, fifth from left) was a Royal Marine Commando in WWII and the perfect candidate to head up the inaugural Special Operations Group. Here he is with some of the original squad.

dallystreetimages.com

Above: My father was a member of the SOG for eighteen years (1981–98), as a bomb technician, general tactician and later Chief Inspector in charge of the Group. When he wasn't working I took every opportunity to spend time with Dad, particularly when it meant firing new guns at the shooting range.

Above: Me with Dad, my one and only hero.

SOG intake training is gruelling and exhausting, yet hugely rewarding. It's also a great bonding experience for the aspiring Sons of God.

All images courtesy Victoria Police

SOG training is as much mental as it is physical. Firearms training requires great focus and concentration, with trainees expected to shoot with precision while displaying split-second decision-making skills. Like all components of the SOG intake process, failure is not an option and the slightest mistake will often result in instant dismissal from the course.

All images courtesy Victoria Police

The blast from the ferocious Russell Street car bombing on 27 March 1986 destroyed parts of Victoria Police headquarters, seriously injured dozens of people and left twenty-one-year-old Constable Angela Taylor dead – the first Australian policewoman killed in the line of duty.

Neale Duckworth / Fairfax Syndication

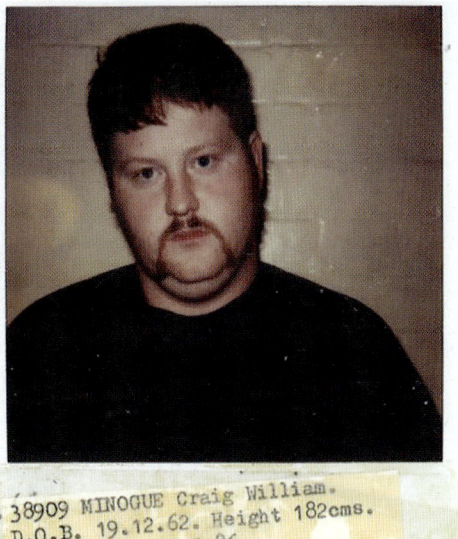
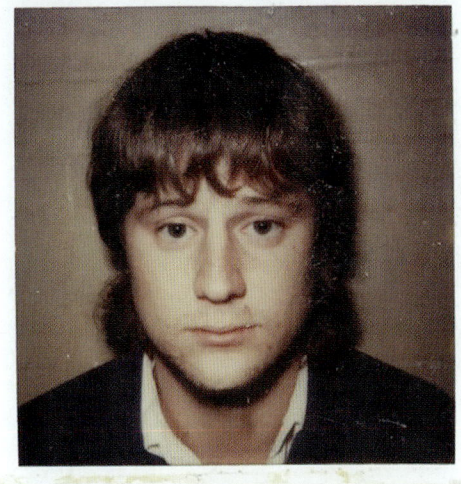

Courtesy Victoria Police

38909 MINOGUE Craig William.
D.O.B. 19.12.62. Height 182cms.
Photo Taken 31.5.86.

16492 MINOGUE Rodney Joseph.
D.O.B. 11.11.65. Height 178cms.
Photo Taken 2.6.86.

Russell Street suspects. The notorious Minogue brothers put up little resistance when Dad and the SOG hunted them down. Craig (above left) and two accomplices, Stan Taylor and Peter Reed, were eventually found guilty of the bombing. Rodney (above right) was charged but acquitted on appeal.

News Ltd / Newspix

Hidden in a stolen Holden parked outside, the Russell Street bomb sent shrapnel ripping through the lower floors of police headquarters.

The SOG lock and load, ready for action.

Courtesy Victoria Police

Above: Detectives point to bullet holes in 'Viper's' uniform after he was shot twice during a violent gunfight with neo-Nazi Tommy Messinger.

Right: Tommy Messinger was part of an underworld sect training to wipe out the SOG. Evidence seized after the shooting showed his obsession with Nazi propaganda and violence.

Courtesy Victoria Police

News Ltd / Newspix

A woman leads children from a Hawthorn kindergarten after Serafettin Huseyin took several four-year-olds hostage and doused them in petrol. The SOG moved swiftly and decisively.

have a go at us like that, so it caught us all off guard a bit. It wasn't meant to happen that way.

—

With detectives and paramedics on the scene, Viper and Kek were debriefing in the lounge room when they noticed something peculiar.

VIPER: Kek looked over at me and said, 'There's a hole in you!' He pointed right at my left pectoral area and slid his finder inside the tear in my uniform. I replied, 'Oh, shit!' and started removing layers of equipment to unzip my black jumpsuit. We eventually found a bullet lodged in all the layers – the one that had clipped my radio. It had come through my Kevlar vest sideways, dropped down and was sitting in the first couple of layers of my vest, right up against my sternum. There was another hole in my right sleeve where the other round had sliced its way through between my top pocket and arm.

—

Viper was checked over by a doctor but, miraculously, there was barely any bruising to his heart and chest. Viper returned to work the next day and, in typical SOG fashion, he refused, and still refuses now, to admit that Messinger shot him once, let alone twice.

VIPER: Technically, he only put two holes in my clothing. I'd been hit with rounds, but nothing penetrated my flesh and there was no blood. It didn't hurt and, at the time, I didn't even know it had happened. It was only that we found the holes in my uniform and found the bullet in my vest after the fact. When I realised I'd been hit, I didn't fall over and faint. So I like to refer to it as being 'shot at', not 'being shot'.

—

After the shooting there were rumours that Wilson and his crew were seeking retribution against the SOG.

VIPER: There was talk that they wanted to grab Kek and me and push us out of a helicopter. So there was some heightened awareness on our part in terms of looking after ourselves in the wash-up, but we weren't afraid of them. If they had tried to come for us, we would have dealt with them accordingly – don't you worry about that.

—

As it turned out, Wilson never got the chance to enact revenge on the SOG. While on bail, he allegedly tried his hand in the illicit drug trade, and, after slaying two of his drug mules during a picnic one afternoon, he was later ambushed and shot in the chest at point blank range. The hit was carried out for a reported $5000.

When the ensuing coroner's inquest into the Messinger shooting concluded, Viper received a call from a homicide detective, Garry Landy, who offered him a small memento.

VIPER: He'd taken possession of the bullet that was lodged in my vest after it was released from evidence. I kept that bullet as a good-luck charm. I put a cap on it and threaded it with a gold chain and wore it around my neck for years, until recently, when I gave it to my son on his graduation into the army at Kapooka. 'This bullet couldn't kill me,' I told him. 'Wear it round your neck and it might save you too.'

8

JUDGEMENT DAY

For judgement is without mercy to one who has shown no
mercy. Mercy triumphs over judgement.

James 2:13

Peter McEvoy dropped to the floor and crawled along the carpet on his hands and knees towards the phone in his lounge room. Known as 'Bubble Brain' for his stupidity and ugly, oversized head, he started to shake profusely as he heard the sledgehammer crack into the lock on his front door. Although dumb, he wasn't silly enough to arm himself with a weapon because he knew exactly who was trying to get in.

Despite his fingers trembling uncontrollably, he somehow hit every intended number on his phone pad and waited for his lifeline on the other end to pick up the receiver. 'Hello?' the solicitor answered. 'Ah, thank God!' McEvoy blurted out. 'They're here. They're here now! They're coming in the door right now!' Seconds later, a team of SOG crashed through the front entrance.

DANE: When I got through the door, the first thing I saw was this supposedly big, tough, bad-ass enforcer, alleged police killer and bank robber, down on his knees blubbering. He had one hand on his head and the phone in the other. He was saying 'they're coming to get me!' to the person on the other end of the line. He thought we were there to kill him. He was as dumb as they come. He used to do armed robberies and would wear a stocking over his head as a disguise. The Armed Robbery Squad would pick him out on the surveillance footage with no worries, because of the abnormal size of his head. He was never smart enough to realise what he was doing and why he'd always get arrested.

—

McEvoy was on the police radar ever since the mid-1970s, when he was involved in a number of heinous rapes of girls as young as thirteen. The SOG was after him on this occasion for his links to the slaughter of two young policemen, Constables Steven Tynan and Damian Eyre, who were shot dead in Walsh Street, South Yarra, in 1988. McEvoy was later acquitted by a jury for the murders after the Crown's key witness sank the case by flipping and committing perjury.

OSCAR: After we arrested him, he said to me, 'So, am I off or what?' When I said, 'What do you mean by "off"?' he replied, 'Are you guys going to kill me now?' I laughed and said, 'Nah, we don't do that.'

—

The SOG has developed a formidable reputation among the state's worst criminals as being an unforgiving and uncompromising unit of men prepared to go to any length to carry out an operation successfully. Some even considered the members of the SOG to be more crazy and dangerous than them. The level of training, speed, aggression and force the SOG used when making arrests meant even the bad guys were left in awe.

LIMA: Most of the time when the crooks realised it was us at their door, they'd just lie down on the ground and give up. We have a fearsome reputation. Word was, if you want to do business, go to another state, because Victoria has a zero tolerance. That was the reputation we relied on, and it wasn't given to us; we had to establish it. We made it through hard work, and by being straight and ruthless.

We tracked various Walsh Street shooting suspects all over the place and were one step behind them, but if they felt we were close to catching up with them, they would do their best to avoid letting us get them inside a house. They would either turn themselves in to police or, if they knew they were running hot, they would surrender in a car park somewhere or walk out the front of a building they were holed up in with their hands up.

DANE: I actually think it's a good thing that we have that reputation and there is that fear there because we have a far safer result because of it, as opposed to it being the other way around. If criminals and violent offenders were happy and willing to take us on, resist our attempts to arrest them and fight back, then that's when someone's gonna get hurt, and it's not ever going to be us. It has to be a far better result when crooks just throw their hands up in the air straight away, give up and say, 'I've been naughty and I've been caught . . . I never want to be caught by those SOG guys again.'

—

According to Dane, one of Australia's most notorious criminals, Christopher 'Badness' Binse, tried to avoid plying his trade (mainly robbing banks) in Victoria because of his fear of the state's SOG.

DANE: We'd arrested him in Daylesford and, because he was such an escape risk, having broken out of two facilities around the country in the space of six weeks, they decided we had to babysit him. I was actually in the cell with him for a period of time. Within the first couple of hours, we started chatting and I said to him sarcastically, 'So, why don't we ever see you down here in Victoria doing business?' He shook his head and went, 'Nup. I come down here and don't do anything wrong cos I reckon you SOG bastards would kill me.' I said, 'Huh? Why is that?' and he replied, 'Come off it, mate! You know why! You blokes are fucking mad!'

MACK: The crooks know not to fuck with us because they won't come out of it too well. That reputation serves us, and the community, very well. They know that we are highly trained and when we come to get them, we will come hard and will have always done our homework on them.

—

Sitting in a house or a building with the SOG coming to get you was an experience the members were forced to go through themselves.

ROGUE: We role-play during our training all the time. It is always one of the worst things that you can do. Whenever I heard the words 'All right, Rogue, it's your turn to be the offender this time,' I'd be thinking to myself, 'Argh, fuck! I don't want to do this,' because it was frightening, it was scary and it was fucking horrible. You'll be sent into a room inside a training house and all these blokes are about to come storming in there to get you. It's weird because you know they're all your mates, and only ten minutes earlier you were standing behind them going through a mock raid with them. But when you're the 'crook' and they're about to come barrelling through to get you, you shit yourself. It can be daylight, in the middle of the day, during the middle of the week and at our own training facility and I still get that feeling deep inside of, 'Urgghhh, I don't like this one bit.' My stomach churns with nervousness and fear.

You could be in the back room and you start to hear the doors getting kicked in at the front of the house followed by lots of yelling of 'Police! Don't move!' then sometimes a burst of gunfire, depending on the scenario. You know they're coming and all you'd be thinking is, 'Fuck! Fuck! Fuck!'

Everyone's reaction is different when we hit them. They might drop to the ground and surrender straight away or they might actually shit their pants because it's fucken scary when we come bursting in. Most people's reactions are like stunned mullets, with their hands in the air, saying, 'Whoa, what the fuck is happening?' Then there are the crazy types who just want to go out with a bang and take as many of us as they can with them. For some blokes who do decide to take you on, Jesus Christ, they are single-minded and only want to cause menace, havoc and trouble for you.

MACK: We had a lot of confrontations and it was unfortunate that a number of them resulted in someone's death, but in some of those cases, it still would have gone that way regardless. I don't believe some of those guys would have ever given themselves up, and without the element of surprise someone is going to get hurt on our side. You're probably going to end up with more injuries and more deaths.

9

DIVINE INTERVENTION

Therefore take up the whole armour of God, that you may be able to withstand in the evil day, and having done all, to stand firm.

Ephesians 6:13

Rayden nestled back into the lounge chair with his shotgun balanced perfectly on his lap and looked over at Lima and Mack and chuckled.

'What are you laughing at?' Lima asked him, confused.

'Can't you see the humour in it?' Rayden replied. 'This is all a bit surreal, don't you think?'

'No, why? What are you talking about?'

Playing on the telly in front of them was the cult-classic sitcom *The Beverly Hillbillies*. It was the fact they were watching it in the lounge room of a gunman who was lying dead on the floor in a bedroom just a few metres away from them that had tickled Rayden's fancy.

RAYDEN: It was at that moment when we realised we'd just survived a gunfight. We were alive watching *The Beverly Hillbillies* on his TV and he wasn't. The irony was that it could have easily been the other way around. We could have been dead. I can vividly remember one of the main characters in the show, Elly May Clampett, looking out at their new swimming pool and asking her father Jed Clampett, 'Hey Pa, can I go swimming in the cee-ment pond?' I found it kind of funny and that line has been stuck in my head ever since.

LIMA: It was very much like, 'What's wrong with this picture?' It wasn't until Rayden pointed it out that we realised how surreal the situation was. Only Rayden could add some light to a shitty situation like that one.

—

Homicide-squad detectives were on their way to the address to conduct interviews with Mack and Lima, because they had discharged their firearms and killed Cambodian stand-over man Vuthy Tep, who also went by the nicknames 'Mr T' and 'Tiger'. Rayden, the SOG team leader on this particular job, was there to make sure there could be no allegation of collusion between Mack and Lima in any ensuing coronial inquest. 'You blokes have got nothing to fear,' Rayden reassured the pair. 'You haven't done anything wrong.'

Vuthy Tep had been making a name for himself in the Cambodian community as a violent robber who was quick to use lethal force to get what he wanted. He'd carried out three armed robberies, each an hour apart, with an accomplice, Veth Ouch, the night before the SOG dropped by to pay him a visit at his Doveton address.

During this night of violence, Tep and Ouch robbed a man and his three daughters in Noble Park using a sawn-off .22 rifle, knife and hatchet. They ransacked the family's home looking for money. Tep fired a number of shots into the ground near the man's feet before fleeing.

The duo next terrorised another father after breaking into his home at 2.00 am. Tep and Ouch demanded money, but when the man said he didn't have any, they stood him up in front of his family and shot him twice – once in the right forearm and once in the left forearm. He was rushed to hospital and was lucky not to have died from the injuries.

In their third and final robbery, Tep shot at a man again, but on this occasion he fired several times, signalling a rise in his aggression and desperation. When Tep missed his intended target and tried to shoot him again, his gun jammed, which enabled the man to defend himself. A brief struggle ensued before Ouch stepped in to stab the man in the shoulder with a knife.

LIMA: The investigators were basically chasing them from house to house as numerous calls came in to police. After talking to the victims and witnesses, they were able to get a clear description of the gun Tep was using in particular, the fact that it was a 'short weapon with red tape on it'. A couple of the witnesses said that, after each shot, Tep would 'mess about and fiddle with the gun'. Now that kind of information is important for us because we established that he didn't have a reliable weapon. For him to shoot, then have to make adjustments to it, shoot and then make adjustments again wasn't ideal. As it turned out, that tiny snippet of information ended up being critical for us and especially me.

–

Following the spate of violent hold-ups, police tracked Tep and Ouch to a small commission house south-east of Melbourne. Knowing they were armed and extremely dangerous, the officers made a request to their superiors to ask for the SOG to come and make the arrests.

MACK: We headed straight out to the house for a look. There was an unmarked police unit sitting off Tep's place keeping obs [observation] on him to make sure he didn't suddenly leave. We did a thorough reconnaissance of the place and took detailed notes. That involved looking at all the streets around the house to identify our 'form-up point' – the place we could form up undetected and then begin our walk up to the house for the raid. We looked for spots out front to place our cut-off teams – they can either be inside the yard or outside. If they're positioned outside the yard, they'll just jump the fence once the assault team kicks the door in.

—

The SOG rendezvoused at the local police station and presented all the information they'd obtained from the reconnaissance to their superior officers, and a plan of attack was then formulated and subsequently agreed on.

The SOG considered sending in a police dog initially, but because there were a number of people inside, the dog would not have been able to identify Tep or Ouch, or distinguish friend from foe. Tear gas was also rejected as an option, as was a 'call and contain' scenario where police would order Tep to come out and surrender.

OSCAR: The number of innocent people inside was problematic. Letting him know we were there would have enabled him to grab a hostage and use them as leverage. A forced-entry raid was the best option, given the information and circumstances. We had to use superior numbers, speed and the element of surprise to try and grab Tep and Ouch before they could access any firearms. We had been told that Tep kept one firearm under his pillow, one in a couch and another in his car. I told the men who were going into the house to maintain firearms discipline, to watch for any knives and to remember their training at all times.

—

Just before dawn the next morning, a five-man SOG assault team formed up a few blocks away from where Tep and Ouch were staying.

LIMA: It was a day job, and we fucking hate day jobs because the chances of being burnt are so much higher. The risks are so much greater than night jobs.

—

At the form-up point, each member of the assault team made sure their kit was in order and carried out final weapons checks.

LIMA: At that point, we will eyeball each other and make sure everyone is ready to go. It's a matter of looking at each member in the team and asking them, 'Are you good?' and getting that all-important nod from them. Then we radio through to the boss at the command post and advise him, 'We're at the form-up point and ready to advance to the move-off point.'

—

The move-off point is the closest position the Soggies can possibly get to the target address without being 'burnt' or seen by the offender. It might be a brick wall or on the other side of the fence of a neighbouring property. The move-off point is where they gather for the final time.

LIMA: At that stage, you take a big, deep breath, get yourself settled and wait for the final guy to join the end of the line or

143

stack. Once everyone is settled, in order of march, the last man in the line will squeeze or tap the man in front, and that will start a domino effect. Each man squeezes or taps the man in front of him to signal, 'I'm ready.' This happens until the man at the front of the queue gets the final squeeze or tap. If the lead man doesn't get a tap, he just waits until he does. He can't afford to look over his shoulder or behind and take his eyes off what's ahead, because he's responsible for covering the team and eliminating any threats. He's one hundred per cent focused forwards at all times. The front man is the cover man for the line and then becomes the cut-off man. He will peel away from the front of the line when we narrow in on the house. There's also a cut-off team at the back of the house, and each cut-off will have a designated side of the house to watch: 'black' being the back, 'white' the front, 'green' the left side and 'red' the right side. A secondary entry point was always established in case there were any issues with the primary entry point.

—

With their firearms at the ready, the black-clad Soggies formed a single file and began a slow but steady march towards the house. Stepping in unison, they increased their pace gradually as they neared the entrance. Only a sudden call to 'Stand down!' from the inspector at the command post could stop them now.

LIMA: The move-off point is the last stage that anyone can make the call to 'stand down'. If the boss has given us the green light to 'Go!', he can't suddenly change his mind and radio to us 'Stop! Stop! Stop!' because it's too late. We're already out and we're vulnerable. We've got momentum and we are punching in. The minute we step away from the move-off point, we are committed to the job. There have been many instances where we've advanced to the move-up point but have then been ordered to drop back to the form-up point because something has happened and the circumstances have changed.

—

In a standard stack of five assaulters, the lead man is focused only on the entry point. The second man is backing up the lead man, and the third and fourth have to cover to the left and right flanks. The last man in the line has to cover to the rear and must keep looking back at 180 degrees for any danger or threats. Depending on the complexity of the job and the roles required, the number of Soggies in the assault team can vary. The most sought-after position of 'No. 1' entry man could be fourth or fifth in the line to begin with, because all the men ahead of him will peel off during the march up. When the cut-off man peels away from the head of the line to take up his position at the front of the house, the next man in the line then takes over as the cover man.

The entry man had to show no hesitation, and go in no matter what. The difference would be when there was an initial burst of gunfire coming from the room before entering or upon entering; there, the SOG member would be forced into an instinctive action of self-preservation and would need to assess the situation and re-evaluate his approach. But for a standard breach, you had to kick the door in and follow the momentum through, into the room.

LIMA: Everyone has their area of responsibility and that's it. The No. 1 entry man must always be the sharpest and best operator available. You want him to be 'the man' and someone everyone trusts. We are trained not to baulk – meaning not to hesitate to go into a room when we are the first in. The thing is about the jobs we do – when we have control – is that they're done at a time when people are in the deepest sleep and at their most vulnerable. We act swiftly and with a lot of aggression. If there was a situation (and thankfully there hasn't been) where someone hesitated or 'baulked', everyone's life would then be put at risk. You can't get to a door and stutter-step – it's too late; you've lost all the momentum and the crook now has an opportunity.

All a crook needs is a split second and they'll seize the initiative from us. It can be the tiniest opportunity and they'll grab it – you never know what they're thinking. They could go for a gun, a knife or even jump out a window and escape – anything. They're creatures of opportunity and they'll take the upper hand if you baulk at a doorway or hesitate. The flow-on effect is enormous when one man doesn't perform his task because it impacts on the rest of the team. You have to make sure the blokes on that entry team are the best of the best. If someone had a tendency to hesitate, we would make sure we found that out about them during the selection and intake process, not when they were on a real-life job.

—

Just before they stepped onto the front porch, the men activated the light systems on their guns to illuminate their path to their target and were surprised to see that the front door was wide open.

MACK: The tension really starts to grab hold of you at that point. You just zero in on that entry. Once we hit the fence line of his property, there was no stopping us. We all knew what each other was expected to do. We had to go in hard, we had to go in fast, and with clear heads.

LIMA: You go into the zone. There are no more distractions. You have an environmental awareness – so you'll see if a curtain moves in a window at the front, for example, but outside of those things you have to be focused and calm. The fact that the door was wide open meant we didn't have to set up there; it was instant access, which was fortunate because of it being a daylight job. The less time we spend idle in one spot in daylight, the better. With a closed door, you have to walk up, set up on either side and you would also need an MOE [method of entry] man with a sledgehammer or a ram or whatever.

RAYDEN: We thought we'd have to break the door down, but instead we just strolled right on in. It was pretty unusual.

—

Rayden (the No. 1) and his cover man Dane headed inside and continued straight ahead down the hallway. Mack was next in, with Lima following him to the left.

LIMA: It was a shitty old house. People were everywhere, sharing hot beds, and there were clearly a few different families residing there. The kitchen looked like a bomb had hit it and the entire joint was filthy. We entered the lounge room through a sliding door and the TV was playing the old children's show with Humphrey B. Bear. Two little kids were sitting there watching it, and a man and a woman – presumably their parents – were sitting on the couch behind them. They were tiny little kids and they were screaming, because we were yelling, 'Police! Don't move!'

We allowed the mum to hold the kids to her, because we quickly established that the adults weren't who we were looking for and weren't a threat. The older man certainly knew what was going on, and he threw his hands in the air straight away and didn't want anything to do with us. They had two guns pointed at them and were told in no uncertain terms, 'Don't move – stay there!' It was sad that the kids were put in that situation, horrible, but it wasn't our doing. The family allowed Tep and Ouch into that house and obviously knew them. Whether they were related or not, I'm not sure, but it was their choice to keep their company, knowing they were pieces of shit. It was a situation of their own making and the kids were young enough to get over it – they were only toddlers.

MACK: As we were checking them for weapons, Rayden and Dane were clearing the rest of the house and had found several other innocent occupants, including some more young children. I called for Bulldog to leave his cut-off position in the front yard and join us inside to watch over the group that we had just arrested.

—

Mack had the family under control, and Lima moved behind him and then to his side at about ninety degrees to provide cover. That angle provided solid and safe arcs of fire and eliminated any risk of crossfire.

LIMA: One of our biggest fears is police accidentally shooting police. It wasn't until I moved to Mack's flank that I realised I was standing in front of another door. It was to my left and was slightly ajar. Out of the corner of my eye, I saw some movement through the crack and a flash of black and immediately thought it was Rayden and Dane coming around, having cleared the rest of the house. I thought they'd gone up the hallway and were sweeping back towards us.

—

With his handgun in his left hand (being a left-hander), Lima reached across his body with his right hand and pushed at the door to open it wider. He wanted to let Rayden and Dane know that he was on the other side and that he and Mack had the lounge room covered.

LIMA: When I pushed the door, it opened up and then slammed back hard on me. I knew immediately, 'I have to go into that room – that's not my team in there and it needs clearing.' I yelled to Mack, 'Closed door! Closed door!' I squared up to the door this time and grabbed the handle with my right hand. As I turned it and cracked the lock [released the catch on the door], I kicked the door with my right foot high up, and it flew open but didn't go all the way.

—

With something stopping the door from swinging all the way open and only a small gap to squeeze through, Lima entered the room with his gun down and pointed at the floor.

LIMA: The room was tiny – only about eight by eight feet. As soon as I went in, I noticed all this shit everywhere, like rubbish and paper. There was a mattress on the floor in the far left corner. I saw that the room was clear in front of me so I then pivoted to my left to look behind the door. I still had my handgun down and turned to find Tep standing on an old sofa with his rifle up in the shooting position aimed directly at me. His arms were fully outstretched, so the barrel of his gun was just inches from my neck. I yelled, 'Police! Don't move!' and then tightened my neck muscles because he was aiming just above my ballistic vest, right at my voice box. I don't know why I tensed up; I can only assume that I was bracing because I was waiting for a round to hit me in the throat.

—

Having heard the commotion in the lounge room, Tep was ready and waiting for the SOG to storm in to the bedroom he was in. He had started pulling the trigger on his sawn-off Ruger .22 at his first glimpse of Lima, but instead of letting off a loud 'POP!' his gun only produced a measly 'click' each time he tried to fire it. Just like in his previous crimes, the weapon had failed on him yet again.

Lima's weapon was fully functional, and he had no trouble defending himself. By the time Mack entered, Lima was backing away and had already put multiple rounds into Tep with his 9-mm handgun.

LIMA: They call it 'vertical tracking' when you shoot someone low on their body and move your shots upwards. I fired nine rounds at Tep from his legs and groin area working my way up to his upper torso, as I was retreating towards the back of the room. At that stage, I became aware of Mack coming around the door.

—

Despite being on the end of Lima's stream of bullets, Tep showed no sign of being shot and was still actively trying to shoot back.

MACK: When I came into the room, I saw Lima firing, but Tep wasn't going down. Everything just happened so damned quick. Tep's finger was on the trigger and he was trying to pull it but nothing was happening. He was making the motions as if to say, 'What the hell is wrong with this fucking gun?' He was confused as to why it wasn't working and there's no doubt in the world that he was trying to kill Lima.

LIMA: Tep's facial expressions didn't change despite the fact I was shooting him. His eyes were locked in on me with the most intense stare and his gun was up as I was firing. I would have thought there would be some sort of facial change as he was being hit, but there wasn't anything noticeable. Because he was wearing black clothing, I also couldn't see if my rounds were hitting him or where they were impacting. I started to doubt my accuracy, and then I had a sinking feeling.

—

It suddenly dawned on Lima that he may have forgotten to swap out the non-lethal rounds the SOG was using during a recent national exercise at the police academy with the SAS. Lima and Mack had been involved in the training and were summoned directly from the academy to help with the arrests of Tep and Ouch.

LIMA: I thought, 'I've still got those fucking blanks in my gun!' We all de-bombed our live ammo when we arrived to start the exercise and bombed-up with FX-rounds, but then got called out and had to repeat the process in reverse. I had no idea if I was hitting Tep or not and assumed there was something wrong, even though I was sure I'd changed them from blanks. I thought, 'I've got blanks! He's gonna kill Mack!'

—

Seeing that Lima was directly in Tep's firing line and in grave danger, Mack fired a single shot from the right-hand-side with his shotgun. WHOOMPF! Nine lead ball bearings exploded out of their cartridge and blew a hole in Tep's shoulder before ripping through his chest cavity and into his lungs. Mack's close proximity to Tep meant maximum damage was inflicted.

MACK: If you're being shot at with a shotty, the closer you are to the gun, the worse it's going to be for you. The grouping of pellets will be tighter as they haven't had a chance to spread apart through the air over distance. They're still travelling as a solid mass. So, for Tep, he was hit with one big slug. My shot went in through his shoulder, took out his spine and the pellets lodged in his lungs. It's a lot of damage at such close range. I shot because Tep still had the gun in his hand and he was still a threat to us, although Lima had already put rounds into him. If Tep's gun had started working, Lima was dead.

When you go into a room like that, it's not as if you are twenty metres apart from each other. This room in particular was very, very small and we were very confined. I would have only been one metre from Tep and two metres away from Lima. The decision to shoot at someone is something you don't take lightly, but one you have to make very quickly. If you've decided to shoot, you're not trying to wound them. It's life or death, and if you pull that trigger, it's a decision you've made to remove a threat. If there's a person pointing a firearm at you or bearing down on you with a knife, he's trying to take your life and you must stop that momentum. To shoot to injure, it's a very hard thing to do. It looks good in the movies when they shoot people in the arm or the leg, but that's not necessarily going to stop any momentum of a person coming forwards. If the threat continues, we are trained to stop the threat, and that means shooting to kill.

—

Tep finally went down after Mack's intervention, and, soon after the shooting ceased, Dane and Rayden arrived.

DANE: I came into the room just after Mack but it was all over. Tep wasn't taken by surprise, because he'd heard us clearing the rest of the house. He made a conscious decision to shoot at Lima when he entered that room. Usually, he wouldn't have had that choice, but because we'd missed that room, the element of surprise had been lost. These people are not kung-fu artists and don't usually react in a split second by grabbing a flick knife and throwing it at us when we crash in. It's always someone standing there waiting for us or where they've heard us coming.

Tep was still alive for a while, but you can imagine the amount of damage a shotgun would do at close range, being shot sideways through your lungs and chest. I think he bled to death.

RAYDEN: We had cleared the other parts of the house and then heard CRACK! CRACK! CRACK! CRACK! CRACK! CRACK! Then a thunderous WHOOOMPF! I pushed my way into the room and Tep was lying there just looking at me, dying, going 'Arrggghhhhhhh.' I could see this massive hole in his side and I thought Lima had hit him several times in the same spot with his 9 mm. 'Nice grouping!' I thought, but then I looked over at Mack and saw smoke coming from the barrel of his shotty and realised, 'Ah, okay. So you got him then.'

The one thing that stood out the most on Tep's firearm was the red tape he had wrapped around the barrel and magazines. He'd taped two mags together end to end, which usually enables a quick reload. It showed that he meant business, but he never got a shot away.

—

Cowering in the corner of the room, jammed between the door and the couch, Tep's partner in crime, Ouch, could only watch on in horror.

MACK: He was packing death. We hadn't even realised he was in the room. When we told him to move out from beside the couch, he was frozen with fear . . . petrified. We had to physically reach in and pull him out and onto the ground.

LIMA: I became aware of Ouch's presence long after Tep went down because all my senses completely shut down during the shooting. I couldn't hear anything, I couldn't smell anything – it's a physiological effect that occurs involuntarily when you're in survival mode. Your eyes are critical to your survival and all your other senses get blocked out. You have to be able to see what the threat is, where the threat is and then act. When things settle and the threat has been negated, that's when your other senses start to return and things start to open up again. Once that door swung open, Ouch would have just curled up into a ball when all the shooting started. He didn't want to get involved, which was a good thing for him.

RAYDEN: He tried to slip between the cracks in the floorboards, I reckon.

—

Paramedics arrived on the scene and worked frantically to save Tep, but their efforts were in vain. Lima wasn't faring well either, although he wasn't injured.

LIMA: When the MICA [mobile intensive care ambulance] unit arrived, I lost the plot a bit. I was fuming. I'm loath to admit it now but, for a moment there, I didn't want the paramedics to save Tep. I wanted karma to take its course. I was in a brutal mindset of, 'He just fucking tried to kill me!' and was also thinking towards him, 'You were the master of your own destiny, mate – it's over for you now.' But they weren't my true feelings – I just lost my cool after a brush with death and my emotions boiled over immediately after.

When Oscar arrived on the scene, he ordered me to go outside to cool down. After I had regained my composure, my thoughts were more sympathetic towards Tep: 'You fucking idiot . . . why did you do that? You didn't have to do that, mate.'

—

Aged just thirty, Tep died at the scene, and, later, his nineteen-year-old partner Ouch was sent to jail on charges of attempted murder, aggravated burglary and false imprisonment.

MACK: When I saw that Tep had died and as a result of my shot, to be quite honest, I didn't feel anything. I try to explain that to my wife sometimes, and she can't understand it and asks, 'But you must feel something?' For me, it all stems from a life in the army and special forces. I was always taught not to show any emotion because it shows weakness, and that's why a lot of guys just bottle it up and, eventually, some explode. That's what happens.

I know that when I've come home after various jobs, I've seemed very distant to my family and loved ones. I think that's a bit of a protection mechanism: that you don't bring what happened at work home with you. We weren't actually allowed to go straight home after a serious job or fatal shooting. There was at least a four-hour unwind period that we had to spend together to talk about the job and what happened, to help come to terms with it. You have dreams from time to time, reliving certain incidents, but that's all part of the process. Those dreams don't ever go away. There are things that come back and revisit you from time to time.

The police psychologists used to get really frustrated with us because we refused to open up to them. 'How are you feeling?' they'd ask.

We'd just say, 'Fine.'

'What's going through your mind at the moment?'

'Nothing.'

'Is there anything you want to get off your chest?'

'Nope.'

Those short answers would really piss them off. We knew they were there to try and help us and to get those various emotions out of our systems and alleviate any consequences that might arise down the track, but we were all the same. We didn't show any weakness. I'm not saying it was the right way or attitude, but that's how we operated at the time. The job affects guys differently. Some go to the gym to work out or go for a long run after a traumatic job while others go to the pub and get shit-faced. We're all wired differently. We also realise that you don't have to be the shooter or one of the shooters to be affected. We have to make sure that all the guys who were there are looked after.

—

In the wash-up of the Tep shooting, and only after they made their statements to homicide-squad detectives, the SOG who were there dissected the shooting. Much of the focus, however, was on Lima's brush with death, or divine intervention for those religiously inclined, and whether or not he was in fact firing blanks.

LIMA: One of the first things I did when it was all over, was to check my mags and see what was in there. I was relieved when I saw the live rounds. It was inconceivable that I would have made a mistake, but in the moment when Tep wasn't reacting to my shots, I just had that sinking feeling that something wasn't quite right.

—

An examination of Tep's .22 Ruger gave another explanation as to why it jammed.

LIMA: It became clear that, prior to our raid, when he was terror-ising people in the neighbourhood, Tep would fire his gun and then have to manually re-cock it. But when he re-cocked it, he got a double feed – which is when two bullets are fed into the chamber. So there's a live round in the chamber and then the slide picks up another one and jams it into one that was already in there. So two rounds were trying to go into the breach.

You start to realise that life's all about choices. Tep made a lot of bad choices. He had a poor choice of weapon to begin with, and then he decided he was going to saw the barrel in half without any knowledge of how a semi-automatic rifle works.

RAYDEN: He'd cut the barrel down too far, and semi-automatic guns like that one need a long-enough barrel to allow a decent build-up of pressure for them to fire. This idiot cut his barrel off way too short, so the slide would only come back partially, and it created what we call a 'stovepipe' – that's when an empty bullet casing jams in the ejection port of a gun, instead of being spat out and cleared to allow the slide to return and pick up the next round. And as for Lima's shots not having an impact – they just weren't hitting the right spots. Nine-millimetre rounds don't penetrate that far. After that job, we started looking for bigger calibre guns to use.

—

Contrary to public perception, gunshots are not always lethal, and sometimes, depending on a variety of factors, are not even as damaging as might be expected. Had Tep been able to fire at Lima at close quarters however, the Soggies knew the chances of survival would have been slim at best.

MACK: Had Tep's gun been working properly, he would probably have killed one or two of us. We were wearing bulletproof vests, but he aimed up into Lima's throat, so we would have had at least one casualty. We would have had a shit-fight if his gun didn't jam. I believe he would have been trying to shoot through the door of that room after Lima pushed at it the first time.

—

At the inquest, Coroner Nicholas Papas said:

> Whether or not Tep attempted to shoot at the police makes no difference in this case. It is clear that when the police officers entered the room, they were confronted by a man aggressively pointing a weapon at them . . . I am satisfied they did what was necessary to be done in lawful self-defence . . . There can be no finding of contribution against the Victoria Police in this case. Having given very careful consideration to the question of what options were available in this case to the SOG, I am satisfied on the balance of probabilities that the correct choice was made. It is clear that Mr Tep had access to a firearm, was prepared to use it and was extremely dangerous.
>
> The decision to deploy the SOG was sensible and called for. To expect police without specialist training to consider arresting this man would have been inappropriate and would have led to potential harm coming to members of the police force and possibly other people.

LIMA: I'm not a religious man, at all. After my little flip-out at the scene, I dealt with what had happened there and then. Had that gun been working, I'd be dead – I know that. But I don't reflect on it at all. The main thing that concerned me was whether the experience of going into a room and literally looking down the barrel of a gun was going to turn me into a 'baulker' – that's what I was terrified of. I was terrified that I was going to let my mates down on the next job, and I was worried that they might all be going, 'Let's just sit back and watch Lima on the next one . . . just in case he baulks.' I never wanted to let the lads down and never wanted to have a bad reputation among my peers.

As it turned out, it wasn't an issue for me. I picked it straight back up like nothing had happened. There was a little bit of doubt on my part in the lead-up to that next job, but once I was there and was doing it, I reverted to the way I was trained.

10

FEAR NO EVIL

*But Jesus said, 'Let the little children come to me and do not
hinder them, for to such belongs the kingdom of heaven.'*

Matthew 19:14

The first person to emerge from the tiny prison was a little four-
year-old girl. The police inspector running the siege would have
recurring dreams of her walking towards him, but he was never
able to reach her.

Haunting dreams would be a shared experience for the survi-
vors of the kindergarten siege. One of the hostages, a little
four-year-old boy, would wake night after night after the event,
screaming. It took a language expert to help the boy's parents
identify the language – Turkish – and the phrase, 'Shut up or
I'll kill you!'

They were the words of Serafettin Huseyin, who only a month
earlier had kidnapped the little boy, the little girl and two other
toddlers, splashed them with petrol and held them hostage in
their kindergarten's tiny toilet cubicle for seven hours.

The first of the SOG members on the scene at the kindergarten, Rogue stealthily made his way into the main room to assess the situation and report back to his superiors. It was 11.00 am, and as he crept quietly over the threshold of the front entrance, he was hit with a powerful smell.

ROGUE: It was petrol, and it was so strong it stung my eyes. I had no idea why I could smell fuel, so it was very unexpected. I could hear the kids screaming up the back of the room . . . they were crying so loudly. I couldn't see them because they were behind a closed toilet door . . . they were so distraught. Then I heard the man for the first time and he was yelling in broken English, 'I have match! I light them all on fire! Everyone get back! Get out now!' I was pretty tense from the get-go.

—

Five more SOG members arrived soon after and joined Rogue on the outside of the door to the toilet where the kids were being held. It wasn't long before they too became distressed.

ROGUE: The fumes started making us all feel really, really sick, and we were in a different room to the kids and the petrol – that's how powerful the smell was. Those children must have been suffering really badly. The smell must have almost been knocking them out and making them vomit.

—

As the stand-off dragged on, the children's screams became faint cries and then tiny whimpers. Although the captives were just metres away, Rogue and the SOG couldn't do anything to save them from the evil man who had captured them.

ROGUE: It was the worst job I'd ever been involved with. Reliving it still makes my heart ache, and the memories are so vivid. I still think about that scene every couple of days. It just pops into my head. I can still hear those little kids. They were so helpless. So scared. So frightened. I used to live near that kindergarten and travelled past it a lot. All I wanted to do was rip that bloke from limb to limb. I wanted to kill him. I wanted him gone from this world. It's the only time I'd ever felt that way about a crook on a job in all my time in the SOG. I wanted him dead for what he was doing to those little kids. I just didn't want him around anymore because what he was doing was just horrible, evil. One moment, we could hear the kids crying and whimpering, and the next, there was silence. You just feared the worst every time it went too quiet in that toilet cubicle.

That was a bad job . . . a really bad job. We couldn't do anything, we couldn't see anything and yet we were so close to them. We were an arm's length from him and the kids, and that was excruciating for us. We're so used to going into situations and being able to have an immediate impact or find a quick resolution, but it wasn't the case this time.

—

The layout of the Manresa Kindergarten in Hawthorn was basic and consisted only of a large main room, where the children played and completed activities, an office and a small kitchen with an adjoining wet area at the rear. The tiny toilet cubicle was right near where the children hung their bags every day, and its door had a gap of about a metre at the top, but was fully closed off at the bottom. Inside the cubicle was a single toilet and small glass window, which the offender, Huseyin, eventually had to smash in order to allow some clean air in because of the fumes.

At the command post, Inspector Doug O'Loughlin faced the biggest challenge of his career at that point. In charge of the SOG, he had weighed up every option available, but quickly realised getting the kids out alive and unharmed wasn't going to be easy, if possible at all. A medical triage was set up, paramedics were on standby and the fire brigade deployed their hoses to the inner perimeter in case Huseyin lit a match. 'The children's lives were completely in his hands, and, to a lesser extent, in our hands,' Doug O'Loughlin said.

Access to the toilet cubicle was problematic, and complicating the matter further was the fact that Huseyin had nailed the door shut and splashed petrol all around. 'There were five people – Huseyin and four little kids – all crammed in there with little room to move,' Doug O'Loughlin explained. 'No matter what we decided to do, it would have been fraught with danger and involved high risk to the safety of the children. It was an inward-swinging door and we were unable to breach it for fear of injuring the kids, as they would have been pressed right up against it. If we put a man up and over the top of the toilet door, where the gap was, and dropped him down on Huseyin, he could have crushed and injured the children. If Huseyin sensed that something was about to happen, he could have lit a match or attacked the kids with the handgun, knife or hammer we were told he had. We examined getting an eyeball [video camera] in through the roof or even through the floor.'

Huseyin held all of the cards, but the SOG had one ace up its sleeve. 'He kept standing on the toilet and was popping his head over the top of the door to speak to police negotiators and try to see what was happening,' O'Loughlin explained. 'I asked Onyx and Rogue if they could get a bead on him with their 9-mm pistols and take him out with a single headshot.' Although it was an option, O'Loughlin said it was very much a last resort. 'If Onyx or Rogue missed or only injured him, he could still harm the children. Add the fact that he could have fallen on the kids or they could have been splattered with brains and blood, and it wasn't a very good option. To me, it was just one option in a situation where I only had few on the table.' While remote, the other concern was that a gunshot or muzzle flash could ignite the fuel and incinerate everyone inside. 'It was a damned if you do, damned if you don't type situation,' O'Loughlin added.

ROGUE: Even though it may have been by accident, Huseyin had set everything up perfectly to counter our every move. He was in complete control of the situation, and we were furious at the thought of what he was doing to those kids in there.

Earlier that day, at 8.30 am, Manresa director Anne Cantwell arrived at the kindergarten and unlocked all the doors ahead of the arrival of her twenty-two energetic and sometimes trouble-some students. Her assistant, Gael Spiers, and duty-mother for the day, Gail Marshall, arrived shortly after, to help Anne with the sudden rush of children that was about to flood through the front gates at 10.00 am.

As the trio started ushering the tiny pupils into the main room to start the day, a strange man wandered into the playground. Cantwell approached him, thinking he was lost, but quickly learnt he was there for a terrible reason. 'I don't want frighten,' he said in broken English and with a thick European accent as he produced a pistol from his trouser pocket. 'I have gun.' Cantwell froze with fear. He raised the weapon in his right hand and pointed it at her mid-section.

Huseyin was small in stature, with a dark moustache and black and grey wavy hair that looked as if it had rarely seen a comb. He was wearing brown trousers and a white singlet under a partly buttoned-up blue and white chequered shirt. In his left hand, he clasped a large black sports bag that had a towel and off-white jacket draped over it. 'They won't listen to me . . . I want my wife out!' he barked at Cantwell. 'They'll listen to me now!' he said in a more raised and threatening tone.

The Turkish-born Huseyin had been clashing with authorities for more than a decade over complications from the birth of his first child. Although his wife, Zehra, had delivered a healthy boy via caesarean section, she complained of severe back pain and aching legs soon after. Despite more operations, Zehra's health failed to improve and doctors concluded she wouldn't be able to have any more children. It was a devastating blow for the couple, who had always planned to have a family of at least five.

Feeling angry, distressed and cheated, the Huseyins went to the Royal Women's Hospital for a second opinion and claimed their obstetrician must have made mistakes during the caesarean. But a physical examination and review of her medical records showed no malpractice, and the family was told nothing could be done.

Zehra became an invalid pensioner and Serafettin began to explore legal action. He gave up work as a cabinetmaker to look after his son and disabled wife. With little progress in their ongoing battle for compensation, the family occupied the steps of Parliament House on two occasions and staged hunger strikes and protests. In all, the hunger strikes lasted for 50 days. Police Inspector Geoff O'Loughlin (Doug's older brother) made frequent visits to their tent, concerned for the family's welfare. He felt obliged to try and assist them. 'I built up some sort of rapport with them,' Geoff said. The Huseyins' now ten-year-old boy, Esin, was who Geoff was most worried about as he hadn't eaten for days. For the boy's well-being, Geoff requested he be removed from his parents' custody. After consultation, Zehra agreed it was in Esin's best interests to be placed under a care and protection application.

With Esin in foster care, the hunger strike continued and so too did Geoff's quest for a resolution. He contacted the Turkish Consulate for help but its representative had little success. He also tried to give the family the media attention they were after by contacting a TV news reporter and spoke with Legal Aid. The advice Geoff received however was that the family was not genuine and were 'gold diggers'. Assistant Police Surgeon Dr Edward Ogden was also involved, and he reported on Serafettin and Zehra, saying:

> It was clear that neither of them required immediate hospitalisation. They both appeared well. They were noted to be drinking soft drinks and one of the police had seen potato chips in the tent . . . this appeared to be a genuinely distressed couple . . . and I questioned the possibility that they may starve to the point of becoming unwell.

Realising the Huseyins were playing games, Geoff O'Loughlin backed off completely. It was agreed that no police intervention was needed as long as the Huseyins' health remained satisfactory. Dr Ogden kept a close eye on them for the next fortnight, and received a concerning phone call from Geoff O'Loughlin advising him that Zehra was holding up a placard declaring she would kill herself 'by fire' at 4.00 pm.

As there was now a genuine threat to life, Dr Ogden rushed back to Parliament and said he observed a marked change in

Zehra's attitude. 'Mrs Huseyin said to me, "I die today. I set fire to myself . . . nobody do nothing, I die." Mr Huseyin said, "She no listen me . . . I say you no die, she no listen."'

Zehra was taken into custody and assigned for compulsory admission to a psychiatric hospital. 'I formed the opinion that Mrs Huseyin was potentially suicidal and certainly capable of setting fire to herself,' Dr Ogden reported.

Serafettin Huseyin was now left alone, and the rage that fuelled his protest was about to boil over. He vowed to get justice and make the world sit up and take notice – and he would stop at nothing to achieve it.

With his wife in psychiatric care and his son in foster care, home had become a lonely and painful place for Huseyin. It was far from the dream he'd envisioned when he decided to migrate to Australia all those years ago.

When Huseyin's solicitor dropped his case, the thirty-eight-year-old tried to track down his address in order to 'do something wrong to the solicitor or to his family'. Luckily for the solicitor, Huseyin was unable to locate his home in Hawthorn despite correctly finding his name and address in the phone book. But, while searching, Huseyin did pass two kindergartens. One was called Manresa, and it sat in front of the bluestone Immaculate Conception Church. He stood for a long time at the front gates and watched the children play in the yard together. The happiness and freedom they enjoyed upset him. He formed the belief these children were from wealthy families and their parents were made up of society's elite – the same people who had denied him compensation. Huseyin believed the rich would never be made to experience what he and his family was forced to go through, so he wanted them to 'taste the harm'.

The next morning, Huseyin caught the train from Springvale to Hawthorn, but this time he wasn't searching for his solicitor's house. He packed a large black sports bag with an imitation pistol, tomahawk, hammer, knife, pliers, screwdriver, nails, steel brackets, torch, drawing pins, hinges, curtain fabric, a box of matches and a can of petrol. His destination: the Manresa Kindergarten.

Gael Spiers was making Mother's Day gifts out of dough with some of the children at an activities table at 9.55 am when she saw her boss, Anne Cantwell, in the front yard of the kindergarten with a man who looked like a salesman. She thought nothing of their meeting initially and watched as they approached the front door together.

Spiers remembers the moment that Cantwell approached her, leaving the man alone in the entrance area of the main room, and told her that he had a gun. 'I thought she may be joking at first and I looked at Anne's face, then I looked at his face and I realised it was serious,' she said in her statement.

From the other side of the room, duty-mother Gail Marshall spotted Huseyin's weapon. 'I noticed the man had a small handgun in his hand, with the bag in the other hand. He was waving the gun from side to side in front of him, pointing it out towards us. While he was waving the gun around, he kept walking further into the kindergarten. I was absolutely terrified and I didn't think any of us were going to escape from him,' she recounted to police.

Cantwell bravely made her way back to Huseyin. 'He said he wanted all the children inside, so I proceeded to go out the open door to get the children from the front yard.'

With Huseyin acting erratically, the children sensed danger and started to panic, according to Marshall. 'He was still pointing the gun at us and kept saying, "Me no want to fright . . . children must stay . . . My wife must come." Then he kept pointing to the kitchen area: "Children in there, sit on floor." Gael and I started taking the children into the kitchen area and they were becoming very distressed. All of them were crying. The area we were ordered to take them into is very small, and they were all very squashed up.'

Huseyin began to manhandle the children, according to Cantwell. 'It was at this stage he became very agitated and the children started to scream. He was pushing some of the children to the floor in the kitchen area. He seemed to want to have them in a small group.'

With Cantwell on the other side of the kitchen bench, Huseyin began barking more instructions. 'You go in there . . . in ten minutes you ring Channel Nine. Don't touch phone until I say!' he ordered.

Spiers attempted to settle the children down by offering to make some fairy bread if they stopped crying. Despite her good intentions, the idea almost backfired. When she opened a drawer to retrieve a knife, Huseyin screamed, 'No knife! No knife!' He then reached into his sports bag and grabbed a hammer and began waving it above the children's heads.

With Huseyin distracted by trying to get control of the hysterical group, Cantwell made a daring move. Briefly out of his line of sight, she made a run for freedom and headed to the neighbouring church for help.

Unaware he'd just lost a hostage, Huseyin pushed a small group of children into the toilet cubicle, away from the protection of their guardians. Desperate not to let the kids out of her sight, Spiers forced the door open. 'At this time, I noticed what looked like a gas bottle on the floor,' she described. 'He also had a box of matches in his hand.' Spiers screamed at Huseyin, 'What are you doing to those children? Don't do that, you're frightening them!'

With Huseyin now in the toilet cubicle, Spiers too made a brave move. 'At this time, I was about three metres from him. I have then yelled at the children, "Run!" I yelled at Gail Marshall, who was hysterical. "Run! Run!"' The pair grabbed as many children as they could, pulling them to safety by their arms, legs and hair.

After raising the alarm with police, Cantwell ran back to the kindergarten but didn't make it back inside. Spiers and Marshall were already in the car park next to the building with a large group of children.

The three adults were relieved after escaping Huseyin's clutches, but they soon knew the ordeal was far from over. Spiers reported that she had to leave a few of the kids in the toilet cubicle with Huseyin. When she did a head count, her heart sank. Four children were missing.

Hours into the siege and with the welfare of the four children weighing heavily on his mind, Doug O'Loughlin knew he needed to take control of the situation and find a resolution. Food and drink was offered but Huseyin refused. 'Do the children want a lolly or something, Huseyin?' a negotiator enquired.

'No! You bring my wife now!'

'But I want a lolly, please,' a tiny voice protested in the background. Huseyin then demanded of police negotiator Greg Goullet that officer O'Loughlin be brought to the scene which caused confusion given the fact that Doug O'Loughlin was already there.

Detectives conducted a background check and found out about Inspector Geoff O'Loughlin's links to Huseyin dating back to the Parliament House hunger strikes he staged with his wife. Realising it was Geoff O'Loughlin that Huseyin was calling for, a decision was made to summon the older O'Loughlin to the scene. 'Huseyin was demanding we bring his wife and Geoff to him and that the media be allowed in to interview them. If we didn't comply, he threatened to kill the kids,' Doug O'Loughlin revealed. It was a complex situation for Doug O'Loughlin to control. He knew that if he met Huseyin's demands, every rule in the book would need to be broken. The SOG's inner perimeter was sacrosanct and fiercely protected. Only those with a specific need to be there were allowed inside. Doug O'Loughlin knew that bringing Huseyin's wife to the scene, after she was recently certified, was fraught with danger. He had to act on instinct and his decisions were every bit life or death.

Inside the kinder, Rogue knew time was running out. 'It got to the stage where we thought the kids were unconscious,' Rogue said. 'We just had to get them out because it was getting to that point where it was becoming really dangerous for them in there.'

Far away from the horrors that were unfolding, Geoff O'Loughlin had just been to a funeral and stopped by his mother's house in Watsonia before heading into work. When he arrived, the greeting he received from her wasn't what he expected. 'Mum was absolutely frantic and extremely stressed out,' Geoff vividly remembered. 'She told me that my police commander, Phelan, had been ringing around and was desperately looking for me.'

Without hesitation, Geoff returned his call. 'I had a sinking feeling in my stomach and knew something had to be drastically wrong for someone that high up the chain from the force to ring my mother,' Geoff said. 'I immediately thought of a horrible call we'd received in the same house at 2.00 am in 1972, the day before I married my wife Carol. The voice on the other end of the line that time told us my brother Barry had been killed in a car accident.'

Geoff soon learnt that the call was not about his family but about one he'd been trying to help over the course of the last ten weeks.

One of the only known people who had a relationship of any kind with Serafettin and Zehra, Geoff was a potential resource for the SOG, and his presence at the kinder siege was urgently required.

Commander Phelan asked Geoff if he knew Serafettin and he replied, 'Yes, that idiot on hunger strike at Parliament House?' After Geoff's knowledge of the family was established, Phelan instructed Geoff to head to a local football oval just a few kilometres away and await transport to Hawthorn. But, much to Geoff's surprise, the car park was empty when he arrived. 'I started to think I may have misunderstood his instructions. Then I heard it in the distance; it was like thunder slowly approaching. I knew what it was immediately.' The rotor blades of the police airwing sliced through the air and cast out a distinct sound over the suburb below. 'I watched in disbelief as the helicopter suddenly banked and headed towards me. I thought, "So here is my ride!" Never in my previous twenty years in the job had I been picked up by the police chopper.'

After a brief flight, the airwing landed at Glenferrie Oval in Hawthorn, but it was still some distance from the kindergarten. 'The door swung open and a uniformed police officer took me by the arm and said, "This way! We have to run, sir! We can't get through the roadblocks by car!"'

Geoff knew he should have been on the verge of collapse after the kilometre-long dash, but adrenaline kept him upright and right on the tail of his special escort. Eventually, the policeman he was chasing slowed to a walk, and as they reached the command post, Geoff began to take stock and catch his breath. 'My heart rate should have been slowing down, but it did the exact opposite when I saw all these police dressed head to toe in jet-black uniforms,' he remarked. It was organised chaos. The fears Geoff had about the seriousness of the situation were realised when he saw SOG members in position all around the kindergarten. 'At that point in time, I fully comprehended just how bad things had to be. You don't call the Special Operations Group out unless it's "situation critical". They're our last resort, and one which we only ever call on in times of utter desperation.'

But the surprises didn't stop there. A familiar face emerged from the crowd and walked towards him. His younger brother Doug approached but there was no time for pleasantries. 'There was no real recognition of family from him, just extreme professionalism. It was something I expected from the SOG boys. When Doug told me what was happening, who was involved and that I'd need a flak jacket, I knew immediately that I was going to be sent to the front line.'

'I didn't see him as my brother,' Doug O'Loughlin said. 'He was just another police officer and one we hoped might be able to help us.'

The area outside the kindergarten became even more chaotic when hysterical parents of both the freed and trapped children began to arrive. The sensitivity of the situation was also highlighted by the surprise attendance of Chief Commissioner Kel Glare and Assistant Commissioner Frank Green. It was Green, though, who had the unenviable task of advising each couple whether their child was safe or not. For most, the news was good, but four sets of parents began to live out their worst nightmare. 'Together, we will win,' Green assured them. But deep down, he wasn't so sure the day would end well. 'When you have to convince the parents that you are doing your absolute best for them and give them a ninety per cent guarantee that you will return their kids safely, you have looming in the back of your mind that you may not.'

Police negotiators had been going back and forth with Huseyin for hours, but there was little progress. When Geoff O'Loughlin arrived at 1.30 pm and started talking to him, he too became frustrated with Huseyin's refusal to cooperate. 'I had nothing but hatred and contempt for Huseyin but in my role along with Greg Goullet, I had to befriend him, coax, console, appease and do whatever it took to get those kids out alive. We were searching for the key or action that would resolve the situation. He still wanted to see his wife,' Geoff recalled. 'And he was desperate for media attention so he could air his grievances to the rest of the world. He would cry, then become aggressive and assertive. Each time the children spoke, he'd tell them to "be quiet".'

Geoff and the negotiators tried all sorts of tactics, and when it was clear Huseyin wouldn't let the group of kids go all together, they worked on securing the release of one child at a time. A common tactic for negotiators was to try and give something in order to get something in return. 'You have to show you are sincere, you are good man,' Geoff said to him in broken English. 'You let one child go, everyone say, "He good man. He not hurt, he want to talk to wife, he can be trusted." I stand back, you let one girl out, she run away, it shows my boss you are good not bad man.' But Huseyin refused to release anyone and kept referring to his lengthy hunger strike. 'I am good man. Don't think I am stupid,' he fired back angrily. 'We wait more than eight weeks!'

Geoff tried to get an understanding of the welfare of the children in the cubicle and asked Huseyin, 'Tell me what you see down there. They all right? The children, they all right?'

'No [not] bad. No [not] bad,' Huseyin replied bluntly. 'No [not] sick. Just crying, upset . . . If not bring my wife, I will kill all children here!'

Geoff recalls becoming increasingly frustrated by Huseyin's stubbornness. 'Regardless of what we said, he was totally rigid and uncompromising while the children were continually whimpering in the background. It was making us all extremely angry inside but we couldn't afford to show it or let our emotions boil over.'

After a long period of solid negotiating, the O'Loughlin brothers came back together at the command post to discuss the next move. At 3.05 pm, five hours into the siege, it was agreed that Huseyin's wife, Zehra, should be brought to the scene. However, the plan almost backfired when she saw the heavily armed SOG. 'She became too emotional,' Geoff said. 'She had to be taken away because she was endangering the children. She told her husband that men in black clothes were waiting outside to kill him.' Huseyin was angered at the thought he was about to be gunned down and stopped raising his head above the toilet door for fear of being shot. At a loss, police resumed negotiations, but no ending was in sight. 'An assault on the toilet was still the furthest thing from my mind,' Doug O'Loughlin said.

Around six hours after the siege began, hopes for the safety of the children were fading fast. 'I still believed that Zehra was the key to solving the problem,' Geoff said. 'It was extremely risky to send her back in, but we had to try. If it failed, there was a very real chance he would get more agitated and kill or hurt the children. It was a very sensitive situation, and if anything went wrong, we'd all be to blame.' Some SOG members were against the idea of reintroducing her and Doug had to make the final decision and put it to A/C Green. Geoff had little trust in the couple. 'They were both callous, unyielding and totally unpredictable.'

Green approved the move to take Zehra back in. Having worked with Barry and Robert O'Loughlin in the consorters, he said, 'Do what all O'Loughlin's do . . . rely on your good instincts and act on it.'

Willing to have another go at convincing Huseyin to give in, this time Geoff took Zehra and a news reporter to the front line as well as an interpreter, who was there to ensure the couple didn't devise any sinister plans in their native tongue. A letter guaranteeing Huseyin his long-sought-after day in court was also drafted. 'While having a brief break, police surgeon David Wells approached me and said, "If he wants his day in court, let's give it to him." We thought if we promised him what he'd been after for all these years – a chance to stand before a judge – then he'd surrender,' Geoff added. 'Well he got his day in court, but it wasn't under the circumstances he was expecting, of course.'

The letter read:

Dear Mr Huseyin,
The undersigned, Dr David Wells and Assistant Commissioner Frank Green, guarantee your appearance before Chief Stipendiary Magistrate at the Melbourne Magistrates Court tonight (9th May) and guarantee you a hearing on matters of concern to you, your wife, and family.

We regret that you have taken this action as a necessary step to have your problems aired before a court.

Doug O'Loughlin knew that allowing a family member into a hostage/siege situation once was an absolute 'no no', but twice was unheard of and against every rule in the book. 'They were the only cards we had in our hand and we had to play them,' he said. 'Using the media was also out of the ordinary, but I was determined to try everything we could to get those kids out safely.'

The interpreter read the letter out loud and despite having all his demands met, Huseyin still refused to surrender, because he feared that he'd be shot. He began demanding that the courts prematurely ruled in his family's favour. Doug O'Loughlin told Geoff to go back inside with Zehra and 'stand at the door and just keep badgering him, without giving up'.

As instructed, Geoff O'Loughlin and the negotiators pressed harder for Serafettin's surrender, but Zehra was still hampering their attempts. 'The television cameras are all up the street. We will talk to you there and then,' Geoff told Huseyin, only to be cut off by Zehra, who said, 'You are a liar!'

'I am not a liar. Trust me, for Christ's sake. Tell him!'

'People all time lie!' Zehra snapped back.

'I know that,' Geoff replied. 'You have got to trust someone. Tell him . . . tell him!'

The negotiator interjected. 'Are you going to come out now, Huseyin?'

'C'mon, don't be silly,' Geoff added.

'Huseyin. Come out now. We have no guns here. I have no gun, Geoff has no gun,' the negotiator pleaded.

At 5.15 pm, some seven-and-a-half hours after the siege began, strange noises started coming from inside the cubicle and an object was thrown over the top of the door. 'This one plastic pistol,' Huseyin told police as he tossed out the toy gun he'd been using. There were more noises, and the SOG assault team outside the cubicle door thought Huseyin was hurting the kids.

ROGUE: We had no idea what was going on in there. It was a really tense time and we had to relay all the information to the command post and await instructions on how to act. When we heard all this loud banging from inside, there was a bit of panic, thinking he was inflicting even more pain on those kids. After a few seconds, though, we realised he was pulling the nails out of the door.

—

The four-year-old girl emerged from the tiny prison. 'Here they come,' a relieved Geoff O'Loughlin can be heard saying on the official police recording of the incident. 'Come on, kiddies. Come on, love!' In his dreams, Geoff could never get to her.

Huseyin followed the little girl out with his hands in the air as instructed by Geoff. The SOG pounced hard and threw him to the ground. The three other children remained in the cubicle and were unable to walk out.

ROGUE: They were all unconscious, floppy from limb to limb and not really with it at all because of the fumes and conditions they were forced to endure. We had to carry them out delicately, one by one. That made us even more furious, seeing the condition the kids were left in. They all had massive burn marks – like welts or blisters – all over them. Their skin was all burnt and red. They squealed when we picked them up, they were in that much pain. It was absolutely heart wrenching.

—

The children were taken to the triage and were assessed by paramedics, with their distressed parents watching on. The worst of them was one of the boys, and he had chemical burns to at least thirty per cent of his small body. 'Word was given that the children had been released, and my wife and I went outside and were ushered into an area where a temporary medical relief centre had been set up,' one of the fathers said in a statement. 'There we found our son lying down and being attended to by medical personnel. They [his clothes] were wet and smelt as if they were saturated with petrol.' One of the mothers described her daughter as being 'very drained and dazed . . . I hardly recognised her', while another said of her son, 'I saw that his skin looked like it had peeled away.'

The victims arrived at the Royal Children's Hospital at 6.15 pm and were met by Director of the Burns Unit John Solomon. He said of the girl, 'She was grossly disturbed and in pain . . . Some areas [of her body] were discoloured, but other areas were grossly blistered, and sheets of skin had separated. An intravenous infusion was commenced, and she was resuscitated and sedated. A morphine infusion was necessary because of the pain, and the petrol had entered the right eye, causing a burn to the cornea through which she could not see because of the slough.'

In custody, Huseyin showed no remorse for his vile act and claimed that he only intended to spill petrol on the floor, not on any of the children. 'One of the kid's, um, arm touched the t – er – tank and more petrol spilt,' he told detectives after his arrest. 'Petrol can fell on . . . fell off my hand.' When he was asked why he brought the petrol with him, he responded, 'To prevent myself from being shot by police,' and when quizzed about the box of matches he had, he revealed his sinister plot: 'If I was shot by police, I would – er – light the petrol with the match.'

Huseyin was jailed for twenty-one years on thirty-seven charges of false imprisonment, intentionally causing serious injury and kidnapping. After his release, he was arrested and jailed again for attacking his wife in her sleep with a tomahawk.

'I still consider that the most difficult job I ever attended,' Doug O'Loughlin reflected. 'We just did what we had to do. This particular job didn't call for our immediate intervention; it was just negotiation, negotiation and more negotiation. It was never a case of us saying, "The SOG is here, everyone stand aside!" I took various people's advice throughout the ordeal and weighed up all the options available, and we achieved a peaceful outcome.'

11

THE FALL

For dust you are and to dust you will return.

Genesis 3:19

The sliding door to the back of the van was thrown open with force, flooding the SOG's once-darkened hiding place with sunlight. Their vehicle was slowing to a halt, so Sarge wedged his foot on the door rail to stop it from sliding back on him as Dexter slammed the brakes on. Sierra grabbed on to Sarge's vest to keep him balanced as the vehicle came to a halt and the pair prepared to leap out and stop a multimillion-dollar daylight robbery at Melbourne Airport.

Sierra is a high achiever in every sense. When explaining his motivations for joining the SOG he once told me, 'Why wouldn't I want to join the SOG. It is the best there is.' He is one of the most intelligent and driven members the group has ever known. Sierra was in the middle of completing his helicopter pilot's licence when he joined the Soggies. To him, there is no worthier cause than risking your life to protect others. In his words, 'Someone has to do it, so why not me. Oh, and I hate coming last in anything. If you're not first, then you're last.'

On this day out at the airport, there was no way he was going to come last.

SARGE: I remember stepping on to the bitumen and seeing the white panel van that the crooks had arrived in right before my eyes. The driver was still behind the wheel and I called on him, 'Police! Don't move! Police! Don't move!' His eyes nearly popped right out of the mask he was wearing and he froze. We'd been hiding in an unmarked van, so, from his viewpoint, he would have just seen our doors suddenly pop open and two heavily armed men in black jump out pointing 12-gauge shotguns. It's a wonder he didn't shit himself!

SIERRA: At the time of our intercept the driver was turned, looking into the back of the van. We called on him and he spun around and panicked.

—

At the rear of the panel van, two armed robbers, Stephen Barci and Norman Lee, were loading three heavy bags of stolen cash on board and were unaware the SOG had ambushed their driver at the front of the vehicle. After throwing his red cash collection bag inside the van, Lee hopped in and pulled in Barci's two. Barci then spun around and sat on the rear bumper with his legs hanging down towards the ground. Lee grabbed the collar of Barci's jacket to drag him inside further but the panel van surged forwards unexpectedly. With the rear barn doors left wide open, the pair spilt onto the ground.

SIERRA: It was just sheer luck, or divine intervention depending on what you believe in, that they fell out of that panel van because in the back with Barci and Lee were some pretty serious high-powered guns, including semi-automatic assault rifles. There's no way we could have countered their firepower with our shotguns, had they been able to access them. Their unexpected fall saved us from a more serious gunfight.

—

The panel van's tyres screeched as the driver, Stephen Asling, slammed his foot on the accelerator when he saw the SOG suddenly appear in front of him. The van thundered towards Sarge. As it cut across in front of him, Sarge quickly established that Asling was unarmed. So, instead of shooting him through the driver's side window, Sarge put the muzzle of his shotgun to the back left tyre of the van and fired, to try to blow the tyre off the wheel.

SARGE: If I'd seen that he had a gun as he drove at me, I would have probably shot him through the window. A 12-gauge round into the tyre would normally take the rim off a car, but it didn't work for some reason and Asling managed to drive off. It was fight or flight from his perspective, and he just took off, looking after 'number one'. He didn't care about the other two he'd left behind in the dust.

—

Rogue had exited the SOG's van via the back door with another member, Khan, close behind him. Barci and Lee got to their feet after crashing to the ground and chased the fleeing getaway vehicle, yelling, 'Stop! Stop! Stop!' but Asling ignored their pleas made a bid to escape the SOG's cordon.

Armed only with handguns, the abandoned Lee and Barci were fully exposed. There was nothing between them and the four members of the SOG: Sarge, Rogue, Sierra and Khan. As they followed the path of the fleeing panel van, they unintentionally ran straight into the assault team. Barci was five metres ahead of Lee and ran across the back of the SOG's van just as Rogue stepped out.

ROGUE: I yelled, 'Police! Don't move! Drop the gun!' As I brought my shotgun up, he let a shot go at me, which went down between my legs and into the ground just in front of me. The first round I fired was straight into his shoulder, and it was just rapid after that: BOOM! BOOM! BOOM! BOOM! He was running past me and had turned and taken a shot at me as I jumped out of the back of the van . . . When I shot back, he sort of spun around and I gave him one last one fair and square in his shoulder-blades.

The plan to pull off one of Australia's largest heists took years to come to fruition, with career criminals Norman Leung Lee, Stephen Michael Barci and Stephen John Asling patiently plotting their violent 'get rich quick' scheme for more than two years.

Before recruiting Lee for their million-dollar grand finale, Asling and Barci operated as a tight-knit pair with a penchant for cash-laden armoured trucks. They once ambushed two Brambles security guards who were sitting down having breakfast at a cafe in Port Melbourne, and they stole their revolvers. The guards were taken hostage and forced into the back of their armoured van at gunpoint. Asling and Barci drove them to a nearby warehouse, where their hands and feet were bound. A warning shot was fired into the air as the criminals fled with a decent cash booty of $426,000.

Any experienced detective knows that, more often than not, jobs like that involve an inside man, but with no leads initially, the case went freezing cold and the crime remained unsolved.

Two years later, a break in the case finally came. ARS detective Rod Keuris was at his desk when he received a message from an informant telling him a man by the name of 'Steve' was involved in the Brambles robbery and that a certain security guard was the inside man police were looking for.

Keuris was informed the young, green guard had been duped by the perpetrators, and instead of getting his cut of the $426,000 in exchange for his inside information, he received a second-hand Ford Falcon as his payment. The old saying, 'There's no honour amongst thieves' immediately came to mind for Keuris, and he had a good feeling that the tip-off he'd received was good enough to act on, so he tracked the inside man down.

Accompanied by another detective, Keuris waited for the guard to leave his grandmother's house in Brunswick one morning and plucked him off the street. On the way back to the station in the police car, the inside man was told in no uncertain terms by Keuris that he was expected to spill the beans on his involvement in the Brambles job in Port Melbourne or face the consequences.

KEURIS: We put the fear of God into the kid. We told him, 'You're off to the big-house, mate! You'll be put behind bars for at least thirty years!' and all of that type of stuff. It didn't take long before he cracked under the pressure, and even before reaching the police station he'd already declared, 'They made me do it!' and gave up the names of Barci and Asling.

—

As a result of the new information, a special task force code-named Operation Thorn was set up to gather information on Barci and Asling. It included sixteen-hour-a-day surveillance as well as phone taps and multiple listening devices. The ARS's timing couldn't have been better. Soon after the surveillance teams began listening in on Barci and Asling, it became apparent they were already planning their next big job.

KEURIS: We were on them like white on rice. We were all over them. The more we observed them, the more we realised a lot of stuff was going on. It went on for months. They were colluding with known underworld figures Jason and Mark Moran about certain stuff, and we knew the Morans were major players. They were planning to knock a 'joint' over in Greensborough. They were trying to get some guns and were wanting the Morans to supply them with some pretty heavy weapons.

Mark Moran was trying to get his nose in the trough by asking how much of a cut he was going to get if he helped them out. Barci would appease him and guarantee that the Morans would get a taste, but would then complain to Asling and say, 'Can you believe that prick? He reckons he's gonna get some! Fuck 'em! Who do they think they are? Those bloody Morans!'

—

With the operation threatening to become a logistical nightmare due to the increasing number of notorious criminals involved, the detectives had to narrow their focus on Barci and Asling to avoid biting off more than they could chew. The Morans would live to fight (and die) another day. But despite investing many man-hours and resources into Operation Thorn, the detectives were blindsided by another robbery committed by Barci and Asling right under their noses.

Late one night, and coincidentally after the surveillance team had clocked off and powered down all the listening devices, Barci and Asling held up a McDonald's restaurant in Greensborough. Two customers had guns held to their heads while other patrons were forced to lie on the floor in fear for their lives.

The store manager was taken out the back and ordered to open the safe at gunpoint but was so terrified he couldn't remember the combination. A security guard had his Magnum .38 revolver and company car stolen. While the violent nature of this latest crime was alarming, most concerning to the ARS was the fact that Barci and Asling were prepared to go to such lengths for a measly $3500 in cash. It showed just how desperate they'd become for money.

Although Asling and Barci were the main suspects for the crime, detectives didn't have enough evidence to arrest them. Before too long, it became evident that the McDonald's hit was just a rehearsal for something much, much bigger.

While always careful about what they said, the pair was heard over surveillance constantly singing 'We're in the money' – it became a little ditty used whenever they were trying to get excited about their next crime. It was a pre-celebration song of sorts.

For the detectives, there was no room for error this time around, and the decision was made to call in the SOG, because they specialised in planning and executing high-risk arrests. As word quickly spread through the SOG's headquarters about Operation Thorn, soon enough the tune 'We're in the money' was also being sung by the Soggies, accompanied by a knowing look and a wink.

The SOG committed an unprecedented amount of support to Operation Thorn, but little did the group's superiors know, it would require several weeks of painstaking time, effort and money. Barci and Asling were actively scoping out a variety of new targets under the watchful eye of the Dogs (a nickname for police surveillance teams) and the SOG, but they were patient and calculated, electing to wait for the perfect opportunity – never really showing their hands to police. It was clear they were not going to simply act on a whim.

One of the sites they visited regularly was a Freight Terminal at Melbourne Airport that received weekly deliveries of cash from an Armaguard van. It prompted Sarge to make enquiries with the then head of Armaguard, Bob Bruce, to ask what the van was carrying and whether he knew of anything else that would be of interest to the criminals. Bruce couldn't identify any specific deliveries of cash, valuables or drugs, and that left the SOG and detectives perplexed as to why the van was a potential target. But the airport wasn't the only concern, as Barci and Asling also took an interest in various businesses in Sandringham, a Bank of Melbourne branch in Essendon and a Tip Top Bakeries factory in Brunswick that also received regular Armaguard deliveries.

Barci and Asling were observed taking notes on different armoured truck routes, drop-off and collection schedules and the shift times and movements of the guards. Asling began socialising at the Golden Fleece hotel in South Melbourne, a popular drinking hole for Armaguard employees. After plying one particularly outspoken guard with alcohol over the course of several weeks, Asling was able to get close enough to him to ask about the company's protocols and processes out at the airport. He was told that Armaguard employees were prohibited from carrying weapons into any building that had an access point to the tarmac and the planes. Following the same method as the Brambles job two years ago with the help of their previous inside man, Asling offered this Armaguard big mouth $100,000 in exchange for more information, but he declined. The guard decided not to go to the police for fear of retribution and the loss of his job for already disclosing too much sensitive information to an outsider.

While Asling and Barci continued to plot their heist, SOG members were ramping up their activity and began conducting reconnaissance missions at the airport and the Tip Top bakery. On one occasion, Sarge went undercover as an Armaguard employee and visited the bakery to gather more information about the site.

SARGE: I had an official Armaguard name tag and uniform to look one hundred per cent genuine. I went into the payroll area where all the money was actually being delivered and collected and took every step to try and work out what Asling and Barci were planning. We wanted to go one better than them and figure out what their exact plan was so we could try and emulate what they'd do. There was a hell of a lot of cash being delivered there; I just don't know how much. It definitely would have been a big payday for them if they had knocked that bakery over.

—

Sarge also went inside the Freight Terminal and went under-cover as a customer wanting to send some packages interstate. He examined each premises and looked at all the entry points, windows, locks, bolts, hinges – even the way the doors swung open. At each location, he put himself in Asling and Barci's shoes in an effort to better understand how they might carry out the job.

While time-consuming and often considered boring, recon-naissance is a vital component of the SOG's work. The members often spend days checking out a suspicious house, property or drug crop to gather essential information about the premises, and its occupants' movements and habits. More often than not, it means very early start times.

SARGE: There might be a situation where an offender gets up at 3.00 am every morning, grabs a gun, switches on his lights and does a patrol of his property or crop because he's paranoid about enemies. If we didn't know that and planned to do a raid at that exact time, it would completely compromise us. We have to know everything that might happen and when, as well as the layout of the building so we'll know where to look once we are inside.

—

Time after time, the SOG was on standby to make an arrest, with ARS detectives sensing an impending robbery. A SOG incident report reads:

> The suspects were again followed to the vicinity of the Tip Top bakery in Weston Street, Brunswick. They were observed to conduct a detailed reconnaissance of the area and also were observed watching the movements of an Armaguard van inside the yard of the bakery . . . The suspects did not commit an armed robbery at this time. The actual target of the armed robbery still was not known.

With the SOG in place and ready to pounce in Brunswick, the order came through to 'stand down' and return to headquarters.

A similar situation unfolded a week later, according to another incident report, which stated:

> members of the Special Operations Group were required to perform surveillance and provide an arrest capability for a possible armed robbery. The armed robbery did not eventuate. Members deployed to areas of responsibility then recalled as information came to hand to suggest the robbery would not happen on this date.

Barci and Asling continued to frustrate the SOG and ARS detectives by being extremely patient and cautious. It was clear that they'd identified their preferred targets, but, for reasons not known to police, they continually decided not to make a move on any of them.

Operation Thorn was beginning to drag on and on, and was at risk of being disbanded. Detectives had to retain the SOG's interest in the case and were aware of the job's strain on resources and funding. Daily briefings and constant updates were set up to keep the SOG on the hook and in the loop.

The Soggies were sent out on several more occasions to make the arrests but, again, there was no action from Barci and Asling. Police were still in the dark, according to a SOG member's incident report, which said:

[We] were again deployed in the vicinity of the Freight Terminal at Melbourne Airport. It was believed that the suspects were planning to commit an armed robbery in this location on this day. The exact time and target of the armed robbery were not known to police. The suspects were observed to place a vehicle at Gladstone Park Shopping Centre early in the morning. Later they were observed to place a stolen vehicle in Derby Street, Tullamarine, before proceeding to the vicinity of the Freight Terminal. They were observed to remain outside the terminal in a stolen white Ford panel van for some fifteen minutes. They were spoken to by a Skyroad Express courier for a short time. The suspects then left the area and collected the getaway vehicles. The courier is not suspected as being involved in the planned armed robbery.

Unbeknown to the courier mentioned in the incident report, he had in fact foiled a big robbery that was about to occur. When the suspects had parked outside the Freight Terminal, they needed an excuse to be there in case any airport security officers, police or AFP viewed them as being suspicious and moved in to ask questions. So the pair devised a plan that involved getaway driver Asling getting out of the van and lifting the bonnet into the locked position as though he had broken down. Therefore, if they were approached and questioned, they could just use 'engine troubles' as their reason for being parked there.

But the idea had backfired. The Skyroad Express courier pulled up beside them after seeing Asling pop the hood and offered some jumper leads to get them back on the road again. The men thought they had been 'made' by the courier and couldn't possibly continue with their planned robbery, so they pulled the pin on the job. They promptly left the scene, collected their strategically placed getaway vehicles, and later that night burnt the white panel van to destroy any evidence. They had to steal another panel van and start over.

Surveillance units continued to observe Asling and Barci as they returned to the Tip Top Bakeries factory. That act left detectives unsure of exactly which target was going to be hit and when. ARS detectives had also discovered the suspects were using a 'safe house', which was located in Avondale Heights. They sent the SOG there to conduct reconnaissance missions and observe any suspicious activity at the address.

In addition to these duties, the SOG conducted intensive training sessions specifically for Operation Thorn. At their secret training base, the elite group ran through all the likely scenarios that could unfold. But it wasn't all smooth sailing. During one shooting exercise, a bullet ricocheted off a static metal target and sliced into Rogue's leg.

ROGUE: I just thought it was a nerve in my leg that reacted to something. 'What the fuck was that?' I remember thinking at the time. We kept training and shooting, and about five minutes later I felt that there was something wrong with my foot. I started feeling all clammy and shitty, so I took my boot and sock off and they were just full of blood. 'Ah, what the hell's happening here?' I thought. 'Where did that come from?' I sat down and realised it was the jacket of the bullet . . . the whole jacket had come back and slung into my knee.

—

Rogue wasn't the only member to be hit with friendly fire. Lima also copped a stray casing to the side of the head and hand. It turned out that the ammunition the SOG was using was substandard, and the group immediately swapped its supplier.

ROGUE: I was shitting myself that I wasn't going to get a guernsey on Operation Thorn after all the work I'd done on the case. I thought that the bosses wouldn't let me do it because of my leg injury. But, as it turned out, they were able to stitch me up and I was right to go.

—

It was at this time the Dogs reported that Barci and Asling had taken a trip to Bendigo to test-fire some military-grade firearms on a large property. Something was about to go down, and the mood among the SOG members quickly changed.

SARGE: That gave us the impression that they were prepared to shoot it out with us or use their weapons on others if they were caught or impeded. I mean, if you're not planning on using any firearms, there's no need to test them or practise-fire with them, is there? All of our men needed to be aware that these criminals were to be treated as serious and extremely dangerous. They would use their weapons against us – there was no doubt about that. We're not talking about shoplifters who are non-violent.

These guys already had a history of carrying out big, dangerous jobs, but now it's escalating to the point where they're in possession of live, fully automatic weapons, rifles and handguns. They were rehearsing and practising to use those weapons against someone, and most likely it was us, the coppers.

—

A week to the day after the Skyroad Express courier foiled Barci and Asling's planned robbery, the SOG was again placed on standby, according to another incident report: 'it was believed that the suspects would again attempt to commit an armed robbery in the vicinity of the Freight Terminal. It was not known what the actual target of the operation was.' Police were convinced the offenders would stop at nothing this time around. And they were right.

Twenty-one SOG members met at Victoria Police headquarters at 7.30 am and updated their arrest plans during an hour-long, exhaustive briefing. The group rendezvoused at the nearby Essendon Airport at 8.30 am and split up half an hour later to take up their designated positions around the Freight Terminal area at Tullamarine. Due to the environment, likelihood of close-quarter combat and amount of civilian activity, the SOG's assault team elected to use shotguns for the job as opposed to semi-automatic firearms.

SIERRA: Shotguns are high powered but they travel less distance and are good for in-close jobs where there are no hostages. We always selected weaponry that we felt was most suited, and shotguns suited the likely scenario that would play out with these guys on this particular day.

—

SOG members blanketed the cargo areas of the airport. At the rear of the Freight Terminal, a team acted as observers and airside cut-offs while several others waited in vehicles along Melrose and Depot Drives in mobile cut-off teams. The assault team, which comprised Sarge, Sierra, Rogue, Khan and driver Dexter, crammed into a van and parked closest to the terminal. They would be the ones making the arrest.

SIERRA: We had to make sure that we were positioned in an area that if we wanted to move, no one could block us in. We were in a great position for observation. We relied on eyeballing the target vehicle at all times. We had people all over the place in plain clothes and all around the perimeter of the airport.

—

The five SOG men on the assault team sat patiently in the white Mitsubishi Express van. It looked like a legitimate tradesman's vehicle and had its windows heavily tinted. The SOG used it often, but most members' memories of it aren't too fond.

ROGUE: Trying to get relaxed in the back of that van there – not that we are all massive men, but when you're all bulked up with gear, guns and vests and all that crap, it's bloody tough.

SIERRA: You get to learn everything there is to know about each other when you spend long periods of time in cramped conditions like that. You get to know all their bodily functions, including what they've had for dinner the night before. It was hot and sweaty and we were wearing thirty to forty kilos' worth of equipment each, including body armour, spare weaponry, ammunition and various tools we might need for the operation. I'm talking heavy fabric uniforms that have got chemical treatment and fire retardant on them . . . so they're not the most comfortable type of clothing or attire, that's for sure.

You're crammed in, it's boiling hot, you're sweating like a pig and you can't really move because the van might rock, which would look suspicious from the outside. So we had to stay very still in there and keep quiet. You can't do a lot, and there are some long and boring stretches like that in the job. You just sit there, but despite how bad it is, you'll never find a team wanting to hand over to another group to take control of the job. We wanted to be there when the job went down . . . you don't ever want to miss out.

—

The assault team drove to the south-east side of the Freight Terminal and parked diagonally across the road. They were about 400 metres from where the suspects had pulled up the last time they'd visited. The distance between the SOG and the target area was critical for safety. The last thing they wanted was to have their lives put in danger or become the brunt of a police joke. As one famous story goes – some crooks held up a payroll office at the Spencer Street Station. A police van with some detectives inside parked too close to the scene and one of the offenders urinated on their vehicle. It became an infamous incident with a surveillance cameraman audible on the footage of the operation commentating, 'Look at this . . . the crooks are pissing on the coppers!'

With the need for a safe distance in mind, the assault team was careful not to position itself too close to the centre of any possible action, but not so far away that the team couldn't react quickly.

Operation Thorn was classified as 'Top Secret', and even the Armaguard and Freight Terminal employees were unaware they could be thrust into the middle of an armed robbery.

SARGE: If one of the employees had been hurt or shot, I would never have been able to live with it. But, at the end of the day, we didn't have enough information to warn them of any impending danger. Keep in mind, there was also the belief that one of the staff could have been in on the job, so the risk was too high. After their Port Melbourne stick-up, it was proven that a Brambles employee colluded with Barci and Asling, so we were very conscious of that on this job. We couldn't tell anyone or trust any staff members in case they were involved in some way.

—

With the SOG in position and ready, news came through via the Dogs that one of the suspects had parked a stolen BMW at the Gladstone Park Shopping Centre, just like what had transpired on Barci and Asling's run-throughs.

At 1.00 pm, a stolen Toyota Corolla and stolen white Ford panel van was tracked travelling in the direction of Melbourne Airport. Following the routine that had previously been observed by the Dogs, the Corolla was left parked close to the airport in Derby Street. The panel van, driven by Asling, stopped briefly as the Corolla was abandoned.

At 1.20 pm, the panel van rolled into the cargo area at Melbourne Airport and parked near the Freight Terminal. Its windows were blocked out with white paint, and it displayed false numberplates. Asling got out of the van and lifted the bonnet. Although the broken-down-car scenario backfired last time, he and Barci had decided to give it another go. In the back of the van, Barci waited patiently with a new addition to the team, Norman Lee.

No stranger to large-scale crimes, Lee was alleged to have been a key figure in the Great Bookie Robbery in 1976, when an estimated $14–16 million was stolen from bookmakers after six armed offenders raided the Victoria Club following the Easter races. Although Lee was the only one arrested for the crime, he was later released without charge due to a lack of evidence. Looking to lie low, he chose to live in Singapore for a short time, and when he returned a few years later, he re-established himself on the wrong side of the law.

Barci and Lee in particular were well equipped and prepared for a shootout. As well as their handguns, they had two high-powered Armalite assault rifles in the back of the van with them. One was a .223 AR-180 and the other was a 7.62 AR-10. One of the guns had two fully loaded magazines taped end to end inserted in it.

At 1.40 pm, the Armaguard van arrived at the Freight Terminal to make a delivery.

SARGE: I remember talking to my inspector and saying, 'The Armaguard van is here,' and he basically said, 'It's over to you, mate. You move in when you're ready to.'

ROGUE: I looked out and I could see the crooks; they were pretty much ready to go. They were in position and they were getting a little agitated . . . you could see these short and sharp movements they were making. I thought, 'Hang on . . . it's definitely gonna go down this time.'

—

The Armaguard van reversed up to the loading dock, and two guards removed several large red bags full of cash, bank cheques and other valuables from the rear. Both adhered to airport protocol and left their pistols behind, just as Barci and Asling were counting on. Outside, the SOG assault team watched as Asling suddenly put the panel van into reverse and backed towards the loading dock at high speed.

Sarge knew there was nothing his team could do to stop the robbery from happening. They were too far away to do anything.

SARGE: The van's doors flew open and, the next thing, two men wearing Michael Jackson masks jumped out with guns. It had to get to a point – and people have to realise this, because there was a lot of criticism afterwards, with people asking, 'Why did we let them do the robbery in the first place?' and 'You knew they were there so why not arrest them when they pulled up?'

Well, firstly, we didn't 'let' them do the robbery; they chose to do it at such a frantic, fast pace that we had no choice but to let it all unfold. Our plan was always to intercept them before they committed the armed robbery, but at what stage was the line drawn as to 'Okay, they're there . . . now they're going to do an armed robbery'? We didn't know. There was a white panel van sitting there in the car park. We knew it was stolen, we knew there was one person in the driver's seat, but we didn't know if there was anyone else in the back. We assumed there was, we assumed they had weapons, but we didn't know for sure. Keep in mind they did this the week before and didn't do anything. So imagine us jumping out of our van yelling, 'Police! Don't move! You're under arrest!' They'd be like, 'What for? No standing?' We would have blown the entire operation and, with that, weeks and weeks of work and taxpayers' money.

—

The decision was made to let the armed robbery run its course. The SOG had to hope there'd be no staff harmed or hostages taken inside the terminal. Seated on the steps outside, a Freight employee was enjoying his afternoon smoko and was looking in the opposite direction when the Michael Jackson look-alikes burst through the doors of his office. He was completely unaware his colleagues were about to be held up at gunpoint inside.

Dexter started the SOG van and began to drive towards Asling in the suspects' panel van. Sarge spoke calmly to the men in the back and prepared them for the high-risk arrest.

SARGE: I reminded them to be safe and to remember our training. I could have been like, 'Oh god! They're doing it! Shit! Let's go, let's go!' but my blokes would be jumping out of the van and would be running across the car park at the offenders. I can remember getting squashed in doorways as a detective for that exact reason. When we'd raid a house back then, some blokes would race to get in first. Everyone just got out of the car and bolted for the front door of the crook's house and, sure enough, me being one of the smaller blokes, I used to get crunched in the doorway. So it was important we executed the job as we'd trained. With calm and level heads.

—

With Barci and Lee inside the terminal, Asling monitored a radio scanner that was tuned in to the Armaguard's frequency, in case a distress call was made. The tension was rising. In the back of the SOG van, Sarge, Rogue, Sierra and Khan were ready for action. Inside the terminal, the hold-up was taking place, and the Armaguard guards were handing over bags full of cash to the armed offenders.

Seconds later, Lee and Barci burst through the terminal doors back out to the car park and ran towards the getaway car still masked, carrying handguns and dragging large red bags behind them. Asling had kept the engine running and was ready to whisk them away.

Dexter pulled in to the car park and positioned the SOG van facing west, at right angles to the terminal and in front of the Ford to try to block Asling in.

SARGE: There was no fear or trepidation among us because we'd planned so much and so well for the job. We were there to support each other, to work as a team, and we were supremely confident that we'd be in total control. The fact that we had the element of surprise and we were superior in number and arms meant we'd win every time.

When Lee and Barci got back to their feet after Asling slammed down the accelerator and inadvertently dumped them on the pavement, they had a choice to make: fight or flight. Barci chose fight. He opened fire on the SOG and his first shot missed Rogue and hit the ground, whereupon he was hit with a volley of returned fire.

ROGUE: They were always up for it. They were always going to fight their way out of it. Barci was falling to the ground after I shot him between the shoulder-blades, but he didn't let go of the gun he had, so I kept firing at him. He finally dropped it after he hit the ground. He did a couple of rolls on the bitumen and he was just screaming in agony.

—

Sarge and Sierra had Lee covered and were also confronted with a life-or-death situation. Lee pointed his silver Magnum towards the men in black but couldn't get a round away before being shot.

SARGE: For a moment, it seemed like he was putting his weapon down, but then he suddenly brought it up again. I can still see it clearly and I remember his exact body movements. He made a slight hesitation with the gun hand by moving down and then, nup, he changed his mind and brought it up and aimed it towards me. That's when I obviously instinctively shot at him. I didn't even think about it. It was just an instinctive, defensive reaction, and I struck him on his left side.

—

Sierra also felt threatened by Lee's actions and fired within a split second of Sarge.

SIERRA: Two of our shotgun blasts struck him in the shoulder and head area, and we blew him out of one of his shoes. A single sneaker was left sitting on the ground, and I'd never seen that happen before. It was just one of those things that you look at and you go, 'Wow!' It just sticks with you. It was pretty weird. Lee was wearing a black jacket, and I could see the stuffing coming out of it as the rounds hit him. We were using SG rounds that contained nine pellets in each cartridge . . . so he would have been hit by up to eighteen pellets by the two shots in the upper-body and head area, and that's what blew him out of his shoe.

—

Lee hit the deck hard. Sarge believes he died instantly, but Rogue says he took a few seconds to pass away.

ROGUE: Lee blew a big, massive blood bubble out of his mouth. It was like a kid blowing a bubble with bubble gum . . . a huge one the size of a little basketball. It was just a huge, big blood bubble and then it popped, and that was the end of Normie Lee. Barci was screaming and carrying on whereas Lee didn't make a single sound. He was lying right next to my feet — I mean right at my feet — and he was gone, just out of it. Their Michael Jackson masks were spooky . . . just spooky. You couldn't see their eyes properly; you couldn't see their facial expressions . . . I didn't know if I was missing Barci when I was shooting him because it looked like he was just tumbling. If I had been able to see his face, I would have probably seen his expressions and an 'Ahhh, fuck! Fuck! . . . that hurt' kind of look. It would have been a lot easier and I thought, 'Am I even shooting this bloke or not?'

SARGE: We formed a tight perimeter around Barci and Lee. When it was deemed safe, I moved forwards and kicked the guns away from them.

—

Under his black jacket, Lee had two layers of clothing, including a white, pinstriped shirt and a navy blue and red-spotted tie. Underneath the shirt, he had a dark-blue sweater with the logo 'MFL – Made For Life – Adrenalin Sportswear' embroidered on the left side. He also had twelve .357-calibre cartridges in his pocket. He was declared dead at approximately 1.45 pm, and it appeared Barci would meet a similar fate after he was shot at least five times by Rogue in his shoulder and back. Paramedics took some time to get to the scene and indicated to the SOG members that Barci's wounds were likely to be fatal. But despite being declared dead on the way to the hospital and two more times in intensive care, Barci somehow survived.

ROGUE: I've seen enough dead people and seen enough people die in front of me to know Barci had already gone past the stage of turning grey. His breathing was rooted and he was gone, in my opinion. I mean he died three times and they brought him back to life, which I'm happy about. But either way, if Barci was dead or alive, it didn't bother me, because he had shot at me. He really had a shot so I knew it was fair game. It was just a game. He was playing his game, and you're not allowed to play that game. So he got spanked for it like a little kid would in the playground for doing something he's not supposed to do. He got spanked really hard.

—

As for Asling, while he managed to escape the arrest team, his freedom was short-lived. Just up the road on the way out of the airport precinct, he ran directly into a SOG mobile cut-off team, seconds after Barci and Lee had been intercepted and shot. As he turned down Depot Drive and accelerated, a SOG intercept vehicle closed in. Inside the white Nissan Patrol that was fitted with a heavy-duty bumper bar was Hawk, Mossy and Elmo.

HAWK: I heard the gunshots in the distance and we started driving down Depot Drive. When we reported the white panel van was approaching us, we were given instructions from our inspector over the radio. 'Stop that car at all costs!' he said. So Mossy increased the speed and jumped the median strip, swerving directly into Asling's path. He just floored it as hard as he could. We had a few other guys in the car, one of which was on his first job with us.

—

Hawk's timing was perfect. As he veered aggressively, Asling had no chance to avoid being hit.

HAWK: We had a massive head-on collision with him. Hawk was given the instruction, 'If you're going to park them, then park them good!' 'Park them' meant stop the getaway car in its tracks and make no mistake about it. We had to stop Asling because, if he got past us, it would have been a high-speed chase on the freeway and the public would have been in danger.

—

The Nissan crunched into the front and the left side of the van and buckled its front wheel. The bonnet folded like a piece of paper and the windscreen shattered while the front passenger door compacted to within a third of its original width. It was a heavy but effective collision, and the SOG members inside were lucky to escape relatively unscathed. Only one team member suffered any injuries, when his head slammed into the windscreen.

Dazed and confused, Asling looked through his smashed windscreen and was confronted by several Soggies with their firearms raised. His .45 revolver had been jolted from under his legs in the collision and he was unable to recover it. He had no option but to surrender.

With the threat now over, one dead, two apprehended, the robbery foiled and $1,025,000 cash recovered, Sierra, Sarge and Rogue started coming to terms with the chaos that had just unfolded and the fact they survived a near-death experience.

SIERRA: You're on a bit of a high from the adrenaline dump after a shooting like that. It's more of a survivor type reaction and pure joy that you've just confronted death and beaten it. It was quite an unusual feeling. That could easily have been my last day on earth and everything because of that was so much sweeter – the sun on my face, the breath of air in my lungs and the taste of food. It all becomes that much more important after you nearly lose your life.

But there was little time to reflect, with the homicide squad on the scene within minutes and taking full control. Sarge,

Rogue and I were quickly separated and told not to speak to one another as an investigation into the shootings would commence immediately.

—

Rogue remembers feeling like he had done something wrong because of the ensuing interrogations.

ROGUE: They swabbed our fingers for GSR straight away, which was fair enough, but in those days we were the ones treated like criminals. They stuck us in the AFP offices at the airport and we were thinking, 'What the fuck's happening here?' They took us in separate cars; we weren't even allowed to walk 200 metres. They drove us over there and we all thought, 'This isn't fucking right.'

—

Homicide-squad detective Johnny Morrish took the statements from the SOG members. Morrish was nicknamed 'The Pope', because no one could lie to him and he elicited more than his fair share of confessions from criminals. More than two hours later, the SOG's assault-team members were finally given permission to call their families.

SARGE: I immediately called my wife and told her, 'Look, you'll see something pretty disturbing on the news tonight, but I'm all right and everyone with me is all right. There's nothing to worry about.' I was always more concerned for her and my kids than I was for myself.

—

From the time Barci, Asling and Lee were intercepted by the SOG to the time Lee was killed and Barci was shot and arrested, just ten seconds had transpired. Asling was apprehended about twenty seconds after the shootings, and the entire incident was over in less than thirty seconds.

None of the SOG members have any regrets about what occurred, but they do resent the criticism they received regarding their actions on the day, even from those directly involved.

SARGE: I wasn't concerned at all about having done what I did. First off, you always ask yourself, 'Was I justified in pulling the trigger and doing what I did?' and I didn't mull over that question at all. I had two other members in Rogue and Sierra that had also fired, and my primary concern was for them, not me. I had to put myself in their shoes. To this day, I haven't lost a night's sleep over shooting Lee.

If you ever face a man with a gun, make sure he's got it in his holster. If he ever takes it out of that holster, you have to ask, 'What's his intention?' In my view, his intention is to use it to shoot you. At the end of the day, there are 101 different ways he can shoot you before you can respond or react in a 'justifiable way'. A police officer has to be so justified when he fires his weapon compared with a solider. The saying 'shoot and let God sort it out' doesn't apply to us, because we have to answer to a coroner. In that hesitation to answer to a coroner, police can get killed.

It's like the instruction you often hear police around the world get told: 'Don't shoot unless someone shoots at you first.' It's ridiculous. It only takes one shot and you're dead, so why give the gunman that opportunity? People suffer from PTSD because they question themselves. They question themselves with things like: 'Did I react properly?'; 'Could I have done anything different?'; 'Could I have died because of it?' And they shit themselves.

That wasn't me. All these people sit in their ivory towers and throw criticism out and they will never, ever come close to experiencing or dealing with the sorts of things we have to. I remember saying to a coroner once, with the greatest deal of respect, 'I was there and you weren't,' and he backed off.

ROGUE: I knew I'd done the right thing in a justified way. I had no interest in ever killing anyone, and, with Barci, I just wanted to stop him. If I had to kill him to stop him, that wouldn't have bothered me at all. I wouldn't have lost a night's sleep over killing him. Don't get me wrong; I'm glad he lived, because he's a good bloke . . . he actually is a good bloke. He just made some poor choices back then. You stop when the threat stops, and he still had the handgun and had already shot at me once. He's doing an armed robbery, he's masked, his mate's got a handgun and they were there to do as much damage as they could if they couldn't get what they wanted, and I didn't want to be damaged. So I was just going to keep shooting until he was no longer a threat, and that's pretty much what I did. That's what we train to do. As he hit the deck, I took my secondary weapon out, my handgun out, and covered him with that. I wasn't convinced it was over, even after shooting him with those five rounds.

—

Barci levelled some stinging attacks at the SOG members during his court case. His defence team claimed he and Lee had fallen out of the van unarmed and were shot in their backs 'like dogs'. Sarge finds the accusation laughable.

SARGE: Lee, I can categorically say, had a handgun, because I wouldn't have shot him otherwise. It's also visible in the surveillance photos from the day. I also back my decision to shoot him with the fact that I chose *not* to shoot Asling, because I believed him to be unarmed when he drove off in the getaway van. I got a good look at him, saw no gun and opted to shoot the tyre out instead. The criticism is just too ridiculous for words. I mean, seconds after the shots were fired, you looked across the road and there was about 250 people standing there looking at us. If we were going to blatantly murder them, we would have had an awful lot of witnesses.

—

Barci also claimed police were involved in a conspiracy to kill him and his own revolver only went off when it hit the ground after he was shot.

ROGUE: He shot at me well before I shot at him . . . it was probably half a second, which is actually a long time in those circumstances. I've discussed it with him since, face to face . . . the two of us, over a fairly long drinking session, and he knows he was wrong. He knows he shot at me first, but he just can't understand why I shot him so many times. I said to him, 'I only shot you five times because I only had five rounds on me, Steve. If I had an extended mag and had had eight rounds, I would have shot ya eight times.' We had a laugh and another beer after that.

—

Sarge argued that, had Barci's gun gone off when it hit the ground, the projectile would not have spiralled into the ground at Rogue's feet and the gun must have been faulty — but a forensic examination proved it was fully functional.

SARGE: I can guarantee 99.9 per cent that it wasn't an accidental discharge from it being dropped and going off. The fact they had live rounds in their weapons, the fact they had serious weaponry and the fact that one of the weapons fired, plus the fact that Lee brought his gun up in a threatening manner, paints the picture pretty well about their mental preparedness to shoot at us. Add to that they'd rehearsed with their firearms prior to the robbery.

Crooks always come out with crazy statements in court and drum up anything they can to take away from the fact that they're the ones in the wrong and they're the criminals. Barci squeezed the trigger; the question is did he do it intentionally or unintentionally? I believe he did it intentionally, as a reflex action. That round had come out as he was running or had been shot and dropped at Rogue's feet. If the gun did somehow go off accidentally, it would have to have been in a cocked position, where the trigger is very light – so if he had it cocked, it points to the fact even more so that he intended to shoot at us.

—

An airport employee who was having his lunch as the shootings took place witnessed the shootout and corroborated the SOG members' version of events.

In the wash-up, detectives established that Barci, Asling and Lee had planned to return to the Corolla they had parked minutes away on Derby Street to remove their clothes, swap vehicles and depart in shirts and ties to look like respectable businessmen who had just flown in from interstate.

The offenders had also planned to use the semi-automatic rifles in the back of the van in the event of a police pursuit. If that had unfolded, Lee and Barci would have set up the rifles on bipods and opened the back barn doors of the panel van. From that position, they would have been able to fire a frightening amount of bullets at any chasing police vehicles.

SIERRA: If Barci and Lee had stayed in the back of the van when it took off and got their hands on those semi-automatic guns, they would have been able to punch holes straight through our ballistic vests, and it would have been a completely different outcome. If things had happened only a split second later than they actually did, the whole situation would have been different and I might not be sitting here today.

Of course, we would have won, but it would have been an expensive win. We probably would have lost myself, Sarge and Rogue, and maybe some of the other guys in the other teams as well. If they had escaped our initial ambush along with Asling, they would have had to fight their way out of the inner cordon, which was made up of all the other teams and cut-off teams, and they would have lost there for sure. But, as I said, we would have lost a lot of police officers and maybe some civilians in and around the airport had they been using that sort of high-powered weaponry.

SARGE: You've got to wonder why on earth they had those high-powered, fully automatic machine guns. There's no doubt they were prepared to shoot at us in pursuit of them. I can guarantee if that had happened, we would have backed off pretty fast.

—

The trio expected to flee with more than $2,000,000 in cash and goods, and although they fell a little short, the $1,020,000 they briefly obtained still ranks as one of the biggest armed robberies in Victoria.

Coroner Jacinta Heffey found Rogue and Sierra did not contribute to the death of Norman Lee, stating:

There is in my view independent evidence of sufficient cogency to support their statements to the effect that Lee was armed and

that the Special Operations Group members made attempts prior to the shooting to command the robbers to surrender. Whether Lee was in fact raising his gun in order to shoot will-never be known . . . The three robbers were in possession of far more weaponry and ammunition than they could need to perform an armed robbery alone.

12

BETRAYAL (PART II)

*And when they were in the field, Cain rose up against his
brother Abel and killed him.*

Genesis 4:8

With prison escapee Archie Butterly still hidden in thick bushes
at Picnic Point near Jamieson, Mouse had little time to react
when he started firing. Rogue, Travis Blackman and Shamus, the
police dog, had leapt headfirst into the blackberries, but Mouse
had to quickly look for cover of his own.

MOUSE: As soon as I crouched low to the ground after Shamus
picked up a scent, the gunman, who I later learnt was Butterly,
opened up and started firing at us. All I could see were muzzle
flashes coming out of the bushes directly ahead of me, and
I thought, 'That's good . . . but they haven't hit me yet.' I don't
know how many shots he fired, but there were a hell of a lot
of bullets coming our way. CRACK! CRACK! CRACK! CRACK!
CRACK! CRACK! When I saw those muzzle flashes, I thought,
'Righto. It's game on now!'

—

The SOG is well drilled and regularly assured by its superiors that, under stress, the men will always revert to the way they've been trained. There are few better drilled teams anywhere in the world. With only a few options open to him under heavy fire, Mouse took immediate action.

MOUSE: All I could tell is that the gun that was being fired was some sort of a semi-automatic. So I've opened up back at the shooter's position and emptied a mag out of my Steyr before I moved to find safety. I didn't see what Rogue and the others did, but my only way of finding any cover was in the freezing water to my right, so I just jumped in headfirst without really thinking. The water was just deep enough to give me enough cover from the shooter, and I disappeared out of sight.

—

What came next has made Mouse something of a legend in the police force, and his incredible actions have become folklore. In typical SOG fashion, though, he has always refused to elaborate on his remarkable act for fear of being perceived as a self-proclaimed hero – until now.

MOUSE: The water was deep and I dived in – I had no other choice. I knew my mag was empty, so I rolled over underwater and flipped onto my back and unloaded my gun. Just by feel alone, I grabbed another mag out of my tactical vest, pushed my gun back above the surface of the water and held it on an angle to let the water drain back out. Then I inserted the new loaded mag. I could see a little bit underwater because it was pretty clear, but I had to rely on my training and, more importantly, the knowledge of the components of my gun to pull the mag change off. I resurfaced and was standing in the water and emptied another mag on Butterly's position. The firing from his direction had stopped at this stage.

I'd never done that manoeuvre before. It was pure instinct. I knew it would work as long as I had my gun up out of the water and on an angle to drain all the water out of the barrel after I pulled the empty magazine out. I knew it would keep firing if I did it correctly. If I pulled the trigger with water still in the barrel, I probably would have blown the gun up – and myself, for that matter.

—

Despite the brilliance of the underwater dive roll, Mouse has never acknowledged it as being anything but a 'split-second reaction necessary for my survival'. But there is little doubt – Mouse's jaw-dropping move saved his life, and also the lives of Rogue, Blackman and Shamus.

MOUSE: At the end of the day, in those situations, you'll do anything to make sure you've got some sort of cover and can avoid being shot and killed. It was a natural reaction. There was no cover for me on the pebble beach, and the blackberry bushes weren't that inviting, as Rogue and Blackman discovered. I went to my right; they went to their left. It is what it is. I don't consider what I did as anything special or heroic; it was a necessary action to try and protect myself and the others.

—

After resurfacing and emptying his second magazine, Mouse stayed low in the waist-deep water and waited for Butterly's counter-fire, but this time there was none. Everything was silent. Even the birds had stopped chirping, no doubt scared off by all the gunfire.

MOUSE: Blackman was in the worst spot of all during the shootout, because he was right up, deep in the blackberry bushes. He was pushed right in there by Rogue and he wasn't coping very well with what was happening, which is understandable. Dog squad members encounter some pretty heavy shit on the job, but this was life or death. He wasn't panicking but he was terrified. He was shaking like a leaf – just absolutely terrified.

—

Minutes went by and there was still nothing coming from the bushes. No shots, no sounds or movement – nothing. Mouse assumed that either he'd shot whoever had been shooting or they'd fled. This gave him time to gather his thoughts, and he knew he was lucky to have survived.

MOUSE: I carry more ammunition than most, and I reckon that's what saved me.

—

In the blackberry bushes, Rogue started to worry about his well-being after remembering he'd been shot.

ROGUE: I had been trying to find out who was shooting at us and where from . . . trying to cover every direction while also covering Blackman and Shamus – who was going berserk. Papa had arrived and I had just remembered that I had been shot in the leg. He was obviously pretty concerned and shocked and said, 'What do you mean you've been shot? How can you only be telling me that now?' and I said, 'I fuckin' forgot, all right?'

Papa crawled down next to me and the look on his face didn't fill me with any confidence. He looked like he was shittin' himself a bit – afraid of what he might find down there, and because he had to move and potentially expose himself to whoever was shooting at us. We were all that fucken worried about exposing ourselves to the gunman. So Papa moved beside me and said, 'Oh, shit . . . there's a big hole in the back of your pants.'

He took his gloves off and put his fingers inside the tear and there was this thick, shitty blood all over them . . . like gooey blood. He goes, 'Oh, fuck!' and I'm like, 'What? What is it?' When he showed me the blood on his fingers and hand, I was like, 'Fuck . . . I'm in trouble here, aren't I?'

—

Papa called in aerial support and a medic. 'Rogue's been shot,' he declared over the radio. He then started calling on the escapees to surrender. 'This is the police! Give yourselves up! Put your weapons down and crawl into the river with your hands in the air, where we can see them!' There was no response.

The police helicopter, with a second team of Soggies on board (including designated aerial sniper Sierra), was already in the air, searching bushland on the other side of Mount Buller. It had flown over Picnic Point earlier, but no one on board at the time had been able to spot the well-hidden Pajero.

The pilot quickly turned the chopper around when news that Rogue had been shot was broadcast over the radio.

SIERRA: We received the information that one of ours had been shot and possibly killed. That info came from the cockpit and was relayed to us in the back.

MACK: We didn't know anything about his condition, only that he'd been shot, so we feared the worst.

TANGO: It was the best helicopter flight I've ever had. The pilot was a gun. He was cutting through the mountains, just hammering it. I don't know what Vietnam was like but I reckon it would have been close. We flew in low-level over their approximate location and came in at about eighty feet [twenty-four metres]. That was cutting it fine for our fast rope, which was ninety feet [twenty-seven metres] long, but we couldn't get any closer to the ground because of the height of the trees.

—

A fast rope isn't for the faint of heart. Normally when the SOG is deployed from a hovering chopper, the men hook on to ropes with a harness and rappel down to the ground. But when time isn't a luxury, there is no harness, no hooking in and no rappelling.

SIERRA: With a fast rope, you just lean out of the chopper and grab hold of the rope with your gloves. You use a double-hand and double-foot grip by wedging the rope between the smalls of your feet and use friction as you slide down to control the rate of descent.

—

This technique enabled the SOG to get multiple men out of the chopper and on to the rope at the same time, meaning a much faster deployment. The men couldn't get to the ground fast enough. So much so, Sierra forgot to put on his roping gloves.

SIERRA: We were under pressure to get to the ground fast and help out, and I just forgot to put my leather roping gloves over my Nomex flight gloves. The Nomex gave me minimal protection but were definitely not suitable for a fast rope of eighty feet, that's for sure.

—

The clock was ticking and Sierra decided to continue without his roping gloves, rather than hold up the rescue mission and risk more SOG being shot or killed. It was a brave decision, as he descended at about eight feet (two-and-a-half metres) per second.

SIERRA: I just jumped out and slid down. My gloves were hot when I hit the ground, but I didn't feel my hands had been burnt or anything at the time because the adrenaline dump was so intense. Somehow, I avoided any serious injury and only had a few blisters.

—

Sierra wasn't the only one who had trouble with the fast rope. Second out of the chopper, Tango had to drop ten feet (three metres) to the ground because the helicopter had shifted sideways and the rope had fallen over the riverbank down to the river and no longer reached the distance.

TANGO: I let go of the rope and hit the riverbank and rolled into the river. I don't know how but I was back on the road before the third man hit the ground! One of the other men saw it all from the ground and thought I should have broken both my legs upon impact, but I was lucky to get out of it relatively unscathed.

—

Desperate to get to the scene, the rescue team carefully made its way up the river. Meanwhile, Papa continued to monitor Rogue's condition.

ROGUE: I knew the boys were shittin' themselves in the chopper. They were thinking I was cactus. They called for the air ambulance to fly me back to Melbourne, and although I told Papa, 'I'm not feeling that bad,' he wouldn't hear it. 'Nup . . . we've gotta get you outta here. Just stay here; I'm going to go back around to find Mouse.'

I refused to stay put. There was no way I was gonna stay there all by myself . . . it's the worst fucken place I'd ever been in. So, I crawled out and followed Papa into the river. Papa was floating with the current and was so focused on where he was going, he didn't realise I was right behind him. He suddenly stopped and I ran right into his back and he absolutely shit himself. He goes, 'Fuck! What are you doing here? Fuck! You should have told me you were coming! What about your leg?' I said, 'It's fine. It doesn't even fuckin' hurt! Let's just go!'

—

The pair returned to the pebble beach where Rogue had been shot and thankfully found Mouse, unharmed. It had been about half an hour since the initial shootout began.

ROGUE: The water was starting to get really chilly now. Papa was shaking and I was shaking. We were starting to seize up a bit, because it was so bloody cold. Trying to move was tough. If anyone had seen the speed at which we were moving, they would have thought we were a pair of eighty-year-old blokes.

—

Mouse was suffering from the cold too, having spent the most amount of time in the water.

MOUSE: I hadn't moved out of the river and couldn't feel my legs by that stage. They were completely numb because of the freezing cold water.

220

The rescue team arrived, and Sierra was relieved to see Rogue alive and still active.

SIERRA: Rogue told me he had been hit and wounded. He was trembling, but I didn't know whether it was because of the gunshot wound or the cold water. I told him I needed to see it, so he lay down and I pulled out my knife and opened up his pants to reveal the wound. Thankfully, the bullet hadn't done too much damage. He took some convincing, though, because it obviously felt a lot worse to him at the time. It was a .223 round travelling at more than 2000 feet [610 metres] per second, but it had only nicked his leg. There's no doubt that it would have felt like a significant blow when it hit him, but, because of the cold, he was pretty numb, and add to that the adrenaline – he couldn't feel how bad it was. He was sure that he'd been seriously wounded, so I had to convince him that he was fine and would 'pull through'.

With reinforcements on the scene, the SOG devised a plan to flush the gunmen out.

SIERRA: We were in a gully, which was pretty abrupt, and there was blackberry bushes to our left after the sandbank and then heaps of trees. To the right of us, there was the river and more trees, and then it got pretty mountainous. We were in a little valley.

MOUSE: We knew someone was either dead or injured in there, so we moved forwards on the shooter's position. I couldn't go, because I physically couldn't move my legs, so I remained where I was as a cover man. Sierra gave me an extra mag of ammunition and I stayed put.

—

The SOG moved off the beach and into the forest area, but the blackberries again proved troublesome. A thick line of bushes sat between the beach and the shooter's location, so Sierra acted as a human stepladder or plank in order to get the rest of the team across.

SIERRA: I lay across the bushes, and Papa crawled over me first and took up a protective position on the other side. Then the dog handler and Shamus went over.

—

Tango took an elevated flanking position on the opposite, high side of the river to cover his team and looked down on the shooter's last-known position. From there, he could make out a foreign shape among the dense foliage.

TANGO: I could see the length of someone or something lying there in the bushes. I radioed a point of reference to Sierra and Papa, using a large gum tree that was right next to the unidentified object.

—

Well established and in a strong position along the tree line, with plenty of cover, Papa and Sierra attempted to elicit some movement or a reaction from the offenders to gauge whether it was safe enough to move forwards.

SIERRA: I threw a nine-banger, which is a distraction grenade, based on Tango's information, and it landed right on the shooter's position.

TANGO: I saw the grenade land right on top of the object I'd spotted. There was no movement whatsoever after it exploded, and I advised the assault team. If there was movement, I had a good shot and could have easily taken them out.

—

A nine-banger doesn't do any physical damage and casts no shrapnel out once it detonates, unlike a regular grenade. It is merely designed to let off nine loud bangs in quick succession, as well as some bright flashes and a bit of smoke. Usually, the SOG would throw such a device into a room before they raided it, in order to surprise, distract, confuse and disorientate any occupants. On this occasion, Papa and Sierra thought it could stir up some movement or a reaction that would allow them to assess the next course of action.

With no change in the circumstances, Shamus was sent in.

SIERRA: Blackman let him off the lead and gave him a command, and he raced off and disappeared into the bushes. All we could hear was the rustling of the leaves and branches and a lot of growling. Then we saw the trees shaking and the growling got louder. He was having a chew on whatever was in there.

—

After a few minutes, Blackman called Shamus back out.

SIERRA: He returned with blood all over his face, nose and jowls. Not many people can take a police dog chewing on them without yelling or screaming or making some sort of indication that they're alive. So we were fairly certain that whoever was in there was more than likely severely injured or dead.

—

Because the SOG had come under heavy fire already, they took no risks. The only way they could move forwards safely was by 'tactical bounding by cover fire'. From his position in the river, Mouse fired five rounds into the bushes as Sierra moved briskly to another tree for cover. Once in position, Sierra fired five rounds, allowing Papa to reposition himself closer. The constant 'fire and movement' is a common tactic designed to make it difficult for the enemy to engage any one target.

SIERRA: We needed to assault forwards. If we didn't, they could have flanked us. In order to maintain the momentum and the initiative, we went forwards with controlled aggression in order to get a resolution. There was no way we were going to let them dictate terms again.

—

With no movement and no further gunfire coming from the bushes, the SOG moved in on the position, confident that the threat had been eliminated.

There, they found the body of Butterly with a fatal gunshot wound to the back of his head, it was later discovered that it had been inflicted by the revolver that was stolen from the police officer back in the city during their escape from the Remand Centre. Butterly had several weapons with him.

ROGUE: When we approached him, he was dead – dead as a doornail. Next to him was a bag full of ammunition, suggesting his last stand had ended a lot earlier than it could have.

—

Back out on the main road, Kek was standing guard and saw two people drifting down the river. He immediately pulled his gun and called on them: 'Police! Don't move!' As they floated closer, Kek realised it was Peter Gibb and Heather Parker. Unarmed, the pair had attempted to escape by drifting down the river, but they were spotted just as they reached the perimeter of the SOG's cordon.

With one dead, two in police custody and Rogue treated at the scene, the violent ordeal had finally ended. But Parker and Gibb weren't done causing headaches for the SOG.

SIERRA: Butterly's headshot was clearly self-inflicted, but people – particularly the criminal element – like to say that we executed him.

—

Rogue, though, believes there was another explanation and voiced his opinion in the subsequent Coroner's Court inquest.

ROGUE: A defence lawyer asked me in the witness box, 'Who do you presume killed Mr Butterly?' It was a stupid question but he had to ask it, I suppose. I replied, 'I believe Heather Parker did it. That's what I think.' I still believe that today. I reckon she did it for sure. The way the round was fired into his head and the way we saw it all when we first turned up there, I doubt that he would have shot himself. It would have been an unusual way to do it.

—

Mouse says that forensic examination of Parker backs up Rogue's claim.

MOUSE: I had obviously put a heap of rounds on him, but he'd been shot behind the ear with a .38 revolver. I assumed that it was either Parker or Gibb that shot him, but apparently she was the only one with GSR on her hands. We assume she shot him. I think they never expected to miss us because we were like sitting ducks for a moment. But once they opened up on us and missed, they copped about sixty to seventy rounds back at them in such a short amount of time, and they've all just put their heads down and thought, 'This is going to be the end of the world!' With Butterly's injuries from the Remand Centre escape, I reckon they decided he was a liability because he couldn't move. They couldn't escape with him so they got rid of him.

—

In a further examination of the scene, Mouse recognised that he and Rogue weren't the only ones to have experienced some early near misses during the shootout.

MOUSE: All the ground in front of Butterly's position was chewed up. He'd been hit in several places. There were gunshots on him, like little nicks from all the .223 rounds going past him. There was a couple of big gashes or bullet channels on his body, so although we had hit him, the fatal shot was the .38 shot just above his ear.

—

One thing that can't be argued is that Butterly was on borrowed time from the injuries he sustained on day one of the escape and wanted to take as many police with him as possible.

SIERRA: Parker and Gibb reportedly told investigators that Butterly was under the firm impression that he was dying. He had jammed wads of toilet paper up his rectum because he was severely haemorrhaging internally. That's why they burnt down the Gaffneys Creek hotel, because he'd left so much blood in the toilet there. He'd been injured when they blew their way out of the Remand Centre, then he'd fallen out of the window and also had a few motorcycle accidents after that. With all the internal injuries to his stomach, he probably would have died from those if he wasn't shot.

—

Some of the SOG claim that luck played a big part in their survival that day, but Mouse believes it was their thorough preparation and skill that saved them.

MOUSE: The way I look at it is that we were trained exceptionally well. None of us panicked. Even though Travis Blackman was terrified, he didn't panic or run around with his hands in the air screaming, or anything like that. We responded exactly how we were trained. We returned fire straight away.

ROGUE: We were all saved by the fact that Shamus picked up the scent and that Travis passed that info on to us quickly and covertly. He didn't yell out, 'Fuck! There's someone here!' Butterly was watching us the whole time, for sure. We were quiet as can be, but, from his position, he would have seen everything. We stood in his bunker afterwards and had a look at the view he had, and there's no doubt he saw us. Of course, there were times when we would have been drifting in and out of their sight in behind trees and that, but they knew where we were, most of the time.

—

Rogue said it wasn't long after the ordeal when the SOG began to relive the shootout with a much more light-hearted view.

ROGUE: We shit-stirred each other about stuff constantly. It was our way of dealing with things. I gave shit to Sierra about the way he fast-roped down, saying, 'You could have got there quicker! I was in danger and could have died!' He'd give it back to me: 'You weren't in danger, you fucking little girl . . . it was just a scratch on the back of your leg from the blackberries, not a bullet wound!' We'd have a laugh about it but, the fact is, it was pretty dangerous shit, especially for that twenty- or thirty-second period when all the shooting started. It was probably one of the worst jobs we'd had at the SOG at that stage, because we were undermanned, we didn't know where the shots were coming from and it was pretty much three against three. We always like to have superior numbers.

On a more serious note, weeks later Papa asked me how I thought it all went. I said to him, 'I just don't know about that bit when I dived into the blackberry bushes with Travis and Shamus. Did I fuck up there?' I couldn't get to a position where I could do much . . . where I was of any good. In the blackberries, there was nowhere to go. It just niggled at me . . . I know now that I couldn't have done anything; I was just being critical of myself. I had Travis in my sights so I was able to look after him. He was a hell of a nice bloke, and we were just thankful to have him there with Shamus.

—

The SOG received a touching surprise in the mail after the event.

I wonder if anyone ever writes to the police to say thank you? I imagine you get abusive and critical ones but rarely praise. Well I am very grateful for the courageous and well-planned apprehension of the escaped prisoners and the woman warder. I am in the Jamieson area in a very remote spot, mostly on my own or with my family, and I was very afraid during their time on the run. I am not a nervous person, you don't live in such isolation if you are, but was well aware how desperate these escapees would be and what ends they would go to, to survive. It is an awful feeling to be an innocent person at risk of one's life, to not be able to go about daily rituals without listening to every sound and watching for danger.

So thank you to all who risked their lives to keep us safe and especially to the policeman who was shot. I understand he is recovering okay. Maybe you could pass this letter on to those who were involved so they know there are people out there who know the work and respect the work done by the police.

Yours sincerely,

S.G. Boisjoux

13

REPENTANCE

Remind them to be submissive to rulers and authorities, to
be obedient, to be ready for every good work.

Titus 3:1

When Toby saw the unmarked black Nissan Patrol with dark, tinted windows pull up out the front of his office, he knew he was in serious trouble.

'Fuck! They've come for me!' he announced to his co-workers.

The usual mundane office vibe had suddenly been sparked to life by the declaration that the men in black had arrived, unannounced. There was a palpable sense of anticipation in the air but, for Toby in particular, also nervousness. He knew exactly what they were there for.

A second four-wheel drive arrived. The SOG meant business.

Within seconds, the elite unit had the building surrounded. Two men, stern looking and heavily armed, walked through the front doors while others broke off and covered the side and rear exits.

Toby knew only too well that his chances of escape were slim, but he wasn't going to go down without a fight. He fled towards the only exit he thought might have been left unguarded.

As he raced through the corridors, his heart began to pump faster and faster as the adrenaline kicked in. The hallways seemed clear, and the longer he went without spotting anyone, the greater his confidence grew of a miraculous getaway.

There were now just two doors between him and freedom. He peered through a small window to see if there was anyone waiting on the other side of door number one. There was nothing.

He burst through the door and froze. Standing just several metres in front of him was Dane – one of the fittest and most physically intimidating men in the SOG.

'Where do you think you're going?' Dane asked.

'C'mon, mate. Let me go, will ya?'

'I wouldn't have thought that'd be happening.'

Toby was cornered. He knew by now the others would be sweeping the building and closing in on his location.

Even though he was a lot smaller than Dane, he figured one on one was better than one on eight. Plus, he was nimble and only needed to get past Dane in order to escape. Also in his favour was the fact that he rode to work and still hadn't changed out of his riding gear and runners. In contrast, Dane's heavy GP boots were a weakness.

Toby shaped up. Dane laughed, and the look on his face said it all: 'You're kidding yourself, little man.'

'Catch me if you can!' Toby yelled as he began his sprint with a series of stutter-steps in an attempt to disguise his direction. His runners scuffed the concrete floor beneath him and created high-pitched squeaks – not unlike what you'd hear at a basketball game.

Toby angled left, then right, then left again, but Dane's anticipation was too good, and he protected the final exit like a world-class soccer goalkeeper.

As he latched on to Toby's shirt, he pulled him closer and wrapped him up tightly with a suffocating bear hug. The struggle was brief – as soon as Toby saw that the other Soggies had arrived, he gave up the fight. Instead, he focused his energy on trying to figure out who could have betrayed him and why.

Toby's world had just been turned upside down, literally. Hanging feet-up from a wire fence with his forehead just inches from the ground, blood rushed to his head. The build-up of pressure caused his brain to throb and the veins in his neck to bulge outwards, as though they were going to burst. Every single heartbeat sounded like a large, beating drum next to his ears.

After the Soggies had subdued him, they'd zip-tied his hands and feet and carried him out to the front gate. Then they'd flipped him upside down and secured him to the fence. There was to be no arrest; this was more about ritual, tradition and a little bit of revenge.

'Happy birthday, mate!' Dane said to him in the most insincere of ways. 'Tell Nicole we all said "hi".' As a parting gift, Dane sprayed a tiny amount of mace into Toby's face and left – it was just enough to make him squirm.

At that moment, the penny dropped. Toby's wife, Nicole, must have called the SOG and told them it was his birthday. With unrelenting tears and copious amounts of snot pouring out of every orifice on his face, Toby still managed to see the lighter side of the prank and, strangely, he felt an enormous amount of satisfaction. Codenamed 'Mouse', he'd been out of the group for almost two years, and for the boys to consider him worthy of such an effort was a sign of affection. He was still one of them and part of the brotherhood. The members of the group often used pranks and jokes to alleviate the stresses and high levels of anxiety that they experienced in the job. Also prevalent was a black humour that many used as a coping mechanism and way to reconcile violent or confronting scenes and situations.

MOUSE: You've got to understand, we had a lot of exposure to mace and gas so it wasn't a big deal to us. Yeah, it was uncomfortable but it couldn't kill you. It may surprise people, but I actually got a kick out of it, for sure. It was all about belonging and that unbreakable bond and camaraderie we share. On another positive note, I was lucky they didn't bring a taser!

—

When tasers were introduced to the SOG's standard kit, the pranks went up a level and evolved.

MOUSE: I was sitting on a desk, and Bulldog, a senior sergeant, came up behind me and put a fierce chokehold on me and dragged me off the desk – we were not supposed to put even our feet on the desks, let alone sit on them. He said, 'Mouse! Up to my office!'

I thought I was in the shit for sitting on the desk, but on my way up to Bulldog's office, our big boss, Oscar, called me over and handed me a taser and a pile of papers. 'I think Bulldog wanted these,' he said with a smirk on his face. I walked out of Oscar's office and into Bulldog's with the taser sitting hidden under all the papers, which I handed to him at about chest height. When he reached out to grab them, I hit him in the stomach with the taser. He copped the fright of his life.

I wasn't going to hang around, though, and took off. Bulldog chased me through the corridors and I thought I lost him. I stopped and looked around but he wasn't coming. I waited for a little while and returned back around the corner, where I walked straight into a can of capsicum spray. I could hear it hissing and going off but couldn't feel anything on my face and thought, 'It's not working . . . I should be in tears by now.' Anyway, Bulldog had the nozzle turned around the wrong way and gave himself a nasty dose right in the face.

One man who had more of an insight into the culture of the SOG than most, was police psychologist Simon Brown-Greaves. He spent years with the members of the group after fatal shootings and other challenges and told me the men all had different ways of dealing with the violent nature of the job. 'These men were as good as I had ever seen,' he said. 'They were amazing with respect to the things they did and the pressure they were under to perform at the elite level. I had some exposure to the SAS and when we did dual exercises, the SOG was equally disciplined and professional.'

Brown-Greaves also saw the occasional immature outbursts and pranks within the group as a necessary behaviour. While outsiders would consider the black humour as inappropriate, Brown-Greaves said it is common in such elite groups as the SOG.

BROWN-GREAVES: There were plenty of debriefs after shootings where you could use that well-worn line, 'Too early!' after someone said something untoward. Three hours after a horrible event, the jokes would start but I learnt to understand that for what it was – an effective coping mechanism. It actually makes sense and for them to be able to share a bit of a laugh – there was nothing psychologically wrong with that at all. In fact, it is pretty natural. Some outside perceived it as callousness, but men like the ones we're talking about have a very good ability to rationalise things and come to terms with all the bad things that may have happened to them or in front of them.

But when it came to performing their tasks, Brown-Greaves claimed no-one came close to the SOG. In his professional opinion, the SOG members were unique and supremely talented individuals.

BROWN-GREAVES: They put themselves into situations where none of us would want to be. They were always walking into scenarios where there were lawless people with firearms who were absolutely prepared, and at times committed, to take them on. They stepped into situations that were always high-risk. It was incomprehensible to me in many ways to see how they constantly pushed themselves and summoned the courage to risk their own lives for the safety of others. They were incredibly altruistic as well. While they thrived on the thrill and the challenge, there was also a realisation that they could do things normal people couldn't do and that motivated them too. There was a genuine sense of, 'We really do protect.'

I was amazed by their ability to endure hours and hours of waiting, but having to be focused, alert, ready and focused for a sudden split second of action. I saw things that they did and it was just extraordinary. They had to embrace challenges, manage their fear and make critical decisions during times of absolute chaos.

The most successful SOG operatives were competitive, but more competitive within themselves than with others. They were really motivated to get the best out of themselves in a serious way. These aren't just guys that wear a Fitbit and say, 'I'll do 10,000 steps', these are blokes who said, 'I'm going to take my physicality and psychology to the best it possibly can be', and it was so far beyond what most people could even contemplate. It requires an unusual degree of confidence and emotional strength.

14

DAMNED IF YOU DO

Jesus said to him, 'No one who puts his hand to the plough and looks back is fit for the kingdom of God.'

Luke 9:62

Sierra woke in the middle of the night and his heart started to race. As his eyes adjusted to the soft moonlight, he slowly began to make out the figure of a person standing at the end of his bed, looking down on him. He knew the man's face, but couldn't recall where he was from. Not a word was spoken as the two men stared at each other, expressionless.

Sierra sat bolt upright in bed. He scanned the room for the intruder but there was no sign of him. He had completely vanished. Sierra rubbed his eyes and realised he'd just been visited by the knife-wielding teenager he'd shot dead that day.

SIERRA: He was just standing there, looking at me, staring. The fact that this kid was only eighteen-and-a-half was quite trau-matic for me. It was the first human life I'd ever taken. I'm not proud of it, but I didn't have a choice. It was either him or me.

The SOG's four-wheel drive was thrust into reverse and the tyres screeched on the bitumen road. Smoke poured out from beneath the vehicle as it pulled on the steel chain harpooned into the front doors of the fortified house. Before long, the doors gave way and bounced through the front yard towards the bumper bar. This allowed the assault team to enter the house without the need of an explosive breach. Sierra was the first SOG in the main bedroom, and he made it to the bedside of the wanted man before he could roll out of his sheets.

SIERRA: I dragged him out of bed and onto a glass side table that shattered beneath him. We arrested the targets without any issues whatsoever. The house had huge bags of cash and amphetamines. We completed the job, secured the offenders and everyone was safe.

—

With another mission accomplished, the SOG planned to return to base in the early hours of the morning for a debrief and shift change, but ten minutes into their journey back they were scrambled to a siege that involved a male who had threatened to kill his ex-girlfriend. Already with a prior conviction of rape, he forced her out of her home and remained inside with a male friend. The pair were said to be violent, armed with the suspect's pistol and ammunition, and possibly influenced by alcohol and speed. His friend had prior convictions for assaults.

After a briefing with their commanding officers at a local police station, the Soggies tooled up and secured the inner perimeter of the home. With the front door left wide open, the arrest team was eventually ordered to go in. Armed with two SIG Sauer 226, 9-mm semi-automatic handguns, Sierra was third through the door. The first two men broke left, while he moved down the hallway and into a small bedroom on the right. When the door swung open, a man immediately confronted Sierra with a knife.

SIERRA: He was jumping up and down, using the knife to stab at me in a very threatening series of movements. I was calling on him, yelling, 'Police! Don't move! Drop the knife!' There was a young female lying on the other side of the bed, and she rolled off and onto the floor.

—

With little distance between the knife-wielding man and the passageway, Sierra was in a dangerous position.

SIERRA: He would have only been two-and-a-half metres away from me at the most. He refused to drop the knife and wasn't obeying my orders. He brought the knife down and then up again and lunged at me with it. I went to step out of the room but one of the other guys was right behind me with a shotgun. I had stepped into his line of fire, trying to get away from the knife, and obviously I couldn't withdraw any further. I feared for my life and thought this bloke was going to stab me to death. So I took aim, as per our training, and put the first round into his head. I was aiming between his eyes, just next to his nose. I remember at the time seeing the round actually go in. It's amazing that I could see with that much detail but the experts put that down to a thing called tachypsychia, which comes on as a result of all the adrenaline dumps you get.

—

Usually induced by intense physical exertion, stress or some sort of traumatic event, tachypsychia is a condition that can alter the perception of time and space. It is probably best explained by referring to a scene out of the film *The Matrix*, when the main character, Neo, shows an ability to slow down time in order to dodge bullets and avoid being shot by his enemy. Sierra also experienced auditory exclusion. He recalls hearing his gun go off, but says it wasn't loud.

SIERRA: I tried to do a double tap but his head flew back from the first round and the second round impacted next to him and bounced back past me and out down the hallway. They were solid brick walls and the bullet just ricocheted. I shouldn't have dropped the shot, but I did, and we were lucky one of us wasn't hit by that bullet. I initially thought the second round had hit him, and I tracked down his body because he was still coming at me. I ended up getting a stoppage [empty magazine], as he fell. I yelled, 'Stoppage!' and the SOG behind me yelled, 'Covering!' I dumped the empty mag and inserted a new one.

—

The offender had fallen to the floor but was still clutching the blade. 'Moving forward!' Sierra declared as he stepped closer in a guarded position with his firearm still aimed and finger on the trigger.

SIERRA: I removed the knife from him and checked his vital signs. We gave him first aid as best we could before handing over to the paramedics. We informed the inspector at the command post that we had engaged and the offender had been shot. They'd obviously heard the firing from outside. Later that day, he died from the wounds. Not from the initial head wound, but from the shots that struck him when I tracked down his body. One of the rounds hit him high on the hip and severed a major artery in his leg. They weren't able to save him, unfortunately.

That was the first shooting incident I was in. It's a traumatic incident because you've taken a human life. We're there because we value human life and human rights. We've all got families and friends – some of us have kids. That's why we opted for an altruistic career path. That was the only thing that really affected me, seeing him there in my room like that.

—

After seeing the deceased in visions for several days following the shooting, Sierra slowly learnt to cope with the fact he'd killed someone in self-defence.

SIERRA: My way of coping is to always have a positive outlook. I'm not one for letting a moment in time define my whole future existence. I saw it a number of times with people in the police force and victims of crime, who would forever hark back to a bad moment in time and it would dictate the way they lived the rest of their lives. It was a life experience for me. Yes, it was difficult, but I'm confident that I made the right decision, and the courts proved that I made the right decision. That might be perceived by some as being harsh, but if I let my mind drift towards self-pity, it won't help. I can't change the past.

—

While the vast majority of the SOG's jobs ended peacefully, the few that didn't brought unrelenting media attention and public scrutiny.

SIERRA: On that occasion there were a lot of questions asked about why we went in, and my superior bore the brunt of that. Unfortunately, that's the weight of command. He made a decision to go in, which I supported, and still support even to this day. He had information at hand, and he's made thousands of those types of decisions before, to go in and resolve the situation. We could have snuck in and probably would have had the same result: who knows? It's a violent world out there. You need someone holding the thin black line, so that's what we were doing.

—

In the wake of damning commentary, public pressure and an adverse finding from the coroner that criticised the SOG's decision to raid the property, the police force went on the PR offensive and took several media identities, judges and other coroners out to the SOG's training base to give them all an experience they'd never forget.

High-profile Melbourne talkback radio host Neil Mitchell recalls being put through a dramatic series of controlled exercises that completely changed his perspective on criminals armed with knives. 'I had a marker pen, but I had to pretend it was a knife,' he explained. 'One of the SOG blokes stood just a few feet in front of me and was holding a gun loaded with blanks on me. I was told that he wasn't allowed to shoot me, unless I did some-thing provocative to him first. They told me I had to do something dangerous, like attack him and try to mark him with the pen to show that I was able to make contact.'

The outcome was staggering for Mitchell: 'I stabbed him easily and several times before he could even get a shot off. Time and time again, I was able to stab him without him being able to disarm or disable me. That really stood out in my mind. Even though you've got somebody, you've arrested him and you've got him under control, if they've still got that knife in their hand, you still have to be very careful.'

When the roles were reversed, Mitchell experienced the same

outcome. 'I was stabbed regularly and had pen marks all over me,' he said. 'I had no hope.'

Mitchell said the special, invite-only demonstrations came at a time when the public and media were highly critical of police following a spate of shootings in the 1990s. 'We were going through this argument about police reacting too quickly, being trigger happy, killing too many people, overreacting . . . and what the special demonstrations did reinforce for me was the complexity of it [police work] and the danger of it all. Before it all, I would have thought that if you were holding a gun on a criminal, then you'd be fine and safe. But clearly you aren't. I could see why there was such drastic action being taken at times, lethal action. It gave me a greater understanding of the vulnerability of police and the level of training, expertise and discipline of the SOG. Some people were critical of their name "the Sons of God" because it inferred having the power of life or death, but I thought that was crap. I thought they deserved to call themselves the Sons of God.

'I left thinking, "I wonder could they be a bit gung-ho?" but then when I thought about it I answered "No". Because the level of discipline that I saw with them and the level of control by their superiors was really like the elite soldiers – their willingness to obey directions. And I think there was a similar level of control with these guys.'

With new and more dangerous drugs such as ice flooding the streets and the threat of terrorism ever increasing, Mitchell believed the SOG was a vital resource. 'Oh, you've gotta have them,' he declared. 'The average copper out in the divvy van . . . do you want an overweight fifty-year-old detective from the homicide squad first through the door? Geez no! You need that sort of sharp-end policing, and I think you probably need more of it rather than less . . . I think we'll need them probably a little bit more in the future. With terrorism alone, that's a whole new element. The public is in awe of them . . . they see them as the civilian equivalent of the SAS; there's no question. There's a secrecy about them; there's something clandestine and impressive about them. They love them. Every now and then, when you read something about their training level and some of the things they do, going into some extraordinary situations, it's with amazing success.'

After his unfortunate experience with the knife-wielding eighteen-year-old, Sierra had a much closer call during a raid a few years later. Upon entering the house, he was struck with a machete.

SIERRA: I was first through the door on a raid and, as I stepped into the lounge room, I felt a heavy blow to my chest and it rocked me backwards, such was the force. When I turned, I saw a semi-naked male standing in the doorway of a bedroom that joined on to the lounge room but he had nothing in his hands. I yelled at him, 'Get on the ground!' but he refused and took up a fighting position. I forcibly restrained him by dragging him down and sweeping his legs out from underneath him.

—

Sierra and Rogue pounced on the offender and restrained him after a brief struggle.

ROGUE: He was thrashing about and screaming, 'Go on and kill me, you cunts! Go on, kill me!'

—

When Sierra attempted to radio the command post once the house had been cleared, he noticed his radio's ear cord had been cut in half. After a quick search, he found a large machete underneath the leg of the offender. Realising he'd been struck with a blade, Sierra then noticed a cut in his ballistic vest.

SIERRA: Someone with a knife, or machete for that matter, at close range is just as dangerous as someone with a gun. If their intent is to stab you or severely injure you, they can cross a large area in a very short period of time. If you make a mistake, you die. It only takes a swipe at your carotid artery in your leg or neck and you're dead. We're not paid to take risks and die; we're paid to arrest and let the courts prosecute. So we have that power and we exercise that power only when we need to.

Ninety-nine point nine per cent of the time, crooks react with fear when we come through the door, and they throw their weapons down and surrender. But there are some who are irrational, under the influence of alcohol or drugs, mentally incapacitated or whatever. The eighteen-year-old boy was possibly under the influence and just irrational. He made a decision that cost him his life. Our strategies are always designed to resolve any incident peacefully. No one should get hurt and there should be minimal risk to all parties – the offender, hostages, innocent parties and us, the police. So there's always that dynamic and we're always making decisions on that basis. The decision-making chain of events to use violence is always in the hands of the offender. The offender escalates a situation, and we have to defend ourselves in order to get the right outcome. Sometimes you don't have a choice.

The hard thing about the SOG is that we trained for those scenarios all the time, so you want to sort of test yourself, but at the same time you don't want anything like that to ever happen. You don't wish for it, but you wonder if your training is adequate and whether you're going to have the capability to function under stress, whether you can save a hostage, save your mates and make the right decision within a split second.

Everyone has probably seen hundreds of gun battles in Hollywood movies, but they're designed for cinematic purposes. They're extended and drawn out for all sorts of reasons, but the reality is a shooting or critical path incident happens very quickly and is usually over within seconds. If you're still standing up and you're not wounded, it's a good result. We have regular psych tests all the time to make sure we are all coping with the job and the things we've done and seen, and to ensure that we're capable of functioning and making the right decisions all the time.

—

Trying to send criminals to court rather than to the morgue has led to some phenomenal acts of bravery and courage by many members of the SOG.

ROGUE: In the best circumstances, the offender walks out with his hands in the air and lies face down on the ground. That is the outcome we always hope for every single time we are called out to a job. But it doesn't always pan out that way, unfortunately. I've seen blokes do some extraordinary things to save not only hostages but also offenders from harm.

It's very easy for the public or the media to think, 'Fuck! They've shot the crook twenty times and he's only shot at them once,' or say, 'He only had a handgun . . . he only had a knife.' What they don't realise is that the threat only needs to last for two or three seconds, and if three SOG blokes all react at the same time, each one is capable of getting five rounds off from a pump-action shotgun in under a second-and-a-half. So, if you've got three blokes doing that . . . that's five rounds each with nine pellets inside each SG casing, so that's forty-five pellets from just one bloke, and 135 from all three if they all hit the offender.

In a second-and-a-half, we could fill a bloke up with lead and he still might have his handgun pointed at us and could still be standing there. All he has to do is pull the trigger and one of us isn't going home that night. A second-and-a-half isn't long enough for him to fall over, and we can't afford to wait. He who hesitates dies . . . it's a stupid saying but it's true. You hesitate and go, 'Hang on, hang on . . . is he gonna shoot me? Is he gonna have a shot?' By that stage, you're dead. You can't give him that opportunity. He's about to shoot, he's pointing a gun at you or he's armed and menacing in any way – bang! You shoot him dead. Better to be tried by twelve than carried by six.

So it's not as though you shoot him once and say, 'Nah, he hasn't dropped yet . . . we had better shoot him again,' then have another look. It's not like that. It's more like, 'Fuck! Hang on . . . He's got a gun and he's shooting at us!' Then everyone's like BOOM! BOOM! BOOM! BOOM! You stop your action when he's dropped the gun, when he's put the gun down or when he's lying on the ground and is no longer a danger to you. If he's got a knife and you've got capsicum spray, you'd spray him in the face until he's on the ground and subdued. You wouldn't just spray once and hope it does the job. In saying that, if someone had a knife, I'd use a gun.

I can't say I've ever lost an hour of sleep over anything I've ever done at the SOG. My conscience is clear, and all these things you hear about criminals being executed by police . . . it is rubbish. I've never been a part, or would never be a part, of anything like that. It just doesn't happen, and if people think it does, I'm here to tell them it doesn't.

When we get called out, it's like naughty little boys in the school ground that are playing a game they're not allowed to play, and the teacher comes along and whacks them. You know the rules – you're not allowed to do it. Until you stop playing, we'll keep hittin' ya. Until they stop doing what they're doing, they're gonna keep getting shot, BANG! BANG! BANG! Until the threat is no longer, that's what you've got to do.

—

In the world of the SOG, there are risks and there are calculated risks. On dozens of occasions, when members would have been justified to fire on an armed offender, they have put their own lives on the line to make an arrest. In many instances, they have had to deal with mentally unstable or unreasonable offenders – some of which have had a death wish.

DANE: We are called in because there is a person who is armed with a deadly weapon or is posing a significant threat to public and police safety, and the job is deemed beyond the scope of normal police. We have the necessary skills, the training and the latest equipment to make sure that the public is kept safe.

For much of its history, the SOG united under a chilling black and white motif that featured a balaclava-clad terrorist in the crosshairs of a sniper's telescopic sights, and the map of Australia in the background. Below it sat the Bible quote Matthew 5:9, hand-picked by Mick Miller, 'Blessed are the peacemakers, for they shall be called the sons of God.'

Known as the 'Spook', the logo had been designed by members of SOG's sixth intake in 1981. But its time as the group's unofficial logo was limited, at least publicly. At its height, the Spook was printed on all sorts of exclusive SOG member memorabilia, including T-shirts, mugs, wine labels, belt buckles, stickers, caps and even a special-edition release of port. But in 2001, then chief commissioner Christine Nixon pushed through an unpopular decision to ban the Spook because it didn't fit with her views of policing and could have been perceived to be promoting killing. The move to strip the Spook was not received well by the SOG.

While the Spook disappeared from public view, it never disappeared completely and is still revered and visible in the SOG offices to this day, albeit discreetly.

15

THE ISLE OF THE DEAD

But as for the cowardly, the faithless, the detestable, as for
murderers, the sexually immoral, sorcerers, idolaters, and
all liars, their portion will be in the lake that burns with fire
and sulphur, which is the second death.

Revelation 21:8

Martin Bryant burst through the front door of the Seascape
Cottages screaming in agony. His hair was on fire and his skin
was starting to melt under the intense heat of the flames. As
he staggered into the blinding morning light, he clawed at his
burning clothes and tore them away from his already seared body.
Large chunks of flesh began to peel off his back. Behind him,
thick black smoke billowed from the windows of the once impressive guesthouse that he had barricaded himself in for more than
eighteen hours.

Sierra slowly squeezed the trigger on his high-powered precision sniper rifle and prepared to take down the man who had just
become the world's worst mass murderer. Sierra could have easily
ended Bryant's miserable life with a single, fatal headshot, but,
as he was about to fire, he stopped. His hesitation wasn't out of
mercy, but quite the opposite.

SIERRA: He was still on fire and in agony. My thoughts were to just let him burn to death.

—

It wasn't the first time that Sierra had had an opportunity to kill the psychotic madman. He'd had one other chance to end the horrific scenes that unfolded at the popular Tasmanian tourist destination Port Arthur. Both times though, he wouldn't have been justified in pulling the trigger, despite the fact Bryant had already killed a known thirty-two people when Sierra and seven other SOG members touched down at Hobart Airport.

Sierra was at home with his wife and newborn child when he sat down to watch the evening news before dinner. He remembers the mood in his lounge room growing noticeably tense when the mainstream news bulletins began broadcasting live reports from Tasmania concerning a mass shooting. Knowing Tasmania Police wouldn't have the capability to handle such a complex and delicate situation, he felt that his plans for a quiet night in were about to be ruined.

SIERRA: There were all these stories coming through about this massacre unfolding that was just horrific. I remember saying to my wife, 'I'll be going to that.' Just minutes later, the call came through, and I was summoned to the Essendon Airport for immediate deployment to Hobart.

—

With a new national agreement in place called Police Assisting Neighbouring States (PANS), Tasmania was able to look to its closest neighbour for help when Bryant began his bloody killing spree. Tasmania did have its own fully trained SOG, but, owing to the state's small population and reasonably low crime rate, it was only part-time. Up to that point, the elite unit had rarely been used, according to the group member in charge at the time, Mojo.

MOJO: We had the capability to respond to the scene that was occurring at Port Arthur, which we did, but it was more of a capacity issue for us. This event became too large a scale because it had multiple crime scenes and potential multiple offenders. It was never one hundred per cent confirmed, until we arrested Bryant much later, that he was the only shooter or person involved. We just couldn't possibly cover all those contingencies. There's no way we could have split our unit up and still been able to maintain a cordon at Port Arthur and around the Seascape Cottages site. All these various elements about the situation we were facing were coming together fairly rapidly. We'd already adopted a lot of what the Victorian SOG was doing and had done a lot of training with them. We were very much aligned with them, even down to the way our vehicles were kitted out.

—

Sierra had met Mojo and many of the other members of the Tasmanian SOG at a national training exercise, or 'show and tell', that was designed for interstate collaboration with regard to special weapons, tactics and training. It was also a chance to determine who was the best of the best when it came to certain disciplines such as marksmanship and long-range shooting. Sierra remembers it being like something out of the movie *Top Gun*, with various competitions running to crown the most elite police officer. Sierra held the title of 'Sniper One' – and was one of the best marksmen in the country. He was a highly regarded sniper instructor and had received numerous awards for his long-range shooting ability and deadly accuracy.

SIERRA: I was running a sniper team for a national training course and spent a lot of time with the Tassie team. We got to know a lot about each other's capabilities, so I had a really good understanding of their operation and what they could and couldn't do. I knew that the scenario at Port Arthur would stretch the resources of their SOG. So it was a fair assumption that we'd be called to help, even though it had never happened before.

Martin Bryant's horrific shooting rampage was the largest massacre committed by a single person in the world at the time. He killed thirty-five men, women and children, and seriously wounded another twenty. The twenty-eight-year-old unemployed gunman from New Town, a suburb close to Hobart, had spent the years leading up to the deadly day buying various high-powered weapons and ammunition with money he'd inherited from a wealthy friend.

On the morning of 28 April 1996, he packed several semi-automatic guns into a large sports bag and headed out the door. He drove to the Seascape guest accommodation – a property his father had unsuccessfully tried to buy years before – and confronted the owners, David and Noelene Martin. Exactly what happened inside remains unclear, but those nearby heard several gunshots and police allege Bryant had gagged and killed the elderly couple. Witnesses saw a car reverse up to the door of the property at 12.35 pm and they watched a man unload it, taking various items inside. It was later revealed that Bryant was stockpiling ammunition and guns in the guesthouse.

Bryant locked the doors to Seascape and drove to the historic Port Arthur tourist destination. Along the way, he stopped and told some people that he was going out to the Isle of the Dead (a nearby island that was used as the cemetery for the historic Port Arthur convict settlement) to 'kill some WASPS' (White Anglo-Saxon Protestants). Mojo believes the eighty-odd passengers on the ferry were Bryant's intended victims.

MOJO: Bryant was intent on getting on that bloody boat. He had remonstrated with the ferry operator for a while about the fact that he'd parked illegally, then eventually left and parked his car elsewhere, but, by the time he came back, the boat had already gone. He was never in charge from that point on. He had the Seascape property prepared for a stand-off with police well and truly before he went down to Port Arthur. I believe he pre-prepared all his firing positions. He was going to get on that ferry; that's what he showed his intent was. Was he going to go out to the Isle of the Dead and kill people there? Was he going to ground the boat at the Seascape, go ashore and go back to the property?

That's what I believe. I believe he was always going to go back to the property and what happened was never really meant to happen. He wasn't in charge. He lost control of what he'd planned to do when that ferry left. You don't stockpile weapons and ammunition like that unless you're going to come back there.

—

With the ferry gone, Bryant entered the Broad Arrow Cafe, ordered lunch and chose to eat on the decked area outside. When

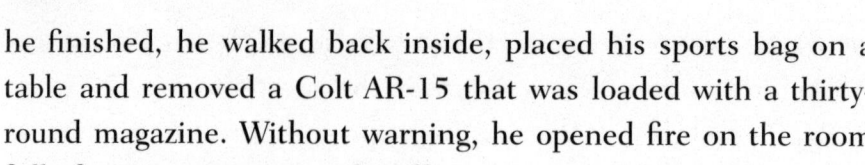

he finished, he walked back inside, placed his sports bag on a table and removed a Colt AR-15 that was loaded with a thirty-round magazine. Without warning, he opened fire on the room full of tourists, visitors and staff.

Some thought the sounds of the shots were part of a re-enactment created for the visitors of the site. But their worst fears came to life when bodies began to fall around them. This was no act. Bryant fired more than forty shots, murdering twelve people and injuring ten in the cafe. He shot at the elderly, children and those trying to shield their loved ones from the danger. When he reached the gift shop next door, he fired twenty-nine more bullets, killing eight more people and injuring a further two. As the visitors and staff fled for their lives to the car park outside, Bryant tracked them down and continued to spray bullets at anything that moved.

He swapped his weapon for another semi-automatic rifle and boarded two coach buses, where many had scrambled inside for safety. He unloaded again, taking the total death toll to twenty-four, with eighteen now injured. Travelling away from the cafe in his car, Bryant stopped to engage a family of four and shot the mother and her two daughters in cold blood. Further up the road at the tollbooth, Bryant killed two men and two women. At this point, he had murdered thirty-one and injured nineteen.

At a nearby petrol station, he slaughtered another woman and took a man hostage by forcing him into the boot of his car. Thirty-two were now dead and twenty injured.

He headed back to Seascape at about 2.00 pm to access the ammunition he'd dumped there earlier. Two officers converged on the property after reports that a car parked out the front was on fire.

MOJO: When he lit the stolen car, it was like a huge smoke stack saying, 'I'm here! Come and get me!' There's no doubt he wanted the police to come to him. He wanted to initiate a shootout.

—

Uniformed police approached the burning vehicle to investigate, and bullets suddenly whistled past them. Under heavy fire, they were forced to retreat and found cover in a nearby ditch. They were pinned down for a number of hours. When darkness fell, they took the opportunity to flee and managed to escape unharmed. An intense hostage-siege situation then began – one that would last more than eighteen hours.

Back in Melbourne, Sierra kissed his wife and baby girl goodbye and headed to the airport. Two turbo-prop jets were ready to rush eight members of the Victorian SOG to Hobart. That particular type of aircraft was fast but had its disadvantages because of its weight restrictions. It meant some vital equipment had to be left behind.

SIERRA: We were making critical decisions as the aircraft was rolling in, like what gear was necessary and what would happen if we couldn't take this or that. We had to try and anticipate what was happening down there in Hobart, without access to much information at all. It was a case of relying on our expertise and experience. We had been called because it was six o'clock and it was getting dark down there. We had thermal and night-vision capability, and the Tasmanians either didn't have it or didn't have much of that type of equipment. Obviously that type of gear was going to be crucial.

—

While information about the massacre was scarce, the SOG knew enough about what was taking place and couldn't get there quick enough.

HAZE: It's a horrible feeling being so far away. We just wanted to get on that jet and down there as soon as possible. Knowing we had a flight and then car ride to the scene ahead of us was excruciating.

—

When the jet finally touched down in Hobart after less than an hour in the air, the SOG was directed to a decommissioned police station near the landing strip. The Victorians had to be sworn in before they could carry out their roles in Tasmania – a legal requirement that frustrated them greatly.

SIERRA: We were wasting time on a silly formality, when we could have been saving lives. It was absolutely ridiculous. Making matters worse, they couldn't find a Bible for us to swear on, and precious time was just ticking away. I tried to tell them we were all agnostic and atheists, but the commanding officer down there wouldn't hear it and insisted we swore on the Bible. I also tried to convince them that a phone book would suffice. After all, it has all the same letters as the Bible in it – they're just arranged in a different way.

—

The Tasmanian Traffic Operations Group officers attempted to make up for lost time on the drive to the scene at Seascape.

SIERRA: It was the scariest car ride I've ever had in my life. It was like all the training these guys had ever had boiled down to this single moment, and this was their chance to show everyone how skilled they were as drivers. It was a really windy road, and they were just hammering along, taking corners at extremely high speeds. I'll hand it to them – they were unbelievably good, because I didn't think we were going to survive. When we got there, the brakes were absolutely cooked. There was smoke coming out from underneath the hood and all over the place.

MOJO: There couldn't have been a better sight for us than when we saw the Vic Soggies rock up. It was just complete and utter relief, knowing that we now had more expertise and resources at our disposal.

–

Shaken but unharmed from their car ride, the SOG collected their gear and received a briefing from their Tasmanian brothers. During the briefing, gunshots continuously rang out in the distance.

SIERRA: We were told there was upwards of thirty people killed, but they didn't tell us that children had been murdered too. We didn't find that out until much later. In hindsight, that was probably a good thing, because we didn't need that on our minds. We had to remain focused on the job at hand. We knew Bryant was heavily armed and alert, because we could hear shots ring out intermittently from inside the guesthouse.

–

The Seascape Cottages were nestled in a small valley flanked by the ocean, rolling hills and forest. The main residence was a two-storey, weatherboard-clad building and was painted bright white. There were two other large cottages on the property, also used for guest accommodation. Bryant had barricaded himself in on the second floor of the main building, smashed all the windows out and thrown furniture onto the ground and awning below.

SIERRA: We knew there was at least one male hostage from the petrol station in there with him, but we didn't know the status of the elderly couple who owned the property. Because it was a bed and breakfast, we didn't know whether there was anyone else staying there at the time or what buildings may have been occupied. We didn't have a lot of information and had to proceed cautiously.

—

Bryant was communicating with negotiators via a cordless telephone, but, when the battery ran out, the critical connection was lost, and the status of the hostages couldn't be confirmed. Sierra and Haze helped formulate the action plan and tried to re-establish a line of communication, but it wasn't as simple as handing Bryant a new phone or leaving one on the doorstep.

SIERRA: There was about 200 metres of clear land all around the cottages. Because Bryant was able to access the top levels of all the buildings, he had an excellent vantage point, which limited the approach routes available to us. That meant we could have come under fire from various high-powered weaponry way before we could get entry to the house. If he had hostages and saw us coming, he could panic and kill them.

HAZE: We had to start thinking outside the square, as all our usual options weren't available to us. The danger to us was very real. We looked at trying to locate a tank or armoured car, even from a museum, but nothing was available. We also considered getting a large bulldozer, with a big steel blade on it, brought to the scene. The idea for the bulldozer was to cover it with as many ballistic vests as possible and drive right up to the buildings, one by one, with the blade raised to act as a shield. We'd position it right up at the front door so Bryant couldn't get an angle on us to shoot, and we'd deploy assault teams to raid all the cottages.

—

In the meantime, plans were underway to have the SOG's special armoured vehicle flown in.

DANE: I was back in Melbourne and was tasked with contacting the RAAF to see if we could use their Hercules aircraft to transport our armoured truck. I wasn't expecting the response I got, that's for sure. They couldn't have been more willing to help. I simply called the base in Laverton and spoke to one of the officers there, told him that I was with the SOG and what I needed the aircraft for, and he said, 'Yeah, no worries. Just drive the armoured truck here and we'll have her ready to go, no problems at all.' It was unbelievable.

—

Intent on killing more people and no doubt police, Bryant continued to relentlessly shoot and in all directions.

HAZE: Over the course of the night, I think there were estimates of about 150 shots – it was probably somewhere between fifty and 150 and the truth lies somewhere in between. What we did recognise, however, is that Bryant, with the elevated buildings and the lie of the land – in that it was a bit of a valley – had a pretty good killing ground and was in a far superior position than us. So if we were to make a deliberate assault or deploy en masse and creep up on the buildings, there's every chance that we would have been compromised.

At the time, we estimated we could have had about thirty per cent casualties by the time we'd be able to get to an assault position – even in the cover of darkness. He had the elevated position and there was intelligence that he may have had his own night vision. There was a lot of misinformation about his weapons and capabilities, and, to some extent, that meant our tactics needed to be ultra-cautious. We had about eighteen SOG operatives on the ground, including the eight of us from Victoria, so we didn't have a lot of people to play with, particularly when you're talking about trying to take down three buildings.

–

Bryant was 'very calculated', according to Mojo, and never really exposed himself.

MOJO: He was standing about a metre back from the windows the whole time and never leant forwards when he was firing. The main building was a beautiful cottage, like a Cape Cod–style structure with attic windows. Because of the distance, we'd only see the curtains move in one of the windows and then we'd hear the crack of a round being spat out. One bullet went over my head and we realised that those loose rounds were eventually going to take someone out. It was only a matter of time before someone copped one and was injured or killed.

We needed to flush him out. We needed him to expose himself and we needed to take care of this problem. Haze and I spoke about putting a plan in place that would lure him out and into the open for a sniper shot, but it meant that we would have to expose ourselves to make it happen – we were prepared to do it if it was required.

—

With Bryant's sporadic and random firing continuing, the forward command post was pushed back to a safer location.

SIERRA: All of a sudden, we heard lots of shooting and one of the Tassie blokes hit the deck right next to me to take cover. I looked at him and said, 'It's a bit late to get down now, mate. You'd already be dead if he was on target.'

—

While most of his shots were random, Bryant did lock in on one particular Tasmanian sniper. He hadn't covered his radio with black tape properly and Bryant could see his red transmitting light flashing away on his vest. He was lucky to get out alive.

The SOG also considered getting the air force to fly low over the cottage with F/A-18s or F-111s and give off a sonic boom to distract Bryant and bring his attention to the back of the property. When the jets flew over, the plan was to send the assault teams in through the front. Another distraction could have come by way of detonating 44-gallon drums full of fuel.

Well into the night, there was no change to the situation. Bryant was still firing shots out the windows as the police were continually reassessing and altering their approach and tactics.

SIERRA: As the night went on, it became increasingly apparent that this situation was going to be difficult to resolve with a direct assault, and I thought personally that the more likely resolution was going to be a headshot from one of the snipers. As 'Sniper One', I felt I was best placed to be in the position to take that shot.

—

Sierra changed out of his black SOG uniform into his ghillie suit (a heavily camouflaged outfit designed to hide snipers and infantry among heavy foliage), and assessed the landscape for the best position.

SIERRA: I went out with a Tassie sniper assistant who was on one of his first jobs. We slowly crawled up through the mountains and positioned ourselves right at the front of the house, about 200 metres away, in the middle with a clear view of the stronghold.

—

The pair was well within range of Bryant's reckless firing but had no choice but to bunker down and hope for the best.

SIERRA: Bryant was still firing randomly the whole time, so we built a little stone wall in front of us to hide behind. We were still within the forest line but well secreted so that he couldn't see us. Rounds would zip through the trees and all around us but we had to divorce ourselves from any thought of being hit. We just had to take cover and hope that we didn't cop one. We knew Bryant had scoped weaponry, and the suggestion that he had night vision was a major concern for us, being so close. Although we weren't entirely safe, we were safe enough.

When we arrived, we had to seek permission to engage Bryant if anyone spotted him. However, our request for a green light was surprisingly denied. He'd already killed thirty people that we knew of, so surely I felt we could take his life, but the then Tasmanian chief commissioner rejected my request, I believe. In my opinion, putting a single round in his head was the only and best way to end it.

What came next was equally staggering, though. If we saw

him, we were told we could shoot at his legs. I had to explain that that's not how things are done. Only a fatal shot to the head would negate him as a threat. If we shot Bryant in the leg or another limb, he would still be able to shoot and kill a hostage or police officer. We couldn't get too frustrated with the orders, though, as this was an education process for the Tassie commanding officers don't forget, and it was quite stressful. No one had seen anything of this scale before.

—

As the night wore on, Bryant became even more careful about his movements and was scarcely seen.

HAZE: We could hear shots ring out. We could hear high-calibre firearms, centre-fire rifles like a .308; we could hear a .22; we could hear a shotgun. These shots were coming from all different directions. All of the sniper positions were being exposed to random firing, and the assault teams that were trying to form up had shots going over the top of them. We figured out, 'Hang on a second. This guy is moving around from building to building to building, and he's setting up firing points in each location.' So, regardless of where he was on the property, he'd have access to firearms and ammunition.

There's no doubt he was trying to confuse us about where he was. He was doing very good siege tactics to some extent by creating the impression that there was more than one gunman. It was difficult for us to be able to pinpoint his location. There might have been an initial brief consideration that there could have been another gunman, but after we weighed up all the information – that one gunman had shot all those people at Port Arthur, one man had stolen the car and taken a hostage, et cetera – everything indicated that there was one gunman.

What we were unsure of was his capabilities, based on information that he had an arsenal of weapons and a massive amount of ammunition. And some police had reported that they'd seen red dots, meaning he may have had high-grade military hardware with laser pointers.

—

Suddenly, there was some movement. A shadowy figure emerged from behind a flyscreen door.

SIERRA: Another sniper had seen a glimpse of him but couldn't take the shot because I don't think he had his weapon in position. When I caught a look at Bryant, all I could see was a silhouette, but at 200 metres away with a twenty-power scope at night, I couldn't see if anyone was with him. I couldn't say with confidence whether he had a hostage in front of him or not. He was standing there firing rounds and I could see the muzzle flashes but I just couldn't be sure enough that he was there alone.

—

Sierra was faced with a choice that would have had enormous consequences. In his sights was Australia's worst mass murderer, and he had the opportunity to take him down and end the madness on behalf of all the victims, their families and the entire country. But to take the shot would have meant taking a huge risk, and disobeying a direct order.

SIERRA: I flicked the safety off and placed my finger on the trigger. I was ready in case he came out with a weapon and started firing, because that would be enough for me to justify taking him out. He would have been a threat to the snipers and compromised us all, so I could have taken a shot and I was fully prepared to. But Bryant stayed behind the thin veil of protection the flyscreen gave him and never came out. I decided not to take the shot and flicked the safety back on because under those circumstances, I would not have been justified.

—

Night soon began to turn into day and it seemed Bryant might have finally run out of ammunition. But he wasn't done with the carnage just yet.

HAZE: We were confident at that point that we were only dealing with one offender. What we weren't sure of in the initial stages was whether the hostages were alive, but, as the course of the evening progressed and negotiations had broken down, we had no indications of any sign of life. We formed the view that in all probability the hostages were no longer alive.

—

Everything was silent just before sunrise when Sierra saw smoke emanating from the building and called it in. 'Sniper One to command,' he said over the radio. 'We have smoke coming from the right corner on level two of the structure. Over.' The flames began to intensify and the fire started to take hold of the cottage.

HAZE: Someone thought a smoke grenade or something had been let off – it was that sort of colour – but then the fire quickly got going. A man was seen leaving the house fully clothed with a handgun, then he went back into the inferno.

SIERRA: We realised that this was all going to resolve itself soon. I called, 'Stand to the action plan!' and the assaulters on the ground closest to the cottages started loading onto the back of the police four-wheel drives, ready for an assault on the property.

—

It was set to be a dangerous trip for the members of both states' SOG units. Two teams had to travel down the road that led to Seascape and then turn into the driveway, meaning they would have been exposed for about 200 metres upon their approach. The sun was also rising, so Bryant's visibility would have been very clear and he could easily see them coming.

MOJO: There was a bit of confusion. What were we assaulting – a burning building? We just didn't know what we had and what we were about to walk into.

SIERRA: The fire took hold, and roaring flames were visible out the windows now and in various parts of the roof. I saw the curtains go up in flames and I called, 'Sniper One to command; the top floor is unliveable and consumed by flames. Over.'

—

The surroundings, combined with the events that had taken place, made the scene surreal. The sun was rising, and it was still and calm. While the crisp blue ocean provided a heavenly backdrop to the beautifully landscaped gardens in the foreground, the smoke billowing from the picturesque cottages was a reminder that something sinister was occurring.

—

The inferno intensified and Sierra told his superiors that the ground floor was now also uninhabitable. Just when it appeared no one would survive the blaze, the front door swung open.

SIERRA: A tall individual, with nothing in their hands and long blonde hair, emerged. I could see that their back was on fire. The person was screaming because the flames consumed them. I took the safety off my rifle again. I was calm and in my breathing cycle and had my scope set to exactly 200 metres. I had this person's head quartered in the crosshairs but didn't know if it was a male or a female or whether it was one of the hostages or actually Bryant. I grabbed the photo of him that was stuck to the little brick wall I'd built and it looked roughly like him, but I couldn't be one hundred per cent sure. All I remember thinking is that this person I was looking at down my scope was quite feminine in appearance.

Then, still screaming and on fire, the person turned to face me and ripped their burning clothes off. I could see a penis and that's when I knew it was a male. I now knew who I was looking at and got a clear view of his face. It was Bryant. I watched his blonde hair burn and singe, and I called through to command that it was the offender and he was unarmed. A lot of things went through my mind, because I had another chance to shoot him. But again, I wouldn't have been justified in doing so.

I remembered the Dunblane school shootings in Scotland that had happened just prior to this, and I'd seen some of the victims' families and parents interviewed on the news afterwards. They were saying how they wished the gunman had survived so they could have had some sort of closure and known what type of monster had taken the lives of their children and loved ones. They wanted the gunman alive, so they could get justice and have some answers.

We don't get paid to take lives in the SOG; we get paid to save them and put criminals like Bryant before the courts. We are ultimate professionals and don't have the authority to make those types of calls. But I have to admit, when I had Bryant's head quartered in my sights and had one-and-a-half pounds of my two-pound trigger taken up on my Robar SR-90, 7.62 accurised Remington 700, with a 6 to 20 inertial scope on it, I was fully prepared to take the shot had it been justified.

—

Once again, Sierra showed restraint and resisted the urge to shoot, allowing Haze, Mojo and the other members of the assault teams to make the arrest.

HAZE: The house was on fire. I've never felt a heat quite like it before in my life. The fire was absolutely raging, and thousands of rounds of ammunition were cooking off inside. When I first glimpsed Bryant, he was a pathetic figure. He was not worth the effort in giving him a belting – he just needed to be taken away and put in a box or hole and forgotten about for the rest of his days. If there was a prison cell three feet by three feet with a small slot to put some rice and a cup of water through every day, then that's all he deserved. He had that wisp of blonde hair and, clearly, he was on fire around the head and back of the neck area. There was skin peeling off him and it was smouldering.

I remember standing there in a semicircle with the others, all with our guns raised at Bryant, and there was this millisecond where you could have heard a pin drop, notwithstanding that we were in the middle of this surreal environment with the house burning down around us, the rounds cooking off. Our heartbeats would have been up around 150 beats per second but there was this momentary period of absolute silence.

He looked dazed and confused. He didn't react when he saw us approaching. He was like a mannequin that was sort of stunned. Everyone knew that this was a guy who had just killed a huge amount of people and it was like, 'Who is gonna go first here? Who is gonna shoot first?' It obviously wasn't going to be him, because he was unarmed and naked. There was a training instinct that kicked in, or some sort of feeling like, 'No, we're better than you.' It only would have taken one of us to stand on a twig and snap it to cause everyone to open up on him, though. It would have absolutely opened up. There was every opportunity for us, or the snipers, to take a shot and kill him.

I yelled to the men, 'Okay! Let's clear the houses! Clear the houses! Get the hostages out! Check for hostages! Go! Go! Go!' Three of the guys moved forwards and grabbed Bryant. They threw him to the ground and strapped his hands together. It was a heavy arrest. I can see the whole thing as clear and vividly as any memory that I have from any job in the SOG.

MOJO: Bryant wasn't even complaining of the burns. It was all a bit strange. He was away with the fairies. Take away what happened at Port Arthur and even just focus on Seascape, I mean this bloke has just come out of a burning building that almost collapsed around him because he stayed in there a hell of a long time – but there was just no substance to him. There was no expression, not even any aggression towards us. I remember thinking, 'Is this the guy that's done all that carnage?' He showed no malice towards anyone, just a stupid, jovial attitude. It was just another day to him. The birds were singing, the sun was coming up and he was just staring at us.

—

Sierra left his sniper position and ran down to assist with the arrest, and there he came face to face with Bryant.

SIERRA: We arrested him like the SOG arrests people. He had just killed more than thirty people, including children, and we weren't about to treat him with kid gloves. You know, you're in the big boys' sandpit when you're in an anti-terrorist unit. You don't have time to muck around, particularly with mass-murderers. He was writhing in pain and rolling around on the ground after the flames had been extinguished, but we didn't make it any more comfortable for him.

I stood over him and he now had his hands strapped behind his back. I looked down and he was just laughing. I remember staring into his piercing, chilling blue eyes. When you look into someone's eyes, you normally see life. You see humanity, you see character, you can see love, hate, sympathy or even apathy. You normally see something resembling that of a human being. But when I looked into Bryant's eyes, they just looked like little pale-blue glass marbles. There was nothing there, just emptiness. I could see straight through him and he was soulless. It was so eerie and disconcerting for me. That's something that will stay with me forever. I looked down at him laughing and I said something to him – I can't recall what. I just pitied him for being the pathetic monster that he was.

—

The police collapsed their perimeter so if anyone was fleeing the scene, they too would have been arrested.

HAZE: The hostages had been killed before the fire even started. The guy from the petrol station was found handcuffed to the bottom of the stairwell of the burning building and his lungs didn't have signs of any smoke inhalation. The elderly couple had been shot very early in the piece, probably the previous morning.

—

Subsequent conspiracy theorists claimed variously that Martin Bryant was framed and that there were two gunmen at Port Arthur that day, but they're just fairytales, according to the men at the scene.

SIERRA: There was never two gunmen. We only ever saw one and it was always Martin Bryant. It was obvious that he was the offender and when we arrested him, there was no one else at the cottage, or at least no one else that got out alive. They found the bodies of the elderly couple and the male hostage that Bryant took from the service station, and that was it.

MOJO: Conspiracy theorists should listen to the people that got shot that day. The victims don't talk about another gunman; they only talk about Martin Bryant. They saw Martin Bryant shoot them. You can't go beyond that. Forget the conspiracies and forget the fact that he shot so many rounds in so many seconds in the Broad Arrow Cafe . . . forget that there were headshots and there was all this precise shooting that Bryant shouldn't have been able to achieve.

You have to remember that he was at very close quarters and he had an AR-15 Colt Commando .556. People have got to get that out of their minds and don't look for other stories. Just listen to the witnesses and the people that faced him when he looked at them and shot them. They're the people that refute every conspiracy theory.

—

For a long time after the massacre, Sierra grappled with his decision not to shoot Bryant on those two occasions.

SIERRA: My own mother asked why I didn't take his life. Nothing was going to bring all those children and loved ones back, and

I've thought long and hard about whether I should have pulled that trigger, but I wasn't justified and wasn't willing to go to jail for that pathetic individual. The better outcome was that we all saw what a weak coward he is. He's just a pathetic waste of space.

If I had taken his life, it wouldn't have been justified. The moment anyone in the SOG steps over that line, all is lost. If you let yourself succumb to revenge and hate, then you are permanently flawed. If he had come out with a weapon in different circumstances and posed a threat, I would have taken him down. It would have been like squashing a bug for me. I wouldn't have lost a moment's sleep over it. Would the outcome have been different? It's a moment in time I can't rewrite. I just don't want to go back there because that's not what happened. I have to live with those decisions and I made the right ones in the end.

—

For Haze, Bryant's rampage had hit very close to home when he realised he knew the mother and the two young girls who had been mercilessly slaughtered.

HAZE: I sat next to Nanette Mikac at a wedding. My best man was Walter Mikac's best man. I knew her but didn't know that she was one of the victims, or that their daughters Alannah and Madeline were victims either. I probably felt more anxiety about this job than another I was involved in where I actually killed a man.

—

Days after the siege, Haze and Sierra were in a car listening to talkback radio on 3AW when host Neil Mitchell began to take calls about the Port Arthur tragedy from listeners around the country.

Courtesy Victoria Police

*When the SOG lock in on an offender, nothing will
stand in their way – even glass doors.*

The SOG is capable of urban and rural operations. Some intensive jobs require long stake-outs in the bush and members to be heavily camouflaged.

Courtesy Victoria Police

Courtesy Victoria Police

SOG members need to have nerves of steel, especially during roping operations that usually involve tall buildings and helicopters. 'Abel' (left) performs a forward run down into a flying angel.

All images courtesy Victoria Police

Taking a 'fast rope' out of a helicopter isn't for the faint of heart. The SOG deploy from a hovering chopper and rappel to the ground. But when time is against them, they skip the harness.

All images courtesy Victoria Police

Getaway driver Stephen Asling made a bad decision when he attempted to flee from the SOG during a brazen armed robbery at Melbourne Airport.

SOG board a chopper to save Rogue and Mouse, who were under heavy gunfire from prison escapee Archie Butterly in the bush.

Courtesy Victoria Police

Right: The Pajero used by Gibb, Butterly and Parker during their daring escape is barely visible, camouflaged on the edge of the Goulburn River in Jamieson.

Left: Soggies on a recovery mission, in similar conditions to what Rogue and Mouse endured on that fateful day.

Below: Prison escapee Peter Gibb is taken into custody after a violent shootout in the bush with the SOG.

Jason Childs / Fairfax Syndication

Above: The SOG Port Arthur crew the day that Martin Bryant, the worst mass murderer in Australia's history, was captured. It was the SOG's first interstate mission.

Below: An aerial view of the Seascape Cottages after Martin Bryant set it alight. When Bryant came out his hair was on fire and his skin was melting. Within seconds, the SOG had him surrounded and enacted a 'heavy arrest'.

Bruce Postle / Fairfax Syndication

Above: My uncle, Neil O'Loughlin (pictured at the rear, centre), was in charge of the Special Operations Group and helped re-form the group in 1983.

Right & below: The SOG practising raids in full kit at its top-secret training base.

There's nothing more
frightening than being
confronted by heavily armed
members of the SOG.

HAZE: People were complaining because we didn't shoot Bryant and only arrested him. We don't shoot naked, unarmed, pathetic individuals. What these people were asking was for us to be the judge, jury and executioner. What's the threshold, in that case? If thirty-five people are murdered, can we be the executioners? Or is it twenty-five people? Thirty? Ten? Or is it one person?

The bottom line is we are one of the most professional organisations there is. We'd been through all these inquests and faced all these issues about the use of lethal force but the community in this instance expected us to use that lethal force, because they now had a threshold. We'd acted in the most professional way, but still got criticised.

The restraint that was shown by our assault teams was fantastic. Had we killed him, I don't think any of us would have been convicted in any court in Australia, because people would have said it was justified, even though it wouldn't have met all the requirements that give you the justification to use lethal force. So when an SOG officer does take a life, people should take some comfort and know that was the course of action that needed to be taken at that particular point of time. This case highlights that. We don't act on anger, grudges or personal benefit; we look at things objectively and deal with them case by case.

—

As Sierra and the men grappled with the shootings, they thought about the victims, particularly the children Bryant had killed.

SIERRA: When I got home, I gave my baby a big hug and it meant that much more.

MOJO: I always wanted to go and see him in prison and tell him that he was not in charge. He failed dismally because he

didn't get on that ferry. That doesn't make it any better for the people who lost their lives or were wounded and their families, but it could have easily been a double headcount had he been able to get aboard that boat.

16

EXODUS

But the one who endures to the end will be saved.

Matthew 24:13

The SOG quietly removed the skylight from the rooftop of the three-storey office building screw by screw. Below them, several hostages cowered in fear in the staff kitchen area – among them a heavily pregnant woman who was in a particularly distressed state. In the room next door, a gunman roamed like a hungry caged tiger, angrily pacing up and down the hallways and office spaces.

RAYDEN: This bloke had separated from his wife and had hired a solicitor to represent him in the settlement, but, despite that, he lost pretty much everything, as I understand it. When the solicitor handed him a large bill at the end of it all, he hit the roof and basically said, 'Get fucked!' When he refused to pay, the solicitor tried to sue him to recover some fees, and, next thing you know, he's just snapped and rocked up to their offices with a shotgun and taken all the staff there hostage.

—

The SOG didn't know it at the time, but the man had packed his shotgun with sabot rounds – a type of round more deadly and dangerous than an ordinary slug.

RAYDEN: If you get shot with a sabot round, you just die. If one of those hit you in the arm, it would just slice your arm straight off. Sabot rounds shoot an ounce of lead that's encased in copper and are normally used for deer hunting. When you see a bloke with a shotgun, you always hope he's using really small ball bearings so they just spread everywhere if he shoots at you. The last thing you want is a fucking sabot round.

—

The solicitor's office was located in Mitcham, beside one of Melbourne's main arterials into the city. Because of the danger to the public, police had to shut down the four-lane highway and its two service lanes – the move created traffic chaos.

DANE: We were told by Force Command, 'No! No! There is going to be no rush on this one. We won't be raiding the building or anything that forces a confrontation. The SOG must take its time no matter how long it takes. Let's just wait it out.' We all laughed and thought, 'Okay, we will wait and see what they say when peak hour starts.' By about six-thirty, it was mayhem on all the roads all around, and they'd had a gutful and said, 'Right. Whatever you need to do, let's do it. Let's send in the SOG and finish it.'

HAZE: We established our forward command post in the back streets near the railway line. When you talk about training in the SOG, it's not just about weapons, tactics and push-ups. A first-floor solicitor's office on a busy Melbourne road and some very frightened hostages, nervously hiding from a disgruntled and pissed off client armed with a serious piece of weaponry needed the command, control, coordination and competency that only the SOG could provide. We trained and practised everything to do with our charter to provide land, sea and airborne tactical policing and counter-terrorism capabilities. Establishing an effective command post and executing a combined urban sniper, mass hostage rescue, elevated ladder assault and forced building entry was a challenge, but was something we had trained hard for.

—

With snipers in position on the other side of the empty highway, the SOG had exceptional intelligence on the movements and whereabouts of the gunman.

DANE: The information we were getting from them was as good as any job I've been on. The snipers were describing everything he was doing and where he was at all times. They were calling things like 'He's put his firearm down', 'He's green side', 'He's walking three-steps away', 'He's heading back towards the office with the gun', 'He's got the gun in his possession again', 'He's sitting down'. So we were getting that sort of detail the whole time in our earpieces, all live and as it was happening. At one stage, he actually came downstairs, walked outside and pointed the gun down the road, but then went back inside.

RAYDEN: This was one of those situations where you know the bloke is never gonna come out with his hands up and surrender. He had so many chances to do that but the more we tried to be peaceful and amicable with him, the more irate he became. It was clear he wanted a confrontation.

HAZE: With the intelligence briefing and situation report out of the way, the SOG Forward Commander did what all good forward commanders do. He asked the right questions and made a quick analysis of the threats and risks, and our strengths and opportunities. Three teams were established: the sniper/observation team, the Emergency Action (EA) team and the Hostage Rescue Team. Planning was prioritised accordingly with hostage rescue, EA and Deliberate Action (DA) in that order. As a sergeant and tactical team leader, I was given the EA to hold whilst the hostage rescue guys went to work on their covert rescue of the hostages and the snipers established their observation posts and sniper positions around the building. It was like clockwork. Snipers across the street, EA held by my team a short distance from the front door and the covert hostage rescue set to be via cavities in the roof. The snipers were fantastic with their precise calls and descriptions that evening. If the offender looked like he was compromising the safety of any of the hostages, then my team would quickly sprint to the downstairs front door and force an entry.

—

The skylight had been successfully removed, and Dane slid down the ladder into the kitchen with the hostages.

DANE: We popped the lid and looked down directly on them and just signalled for them to be quiet. If the gunman came back into the kitchen all of a sudden, they'd be in more danger than they already were. We slowly climbed down, with the snipers in our ear telling us that he was still at the other end of the building. It's strange at a time like that, because all the tension and worry for us was basically about making sure the hostages didn't make any noise. That's the only thing we didn't have control of.

So I wasn't worried about coming face to face with the gunman; I was just worried the hostages might accidentally alert him.

—

Dane moved to the doorway that led to the side of the building the gunman was on. He placed himself directly between the hostages and danger.

DANE: I was very confident with my position and knew I had the drop on the gunman if he decided to come back to our area at any stage. I wasn't worried at all. I was looking through the crack in the hinge-side of the door down the hallway. He had to come down that hallway to get to us. I could see the office that he was in and I could see him moving around. So he would have had to come out of the office he was in, out the door and then down the hallway towards where we were. To get to the hostages, he would have to get through me, and that wasn't going to happen.

—

One by one, the SOG extraction team got the hostages out via the ladder and onto the roof to safety.

DANE: Thankfully, he did not hear a thing and the hostages all did their part. It was beautiful. Once the hostages were out and safe, we stayed inside the building and I gave my recommendations to the inspector at the command post as to what we should do next. We had a great location. Like I said before, we had the drop on him. But our superiors called us out and I was spewing about it. We'd eliminated the bloke's stronghold but he wanted us back up the ladder and out of there. I was whispering on the radio, 'But we've got him, boss! We can finish this right now!' I protested as much as I could, which was only once or twice for fear of disrespecting a superior officer, but I was desperately trying to convince him by saying, 'We won't get a better opportunity than this! We can grab him now!' I even told him to send an extra couple of guys down to our position via the ladder. I said, 'Next time he puts the shotty down, we'll just storm into the room where he is and get him.' I knew his unmanned gun wasn't going to hurt me; only he could. I would have just gone straight for him and arrested him.

When a person doesn't know you're coming, the amount of force you can apply when there's two, three or four of us bearing down on someone, you can't put it into words. It's not like the movies. We would have charged in and front kicked him or tackled him to the ground and strapped his hands before he even realised we were there and knew what was happening. It's just about using the element of surprise, momentum, aggression and pure physical force for us. The psychological effect of it also can't be underestimated. You see people's eyes when they first see you; they're as big as dinner plates. Some of the SOG blokes are pretty big. I'm well over six foot, close to a hundred kilos and wore more than twenty kilos of kit. If I'm running through a doorway and I'm coming towards you, with the sole intent to take you down, I wouldn't even be able to stop myself that quickly. It's like being hit by a freight train. I can't count the amount of times that we've done an arrest and just stuck a knee or an arm up to drop someone – people just don't know what's hit them.

HAZE: It was a brilliant piece of work by the hostage rescue team. As quiet as mice, they had managed to breach the premises, access the hostages and safely remove them, all while an armed gunman was only metres away with just a flimsy hollow core door separating him from the hostages, the SOG team and a potentially deadly confrontation. The snipers played a big part with their ability to put a round on a pinhead from hundreds of metres away. The offender actually came downstairs at one stage and popped out of the front door during the hostage rescue. We almost initiated the EA at that point, but the timing with the last of the hostages being rescued may have placed their lives at risk as he quickly ducked back inside. A sniper-initiated resolution was not justified at that point.

There was now a lull in the situation. Negotiators unsuccessfully tried for a peaceful surrender but the offender barricaded the front door and retreated to the upstairs area of the offices. He then barricaded the hallway door and formed a stronghold in the first floor offices, which faced the street. He wasn't going anywhere. The SOG Forward Commander started to formulate the DA. The tactical team leaders and lead sniper were called back to the CP for a briefing and worked on a way to bring the ordeal to an end. My EA team was to become front entry team using assault ladders to get onto the first floor balcony and force entry through the windows to arrest the offender. The second entry team was to make its way to the barricaded hallway door from the rear and force entry from that side. The two teams were effectively each other's cut-off. The direct opposite pincer movement had some risks but we needed to maximise our opportunities to secure the offender. Prior to the forced entries, the snipers would launch CS tear gas into the room to either flush out the offender or demobilise him. It was going to be a full blown assault in gasmasks at night. It needed coordination; exactly what we trained for.

—

Despite Dane's desire to end the siege while he was inside the building, the SOG instead opted for the unprecedented gas plan.

HAZE: It was such a beautiful night in the middle of a Melbourne winter. The air was clear, crisp, cold and everything was so still. We assembled our ladders and the front assault team silently crept up to a position out of sight under the first floor balcony. The second entry team covertly moved to its position and the snipers awaited their orders to deploy the gas while still calling observations as we got into our final move off positions. All the teams called in their status and we waited for the snipers to launch the gas. 'Standby . . . Standby' crackled through our earpieces. Then Boom. Boom. Boom. Just like RPGs [Rocket Propelled Grenades], CS gas rounds flew across the street whistling loudly with their fire trails above our heads and then Smash. Crunch. Smash. Crunch. Smash. Crunch. One by one, they slammed through the windows and into the offices above us. I was momentarily mesmerised by it all. It was like watching New Year's Eve fireworks. My team was enjoying the show and it was brilliant. Despite the entertainment, we were well aware there was still a job to do. We waited for the gas to do its work and then it was GO, GO, GO.

DANE: I had climbed back out the skylight after rescuing the hostages and was sitting on the roof of the building next door, which was a single storey, and watched as the snipers fired gas canisters across eight lanes of highway and the two service lanes into the building. It was surreal seeing the cartridges rocket through the air with a tail of swirling smoke behind them, and smash through the glass windows of the solicitor's offices. The place was absolutely saturated with gas. One forty-millilitre canister is enough for a twenty- or thirty-metre-square room, and they put at least four canisters in there. I mean, you couldn't see your hand in front of your face.

RAYDEN: It was an incredible plan, and the snipers pulled it off exceptionally well. They absolutely filled the building with gas and hosed him down like a fly with Mortein. We gave it a few seconds of what we call 'soak time' and then the snipers said, 'Yep, he's bumping into walls and cabinets – he's got no fucking clue where he is now. He's now away from the gun and at the other end of the building. GO! GO! GO!' Imagine being in a room with a smoke machine and not being able to see a metre in front of you. That's how much tear gas we put in the joint – it was fucking chockers in there.

—

With the gunman unarmed, disorientated and unable to see, he was deemed to be no longer a threat, so the SOG assault team pulled on their gasmasks and climbed up ladders to the balcony level. Within seconds, they had reamed out the windows and smashed their way into the building.

DANE: He was a blubbering mess and he was arrested very easily. He wasn't in any condition to do anything. He was useless. That gas is not like being hit with OC [capsicum spray] – we're talking about a more potent CS tear gas that causes every single wet membrane in the human body to produce copious amounts of saliva and muck. You can't see, you can't speak – you think you're having a severe asthma attack.

HAZE: The assault went perfectly. We flew up the ladders and onto the balcony, reamed the windows and made our way into a room so thick with gas you could barely see past the nose-piece of your gasmask. But the snipers had done their job and the gas worked exactly as planned. The offender was separated from his firearm, his threat reduced and the odds were put in our favour.

DANE: It was rare that we used tear gas because of the costs associated with it – not of the canisters themselves but of the clean-up that comes afterwards. They had to rip everything out of that office. The only complaint we had after that job came days later, when the decontamination truck driver came to take away the rolls of carpet. He was driving down the highway and hadn't covered it up properly, and people were getting gassed. They had secondary gas exposure on the side of the road, and they didn't know why they were struggling to breathe and were full of tears and mucus all of a sudden.

—

One week after the arrest, the Soggies were pleased to receive a highly appreciative letter from the solicitor's office.

Dear Sirs,
The Partners and Staff at Wainwright Ryan are very grateful to the Special Operations Group. We wish to thank you for your superb handling of an extremely difficult situation.
    Words cannot express our appreciation.

17

THE HAND OF GOD

Greater love has no one than this, that someone lay down his
life for his friends.

John 15:13

The armed man sat in a chair in the front yard of his house on a quiet suburban street and looked for movement ahead. He knew there were uniformed police out there, hiding beyond his fence line behind trees and cars, but he couldn't get a clear shot at them. If he saw so much as the shuffling of black police boots along the gutter underneath the chassis of a parked car, he'd take aim and fire in that general direction, hoping to hit one of the officers.

The man was a Protective Service Officer (PSO) and was under a severe amount of stress for reasons not known to the SOG at the time. He had stolen a service revolver and wanted to cause havoc.

With the sound of school bells ringing in the background signalling the end of the day for local students, the risk to public safety increased substantially, and the SOG needed to act.

DANE: We'd set up a perimeter and had called on this guy, but we weren't going to sit there for hours and let him shoot randomly into the neighbourhood.

—

With the gunman's attention trained on the front of the house, Dane and three other SOG members in the assault team crept over a neighbour's fence and into the rear of the property.

DANE: The detectives and uniformed police were letting us know where he was at all times and that he was still out the front.

—

Dane, the assault team, which included Bravo, and a police dog moved ever so slowly around the side of the house, careful not to make a sound and alert the gunman of their presence. Sensing the time was right for a confrontation, the SOG sent the police dog in, but the plan backfired.

DANE: A lot of the time, an offender has to be animated and aggressive for a dog to attack or do something, but this guy was basically just sitting there with his back against the house with the revolver out, shooting when someone moved. So the dog didn't take any interest whatsoever in him and only caused an unwanted distraction.

—

Following the dog, Dane turned the corner and arrived at the front of the house quickly, realising he'd have to take matters into his own hands.

DANE: The man was pointing the gun straight ahead, out onto the street, and I just remember thinking to myself, 'If that barrel on his gun doesn't turn, the gun can't fire.' So I slung my shotgun to the side and made a move to disarm the offender.

I charged at him and just reached out and clasped the cylinder of his revolver as tightly as I could.

—

Seeing that Dane had the gun secured, Bravo came over the top and landed a heavy blow to the gunman's head.

DANE: He dropped like a bag of shit, and that was the end of it. We took the revolver off him – he was arrested and handed over to the detectives. Quite justifiably, we could have come around the corner of the house and called on him, but he would have turned towards us with a raised gun and we would probably have shot him. Instead, we had a chance to resolve the situation peacefully, so we took it. It wasn't something we trained for, but it was just a spur of the moment action to disarm the gun and him without using any lethal force.

—

This was just one of the resourceful methods that the SOG employed to resolve the incidents they were called to. Contrary to some people's belief, a raid or assault was always the last resort. But there were times when simply waiting for a situation to resolve itself could put members and the public at risk.

Hours had passed and Oscar was growing tried of playing the dangerous game of hide and seek with this latest gunman. The information he'd been given was that the offender had been squatting in a vacated general store and had snapped after being taunted by some local kids.

OSCAR: He was living in a shop and some kids had been annoying him – and had been for some time, apparently. He wasn't mentally stable and obviously just had enough. He took a shot at them with a shotgun and then barricaded himself inside. The kids were probably just annoying the shit out of someone who they thought was a bit crazy and they almost wound up dead. My understanding is that the cat-and-mouse game they were playing with him had been going on for a fair while. They were annoying the hell out of him . . . knocking on his window constantly and all that silly stuff that kids do.

—

Negotiators on the scene weren't able to establish a line of communication with the gunman, but Oscar recalls a man who couldn't be reasoned with.

OSCAR: He kept walking out the back door to where I was positioned. He'd stick his head out and have a look around. I was around the corner with another SOG, and we'd have to quickly hide every time he came out. It was pretty intense, because he always had his gun with him and was clearly agitated.

—

When the gunman retreated back inside, he'd occasionally lie down, which provided the SOG with an opportunity to end the stand-off, but the inspector in charge wouldn't approve the raid.

OSCAR: I kept ordering one of the other men to creep up to the window and look inside to give us an idea of his movements and what he was doing. He was just lying on his bed, and all of a sudden he'd get up and we'd all have to scramble and hide again. It went on like this for some time . . . many hours.

It was a matter of either waiting it out or going in to get him. That's why I had the bloke up at the window to see where he had the gun and whether he was falling asleep and whether we could burst in and grab him before he could get to his gun. That course of action wasn't approved by those higher up the chain, though, so we had to wait it out. We'd also talked about using tear gas. Whether that would have worked or not, I don't know. Sometimes when someone's mad like that, the gas just has no impact.

—

Time dragged on and the gunman was becoming increasingly restless. Negotiators were wearing him down with constant attempts to communicate and convince him to surrender. With little warning, the back door swung open again, and Oscar and the other SOG cut-off men scrambled for cover.

OSCAR: Normally he'd come out quickly and rush back inside, but this time he didn't. We knew he was there, and then all of a sudden I'm standing at the corner and he appeared. With his gun held out in front, I saw the barrel come past the corner of the building first and then he followed. When I saw the barrel right there next to me, I yelled out, 'Police! Don't move!' and within a split second of calling on him I heard a big BOOM! and saw a muzzle flash . . . He'd let go a shot right next to me, and the shot missed me by a few centimetres.

—

The blast brushed the side of another SOG who was crouching down just behind Oscar. As the gunman retreated towards the back door, he was hit by bursts of SOG gunfire from two directions.

OSCAR: I fired a shot from around the corner at him and then stepped out from my cover so I could see where he was. He had just made it back to the back door when we fired again, and our shots sort of bowled him A-over-Z . . . He fell to the ground, just inside the door. We rushed over to grab him and made sure the gun was out of his reach. I know I hit him, and they reckon that the other Soggie's shot ricocheted off the wall as he ducked back inside. He was wounded in the head and was taken to hospital and survived.

—

While Oscar narrowly avoided being shot, his colleague, who was crouching next to him, didn't come away unscathed. A pellet from the gunman's shotgun had struck his leg.

OSCAR: With all the adrenaline pumping, he didn't realise he'd been hit until well after the incident was over. He was patched up by the ambulance officers and was fine, thankfully.

Afterwards, it's always the 'what ifs?' What if we had waited longer? What if we'd used gas? What if we had waited for him to fall asleep? You go through all the scenarios. It stays with you. You're always aware of what can happen. We're trained to take control of the situation and dictate things, not be dictated to. That way, you go into these things with confidence and you feel in control and safe. I couldn't just let him come around that corner and say, 'Excuse me, sir, could you put the gun down, please?' Because he obviously would have kept shooting until one or both of us was dead.

In his mind, he probably thought we were trying to attack him, or upset him like the kids had done earlier. You're dealing with someone who is clearly not rational. Although we made it clear we were the police and wanted a peaceful outcome, he just didn't care or didn't understand. It was one of those situations where you realise action is going to have to be taken at some stage, because the longer it lingered, the bigger the risk to the officers and the public.

Tango and the SOG were called to the home of another armed offender who was more than willing to shoot at police. Even from a distance of twenty-five metres, the SOG officer could pick the type of weapon in the offender's hand, and the sight of it made him shudder. As the man patrolled the front of his property with two hunting dogs, his .300 Winchester Magnum rifle was the only thing Tango was concerned about.

TANGO: The guard dogs didn't worry me so much, just that big gun. That thing was a serious hunting weapon and could punch through a gum tree with no problems whatsoever. We were off his property behind some trees, and he came out with the dogs and yelled, 'Go get 'em! Find 'em!' He knew we were out there somewhere.

—

The gunman was patrolling a large drug crop and followed the dogs onto the property in search of any trespassers, and it wasn't long before he spotted two SOG members in hiding.

TANGO: He was about twenty metres away and he'd clearly seen us. I decided to call on him but I only got to say, 'Police!' when he brought the rifle up to his right shoulder and pivoted towards us in a shooting position . . . As he took aim, without even communicating, we fired off a few shots and both rolled left and right for cover. We were half-crouched and kneeling at the time. He jumped behind a big gum tree and aimed at us again. The bark was flying off the tree as we fired at him, and you could see where the rounds were going. The shots kept him pinned behind the tree.

—

Tango sprang to his feet and ran across open ground to get some separation from the gunman and the other SOG team member.

TANGO: I ran in an arcing movement and heard a few more shots go off. I knew it wasn't the .300 Magnum because you'd know it when that thing goes off – the noise would be very distinguishable. I got to a good position and saw that he was being fired at from the other SOG member. Now we had him in a pincer movement – meaning that if he moved one way, I'd have the drop on him, and if he moved the other way, our other man had him covered.

—

When the firing ceased, Tango called for the gunman to surrender and throw his gun to the ground.

TANGO: I heard the rifle hit the deck, so I advanced with my gun up and ready to fire at him again in case he changed his mind. He could have had a secondary weapon, so I had to be vigilant. As I closed in on him, he got to his feet but was gesturing towards his rifle that was on the ground right next to him. Just from the way he was acting and his movements, it seemed to me he was going to make a play for the gun again. I felt he wanted to create a 'suicide by cop' situation in that he'd lunge for the rifle, forcing us to shoot him dead. He was telegraphing what he was going to do.

It was a tense stand-off, and I kept yelling, 'Don't do it! Don't do it!' to try and dissuade him from reaching for his weapon. I saw that he was going to go for it again so I sprayed him with OC and front kicked him away from the rifle. He was blinded by the spray and we tackled him to the ground and tried to strap him. We probably wrestled for about two to three minutes, because he put up a hell of a fight. We couldn't even communicate to the other members of the team for backup, because we were fighting. It was a violent struggle, and eventually we overpowered and restrained him.

—

Although his intentions to shoot the SOG members were clear, the gunman never got a shot off. The quick thinking and training of the men in black had him well and truly outwitted.

TANGO: When he brought that gun up initially, he had the jump on us and we had to take back control of the situation. That was one of the closest calls I've ever had to being killed – even though he didn't fire a shot. Two or three of our rounds, on the other hand, had just nicked him on the way through, so he's lucky to be alive. We were lucky that his dogs weren't that good at hunting, I suppose.

—

On other occasions, the SOG had to contend with dangerous individuals intent on causing the maximum amount of harm to the group. Oscar and Dane recalled two separate occasions where offenders had decided to self-immolate.

OSCAR: We're always thinking about ways to preserve life, not end life. Even when people wanted to commit suicide and could have easily done so without harming others, we'd try our best to save them. One man, a scientist who had taken news of his failed promotion fairly hard, doused himself in flammable liquid inside the laboratory and was threatening to light a match or burner and kill himself.

—

With the lab saturated with chemicals, Oscar knew that sending in his men would have been fraught with danger. So he had to think outside the square.

OSCAR: I asked for the commander of the fire brigade that was on standby to fill their hoses with their chemical firefighting foam. Viper and a few other men then took the hoses, crept up to the window, smashed it in and filled the room with the foam.

—

The man was covered from head to toe in the thick white foam and couldn't do anything. The SOG moved in within seconds and placed him under arrest.

Dane recalled facing a similar scene with a man who had barricaded himself in a bungalow.

DANE: He had covered himself in petrol and wanted to blow himself up. The fireys have a protocol that prevents them from using their hoses against an individual, but are allowed to give them to us, thankfully.

—

Just as they did with the scientist in the lab, but with water this time, the SOG turned the fire hoses on the offender and blasted him into submission.

DANE: The force of the water coming out is incredible on those hoses and we'd basically turned the jets on and knocked him off his feet and into the wall at the back. We just pinned him to the walls of the bungalow. He was defenceless and our guys just simply strolled in, we turned the hoses off and then they grabbed him. He was like a drowned rat.

18

COUNTING THE COST

*But if you do wrong, be afraid, for he does not bear the
sword in vain.*

Romans 13:4

The two men who entered the real-estate agency in the middle of
the day didn't look like a couple of guys in the market for a new
home or individuals hoping to sell one.

'Can I help you?' the female receptionist enquired.

'Yes, you need to get yourself and whoever else is here out of
the building straight away. Some very bad people are coming,' one
of the men replied.

As Rayden and Sarge safely ushered the staff out of the building
via the rear exit, a white tradesman's van with its windows blacked
out pulled into the car park out the front. The driver switched off
the engine. No one got out.

Inside the van, packed in like sardines, was a five-man SOG
assault team that included Mouse, Merlin, Ace, Orion and Abel.
The men were lying in wait for a pair of violent armed robbers to
arrive and hold up the estate agents' office.

MOUSE: The job had been going all day because these blokes had been running around causing trouble in different locations. We got some late intelligence that they were going to hit this real-estate agency for some reason or another and we only arrived twenty minutes before they did. We could hear the Dogs saying 'They're on their way', 'They're pulling into the car park' and all that sort of stuff, so we were prepared for their arrival. Our task was to stop them going into the building, and the Armed Robbery Squad was planning on charging them with conspiracy to commit armed robbery.

—

Thirty-five-year-old Paul Skews was a known criminal, and he had with him a novice bandit in eighteen-year-old Stephen Crome. Detectives had been following Skews for weeks and told SOG members that he was an 'erratic career criminal' desperate for quick cash to pay an outstanding debt of $4500 he'd accumulated from drugs. Detectives noted, 'Skews has an extreme propensity for violence,' and reported, 'An informer has stated that Skews will not go back to jail and he will shoot it out if confronted by police. Information received and surveillance has confirmed that Skews is a heavy drug user and is irrational in his behaviour. He'd take the police on in a shootout if he had to.'

Arresting Skews and Crome was deemed too high a risk for ARS detectives alone, and the SOG was brought in to assist with the operation codenamed 'Short Time'.

RAYDEN: I met with two of the ARS detectives about the job and they told me they believed Skews was living with his mother in Springvale. He had a long list of priors, most of a violent nature. Skews had been scoping out a few different places and the detectives were convinced he was about to hit one of them.

It was a no-brainer for us to come on board, given the risks that were involved.

—

On bail at the time, Skews had no idea the police were watching his every move.

RAYDEN: After a few days of watching them, it became clear that they were going to make their move at about 1.30 pm on this particular afternoon. Sarge and I were sent around to the rear of the real-estate agency and waited for the crooks to arrive while the others were in the van out the front.

—

Everything was in place for an ambush until an unknown car pulled into the rear car park.

RAYDEN: I didn't know what was going on and approached the vehicle with caution. It turned out to be an estate agent returning to work from an appointment. As he got out of the car, I heard over the radio that Skews and Crome were on their way to our location. We didn't have time to get him out safely, as Skews or Crome could have turned up at any time and parked in the same car park at the rear. I continued to monitor the surveillance unit's radio, hoping they'd use the front car park. To be safe, we retreated with the estate agent in our care to a brick toilet building about twenty metres away from the main building.

—

With their next armed robbery minutes away from occurring, Skews unknowingly parked his Ford Falcon right in front of the

SOG's white van. He grabbed a loaded shotgun and three extra shells and got out of the vehicle. Crome grabbed a large sports bag and followed him closely behind.

MOUSE: After observing Skews and Crome drive past on three occasions, the surveillance guys said over the radio, 'This is it. This is them. Standby, they've now parked the car. The targets are in a white Ford Falcon.' I looked out of the small viewing slot on the side door of our van and could see their car in full view. We were parked tail-in, facing out towards the main road, and they parked almost in front of us, but down the road a little bit. I saw Skews get out and he had a sawn-off in his hand. I thought to myself, 'Yep, it's on.'

—

In charge of the assault team, Ace made the call to wait for the pair to leave the vicinity of the car.

MOUSE: Ace said, 'Okay, boys. Let's just wait until we get a good look at them before we move.' He wanted to wait until they were in a position that suited us to make the arrests – a spot that was out in the open, where they were most vulnerable, well away from their car and everyone else.

—

As Skews and Crome narrowed in on the front doors of the real-estate agency, they increased their pace to a 'purposeful and fast walk', according to Mouse.

MOUSE: We were lined up inside the van in order of exit as per our plan, waiting for the code word 'Cowabunga', which was our instruction to go. We always used a code word that was impossible to misunderstand, easily remembered and not normally used in conversation. 'Cowabunga', from the Teenage Mutant Ninja Turtles, was one of those words we used frequently, and it was perfect for us. The code word always had to be something that was unmistakeable. You can't simply use 'Go', because it could be mistaken for 'No' and vice versa.

One person was always designated to give the code word, and one person only. Sometimes the word was given over the radio by an OP [observation post] and, again, it had to be unmistakeable, in case we had scratchy radio communications.

If Skews and Crome turned up, got out of the car and suddenly turned around and walked away, the call would be 'Stand down'. If we were using the word 'No' instead of 'Stand down', you could have someone mistake 'No' for 'Go' and exit the van and unwittingly put members of the public at risk. They could jeopardise the safety of other members or they could give the crooks an opportunity to retreat to their car and initiate a police chase. In that case, we'd be left standing on the side of the road looking like fools. Another scenario could involve a sniper. If he mistakes 'No' for 'Go', he could take a shot prematurely. 'Cowabunga' sounds childish and stupid but it worked. It was the perfect word because it's so stupid. We never had people stuff up because of that word. It prevented so many mix-ups, muck-ups and cock-ups.

—

Ace called 'Cowabunga!', sensing the time was right to make the arrest and prevent Skews and Crome from going any further.

MOUSE: Three guys exited the van out the back doors and I jumped out the side door with Abel. We were looking directly at Skews and Crome as they ran from right to left of us. As we came out, we all called on them, 'Police! Don't move! Police! Don't move!' They were both wearing balaclavas and overalls. Skews still had the sawn-off shotty in his hand, and Crome had a bag with his right hand inside of it. They both looked at us, and then Skews brought his gun up and levelled it at us. He hadn't seen us come out of the side of the van. It happened that fast – within a split second. I'd stepped out the side of the van, I saw him bring his gun up, and Abel and I fired at exactly the same time. BOOM! BOOM! BOOM! BOOM! BOOM! BOOM! BOOM! BOOM! BOOM! BOOM! BOOM! BOOM!

It's one of the only times I've ever seen a crook bring his gun up after we've called on him. Usually, they will hear us identify ourselves and panic, drop the gun and put their hands straight up. Without any doubt, Skews wanted to shoot at us. Everyone who had a clear line of sight on him fired almost instanta-neously, and fired multiple times, so it's beyond doubt what he was planning. I know those two poor bastards got hit with a truck load of lead, but people don't fall over instantaneously, so you have to fire more than once to ensure they go down and the threat has ceased.

—

Mouse got off nine rounds, Abel fired five, Ace two and Merlin one. The offenders fell to the ground in the quick hail of gunfire.

MOUSE: I'd say it would have been over in about two or three seconds. To this day, I've still got no idea why Skews brought his gun up at us. Both of them got shot within that time. Crome didn't have a gun, as it turned out. He got caught in the crossfire because of his proximity to Skews. The fact they were masked and Crome had his hand in the bag didn't help his cause. You can only make so many assumptions in a split second. We can't make the assumption that Crome isn't holding a weapon that's concealed inside that bag. We've weighed up the fact that he's going to commit an armed robbery and his mate in front, Skews, is tooled up with a shotty. You can't hesitate, because that's when you'll get killed, or one of your mates would get killed. I always made the assumption that the people we were dealing with weren't very nice people.

—

With both men down and the shotgun out of Skews' reach, the SOG members reloaded their weapons and formed a tight perimeter. After the team checked themselves for any injuries, Merlin quickly assessed Skews and Crome for signs of life.

RAYDEN: Sarge and I heard the gunshots and advanced through the building to the front. I saw two men lying close to each other. One of them was lying on his back and I could see a shotgun on the ground about five feet [one-and-a-half metres] away from him. I saw Merlin crouched beside him and I asked, 'How is he?' Merlin replied, 'There's nothing here and there's nothing there,' as he gestured towards the other man lying prone. I looked over at the second man and saw that he'd suffered a wound to the left side of his head and wounds to the front of his body.

—

Paramedics were on the scene within minutes of the shooting, but both Skews and Crome died from their injuries.

MOUSE: Once the dust settled, we all got separated and had to wait for the homicide squad to turn up. There's no emotion. There's absolutely no emotion for me on this job or any of the jobs I was involved with. It's just a matter of doing what we are trained to do and what we are paid to do. We do the job to the best of our ability, and if that means shooting someone who is doing the wrong thing, then so be it. I don't struggle with anything I've done or the group has done, at all. I went home and told my wife what had happened, and then we move on.

—

At the ensuing inquest, State Coroner Graeme Johnstone took the SOG to task over particular aspects of the job and the claim that Mouse fired nine rounds from his shotgun in less than three seconds.

MOUSE: The coroner didn't believe it and I suppose a lot of people wouldn't realise that's possible, especially from a pump-action, because you've got to move your hand up and down with the pump and coordinate your trigger. He made me go and do a demonstration for him to witness it first-hand. During the demo, I got nine rounds off in 2.4 seconds and he was pretty shocked.

That's our training. That's what we do. We know how to cycle a gun faster than anyone. We train probably four days a week and may fire 300–400 rounds out of a shotgun every day. We may fire 400–500 rounds out of a handgun. That's what we do.

The coroner also questioned why so many of us fired and why we fired so many times. We had to explain to him that we couldn't just shoot once and then stop and reassess. If we did that, we would be dead.

—

In his finding, Coroner Johnstone stated that the SOG members were justified in their actions, and that Skews and Crome contributed to their own deaths and to each other's by attempting an armed robbery.

The shooting by the members of the Victorian Special Operations Group was lawful and justified in that all members fired after being put in reasonable fear that their own lives were at risk by both Skews and Crome . . .

The fact Crome was later discovered not to be armed does not, of itself, alter the view of the police response at the moment of the shooting. Skews and Crome – by attempting armed robbery – put themselves, the public and police at considerable risk, and the eventual consequences of their actions would be foreseeable . . . it must be remembered, the outcome was dictated primarily by the overt actions of Skews presenting the shotgun in spite of police commands.

19

A CROSS TO BEAR

Judge not, that you be not judged. For with the judgement
you pronounce you will be judged, and with the measure
you use it will be measured to you.

Matthew 7:1–2

It was 6.00 am on a quaint farm in Wandin North, a small town about forty kilometres north-east of Melbourne, when locals woke to what some described as the sound of 'Chinese crackers' going off. CRACK! CRACK! CRACK! CRACK! CRACK! CRACK! CRACK! CRACK! CRACK! CRACK! CRACK! CRACK! CRACK! CRACK! CRACK!

At the SOG's command post, located on the perimeter of the property, Oscar heard the sounds too but reacted very differently to the concerned residents. 'Fuck! Fuck! Fuck!' he cried, knowing instantly that another police shooting had just taken place on his watch. 'Get me down there, now!' he ordered his second in charge, Rayden.

Such was his confidence in his men and their training, he knew it wouldn't have been one of them who had been shot, but he was not in a good mood.

OSCAR: My initial reaction was one of frustration, not anger. I always knew that if my men made a decision to fire, their hands would have been forced. I always had confidence in them, but I knew I'd have some explaining to do to Force Command, and I was about to leave the group to further my career, so I really didn't want another shooting on my hands for my final job.

RAYDEN: It wasn't the first time I'd been at a shooting with Oscar, and after the shots were fired I looked over at him and said sarcastically, 'See, I told you I was a good luck charm!' It was poor timing on my part and he was not happy. He fucking paid out on me and yelled, 'This is not the time to be a fucking smartarse! I said get me down there!'

Reportedly high on speed and drunk on alcohol, thirty-two-year-old Robert Anthony Hall was known to be violent and unpredictable. The day before he was shot by the SOG on his hobby farm, it was alleged that he attempted to strangle his own mother and threatened to shoot his de facto. Concerned for their safety, his family applied to take out an intervention order against him, but things escalated violently the next afternoon and he needed to be dealt with by police.

A highly experienced detective and policeman, Prime was very familiar with the area, having lived in nearby Upwey for the past ten years. He played football for Gembrook and knew the locals in the region well. Because of his physical stature – weighing in at more than one hundred kilograms and standing six feet and five inches (196 centimetres) – he was an intimidating figure, and at the time of his induction to the SOG at age thirty-five, he was the oldest person to have passed the intake course.

PRIME: I was one of the first of the SOG on the scene and spoke to the local inspector. He told me this bloke Hall had a long history of violence and was also a bank robber. Apparently, any time he was pulled up by police, he assaulted the officers and it always resulted in his arrest – he was just that sort of guy. I was also informed that he'd been involved in another situation where he held police at bay with a machete. This time around, because he was armed and was firing shots inside and outside of the farmhouse, the concern was that he would walk away from the property and go and shoot or kill someone nearby or on a neighbouring property. We couldn't afford to leave things as they were. The question was: if he got outside the police cordon that had been set up, where would he go and what would he do? Clearly, he wasn't thinking reasonably, given he'd tried to kill his partner and was shooting randomly.

—

When the rest of the SOG arrived at the scene just after midnight, it was the beginning of a tense, six-hour stand-off.

PRIME: I was trying to figure out all the information. What was the situation? What was he doing? Where was he on the property? What type of weapons did he have? What did the house look like? It was pretty ugly – we were on the outskirts of Melbourne on a big property that posed many challenges because we couldn't get that close without being compromised. The plan was to 'cordon and call', meaning to surround him and get him to surrender peacefully, so we put the snipers out to try and get eyes on him and provide information back to the command post to then formulate a better action plan. We needed to try and arrest him and end the stand-off. We had a fair idea that there wasn't anyone else left in the house with him from what the girlfriend had told us.

—

In the front yard of the farmhouse, Hall had set fire to a car and watched it burn while clutching his .22 rifle. The phone inside rang continuously as police negotiators tried to make contact with him but he refused to answer it. Oscar, Prime and Rayden devised a plan to use the SOG's armoured vehicle, known as the Pig, to establish a line of communication to the gunman.

PRIME: The plan was pretty simple after we put the snipers out. We were using night-vision gear to try and find him on the property, but it wasn't easy. The snipers were trying to get close enough to the house so they could see him and locate him. We got an arrest team together and a negotiator in the back of the Pig. We had a few options; we could have driven down to the house and thrown a phone out to him, or we could just negotiate over the PA system in the Pig. We decided for the latter to open up the batting.

—

As the sergeant in charge of the arrest team, Prime recalled shots being fired at the Pig as it ambled down the driveway. The snipers reported that the shots came from inside the house.

Back at the command post, Oscar phoned an assistant commissioner to provide an update on the situation.

OSCAR: I informed the A/C that we'd tried to establish comms with Hall without any success. His instructions, and what I relayed back to Prime and the assault team, were to 'keep trying to negotiate with him'. That was the intention and plan.

PRIME: As we neared the front of the farmhouse, Hall suddenly appeared and started attacking the Pig. He was unarmed and was kicking and punching at it, trying to pull things off the vehicle. We didn't know where he'd left his gun. He was as angry as anyone I'd ever seen. He was incensed . . . clearly irrational and full of rage. Because we could see that he was unarmed, I radioed Oscar and asked for the green light to get out of the Pig and grab him.

OSCAR: There was a chance to end the siege then and there with Hall exposed and unarmed, so I gave the green light for Prime to grab him, but unfortunately Hall ran off before the team could deploy.

—

After his unprovoked attack on the Pig, Hall retreated around the side of the house and out of view of the SOG.

PRIME: We manoeuvred the Pig to try and find him again. We had spotlights, IR [infra-red] capability and even thermal imaging on the vehicle. We used the thermal to identify where he was, and after about ten minutes of searching, we located him lying in a hammock. We moved forwards again to try and engage him with comms but, to be honest, I don't think many of us held out much hope because of the level of anger and emotion he had shown. We went around the corner and could hear him yelling out, but we lost sight of him again. We thought he may have moved to the back porch, so I ordered one of the snipers, Amigo, to move up a bit closer. I felt that if Hall was outside and the gun was inside, then we could make a move and prevent him from getting back inside and grabbing the gun.

—

Following Prime's instructions to try to see where the gunman had gone, Amigo began to creep towards the back of the house, but he was forced to defend himself when Hall spotted him.

PRIME: Hall saw Amigo and charged at him. Amigo was calling on him, 'Police! Don't move!' and ordering him to put his hands in the air, but Hall ignored him and hurled a garden chair in his direction. Amigo front kicked Hall in the chest and knocked him down. Hall didn't stay down for long, though, and got up and ran away.

—

Seeing that Amigo was under attack, Prime called for the arrest team to roll out of the Pig and assist.

PRIME: When we deployed, Geronimo grabbed a tank of tear gas that we call the Pratt Gun, named after a cop named Michael Pratt, who was shot during a bank robbery. There wasn't a specific reason for naming it after him that I'm aware of, it was just an opportunity for us to pay respect to him. The Pratt Gun is like a big fire extinguisher. We fanned out into a semicircle as Hall ran towards us. We called 'Gas! Gas! Gas!' and Geronimo hosed him down – I mean absolutely saturated the bloke with tear gas. He was enveloped in a thick white cloud of the stuff.

Now, tear gas normally affects me severely, as it does most people, but we all walked through that gas unmasked like it was fresh air. The problem was: so did Hall. It was just a by-product of that fight or flight response and we were all fighting, I suppose. It was unexpected, though, because CS gas usually renders targets helpless. Hall was covered in it, it was all around him and he still managed to lean down, find and pick up his gun, which he had stashed near the hammock.

Seeing that Hall was now armed with a .22 rifle, Prime and the assault team called, 'Gun! Gun! Gun!' and told Hall to 'Drop it!' But he ignored their orders and ran around the back of the tree to which the hammock was attached, and towards the position of another sniper, Hank.

PRIME: He was headed right for Hank and then levelled the gun at him. We fanned out again to follow his movements just as Hank stood up and started firing. Hank's first shot hit Hall in the chest, his second hit the Pig and the third went into a hot-water tank on the other side of the house.

—

Hank was a deadly shot, but because Hall was so close to him, he was forced to aim and fire while looking over the top of his night-vision device – a feat that's incredibly hard to do.

PRIME: You're talking about a big scope that's emanating a green glow and it was right in Hank's face. Because of the type of gun he had, the fact Hall was moving and at such close range, it would have been impossible to get a bead on him using the scope. It was pitch black and Hank was using instinctive shooting – it was a pretty tough shot but he landed one on him. Hank had to fire. He was in real danger. Hall was coming at him with a raised gun and was ready to shoot him.

—

At the same time as Hank fired, the assault team also opened up, recognising the immediate threat to their teammate's life.

PRIME: Whether Hall got a shot off or was racking the action on his rifle to get a live round into the chamber, I'm not sure. It all happened so fast, but we all started firing. I had a Benelli semi-automatic M4 super 90 entry shotgun and I knelt down and shot him five times with SGs – so I had one round left. The other guys let off a number of rounds too. Either he or our guy would be getting shot in that situation. Him or us.

—

Hall slumped to the ground and let go of the gun. It's not known exactly how long it took for him to die.

OSCAR: I had only just got off the phone with the A/C and agreed on the team getting out of the Pig to grab an unarmed Hall when all the shots rang out. I'm usually good at not showing any emotions but that's when I yelled, 'Fuck! Fuck! Fuck!' and told Rayden to take me down to the scene. I needed to know what had happened and find out how the plan for a peaceful arrest had suddenly changed. The last thing we wanted to do was shoot him, and I was gutted because of that and the fact it was my last job.

—

Oscar soon learnt that Prime and the assault team had no choice but to engage Hall after he attacked Amigo and levelled his gun at Hank.

PRIME: Ideally, we wanted to separate Hall from his gun. If we could achieve that, then we could have used beanbag rounds, gas, batons – a whole range of non-lethal options and superior numbers to overpower and arrest him. The idea was to find that gun. When Amigo's cover was blown, we had no choice but to engage. One on one is never a good option, especially when you've got a guy as mad as Hall was.

We have rules we need to abide by in those situations: superiority in numbers, speed, surprise – all that stuff. Well, we'd lost surprise and we'd lost the option of using speed against him, so basically we had to get out of the Pig and support our man who was being confronted and attacked. That was a no-brainer for me. When he was attacking Amigo, he had empty hands – after he threw the chair, that is. In a tactical scenario, all you're looking for is hands – hands, hands, hands. Because hands kill. I've never concerned myself about taking his life; it hasn't impacted me one bit, because he caused it.

–

In the aftermath, the bullet holes found in the side of the armoured van and hot-water service from Hank's gun were cause for some concern.

PRIME: One of the main things we're really wary of in a scenario like that, and something we train for all the time, is crossfire. So at the ensuing coroner's inquest there was some consternation at Hank firing, with the question being asked, 'Was there a crossfire situation?'

After reviewing everything, there actually wasn't. Hank was shooting across the face of our semicircle, back towards the house. That tachypsychia stuff is so real. Hank's vision would have narrowed down to only that guy and the gun. When you have an armed man coming towards you, nothing else matters – it's time to act. You haven't got the chance to stop and think, because it could be your last breath. You're just reacting to what you see, and that's why we do so much stimulus-response training. No one from our end ever questioned Hank; it was just the coroner.

The only problem was another member, Rove, had moved from the back of the house to the front, and we didn't know he was there until Hall hit the ground after being shot. Unfortunately, Rove didn't radio us to say he was moving, so there was a bit of consternation about that too.

—

In the wake of the shooting, the SOG was contacted by the mother of the deceased.

OSCAR: She contacted homicide squad Senior Sergeant Ron Iddles and asked to meet with me. I called her and spoke to her on the phone and she invited me to her house. I went to see her and her two daughters, along with Ron, to explain what had happened and why. They wanted to know the circumstances and understand why her son had to be shot and was killed. I told her everything that happened and explained that we had no choice. Weeks later, a letter arrived in the mail and it was from her – she thanked us for what we did and apologised for us having to go through the ordeal.

—

The coroner absolved the SOG from having contributed to Hall's death, but the shooting followed members of the group for years to come. Several months after the inquest, Prime addressed a CFA crew from the Wandin area about the growing concern of IEDs hidden around drug crops and lab locations, and in houses with hydroponic set-ups. When properties of that nature catch fire, the danger of volunteer firefighters being blown to smithereens by booby traps is very real. A bomb technician, Prime was there to explain to them what to look for and what to do if they stumbled across anything suspicious. On official duty and wearing his blacks, Prime took questions after his lecture, but his students' fascination quickly centred on the SOG.

PRIME: They were asking me all sorts of questions about the types of guns we use and the damage they could do to someone if they were shot. Luckily, I never answer those sorts of questions with much detail because you never know who you're talking to. It was during the Q&A that the captain of the CFA came forward to introduce me to someone. He said, 'Before you go, I have to introduce you to my second in command here, Mr Hall.' I took one look at the man and the penny dropped. I was like, 'What? Oh my god! Oh no, I'm so, so sorry.'

—

The man Prime had just come face to face with was the father of the gunman, Robert Hall.

PRIME: I really didn't know what to say to him. I mean, what can you say to the father of a guy you've just shot and killed? Once I was introduced to him, I immediately recognised him from the coroner's inquest. I didn't feel sorry for the guy we shot, but I really felt for his family. In those moments, you start putting yourself in their shoes and realise they've done nothing wrong but their lives have been destroyed through the actions of their son. I found that very tough. He wasn't angry, he wasn't emotional and he wasn't aggressive towards me at all. He obviously knew who I was, which put me on the back foot. I was taken aback, that's for sure. No matter how bad the crook was or the fact he tried to shoot one of our guys, it was still someone's son.

—

Former police psychologist Simon Brown-Greaves spent hundreds of hours with members of the SOG during his time with the force and encountered many different levels of emotions following shootings. 'I can't remember a single occasion where one of the guys said to me, "Nah, killing that person has had no effect on me." Even if initially they were frosty and showed no interest in talking, at some point there was always a discussion about the fact that someone had lost their life. The men were surprisingly compassionate one on one. Even the hardest ones would come to me and open up about things.'

PRIME: Taking someone's life and protecting other lives is a pretty big weight to carry. It's the weight of the emotions of the deceased that you carry the most and that sits with you forever. I can think of other scenarios where people have been shot and killed where they haven't been crooks or been bad; they were just mad. Shooting a bad guy that's trying to kill you is justifiable and you can reconcile that easily in your brain, but shooting a mad guy that may have forgotten to take his medication that particular day is a different scenario altogether. You've just taken a loved one away from a family, and that's the weight that sits on a shooter's shoulders. People can't even begin to imagine what that feels like unless they've experienced it and have had to live with it themselves.

—

The ripple effect of a fatal shooting is significant and not limited to the shooters themselves. Not only were the SOG charged with protecting the public, subconsciously they also protected their families and loved ones from the atrocities and violence they regularly encountered. Brown-Greaves said this reluctance to show any emotions or share information often created rifts in the family home. 'People outside the SOG world struggle to understand what these guys go through on a daily basis,' he told me. 'What that does is forces the men within the group even closer together. They start to ask, "Who can I depend on? I can't depend on my wife, I can't depend on my family or friends, because no one gets it." It's a band of brothers, and for many of them that lack of understanding became the reinforcement that the environment within the group was the only one where they'd be truly accepted. So it is fair to say that they did play hard and often, and they were separate and often a group unto themselves.'

PRIME: There's a level of peer pressure and an expectation not to show any emotions because you're in a tactical unit, and we don't show emotions. There's a facade that you put up. It can manifest itself in different ways for different people, and we need to be conscious of that. I remember after that particular shooting of Robert Hall, Ron Iddles escorted me back to my place in the middle of the night and my partner was there wondering why I was basically under arrest. I had to hand over all my clothes and I wasn't allowed to speak to anyone to avoid any accusations of collaborating or colluding with them. I walked in and my partner asked immediately, 'What's happened? What's going on?' Obviously, she was terrified that something bad had happened to me. I made the mistake of saying flippantly, 'I'm under arrest for murder,' and Ron nearly fell to the floor in shock and said to her, 'No! No! He's not, he's not!'

My partner was really worried and you can't underestimate the impact it has on the people closest to you. We weren't allowed to tell her any details and didn't really want to, so, looking back on it, I can now imagine the stress it placed on her.

20

EXPECTING THE UNEXPECTED

For the righteous falls seven times and rises again, but the wicked stumble in times of calamity.

Proverbs 24:16

On top of all the training, meticulous planning and endless hours of reconnaissance for which the SOG members were renowned, perhaps their strongest attribute was their ability to be flexible, deal with unexpected changes and think on their feet to ensure each job was completed successfully. This level of resourcefulness was essential, because things didn't always go to plan.

On one occasion, members of an SOG assault team were nearly trampled on and discovered by the crook they were waiting to ambush when he stopped unexpectedly to urinate on the side of the road.

On that job, an undercover drug-squad operative had arranged a big drug deal involving some 'pretty nasty' bikies. The plan was that when the exchange occurred, a series of simultaneous raids would be triggered across the state – but it and they almost didn't happen.

DANE: It was a huge buy/bust job and I was in charge of putting the plan in place for the first arrest of the wider operation.

The UC [undercover operative] wanted us to lie in wait for the bikie, and I can recall thinking, 'You want us to try and hide on the side of the Hume Highway? You can't be serious.'

—

With little cover available at the drug-deal location, Dane knew that the SOG assaulters would have to be clever if they were going to remain hidden from the bikie in plain sight.

DANE: When I went out to have a look at the location the day before the planned deal, I was relieved to find that the grass was long enough for us to hide in. It was about knee-high, and I knew it would have provided us just enough cover in our cam gear.

—

But the landscape literally changed just hours later, and the SOG was forced to improvise.

DANE: The next day, when we went back to lie in the grass and wait for the exchange, someone had come along and slashed all the grass. So there was no fricken cover anymore! Thinking on our feet, we had to dig in and create some deep trenches below the grass level to lie in. Then we covered ourselves with all the clippings and effectively disappeared.

As it turned out, we were there for ages, because druggies are so reliable when it comes to punctuality – not. If they say nine o'clock, then it's more likely to be twelve, one or even two in the afternoon before they'll bother to show up.

—

The undercover police officer had instructed the bikie with the drugs to pull into a service road next to the highway to do the deal. But instead of doing what he was told, the bikie pulled over further down the highway and got out of his car right behind the SOG's position.

DANE: He walked between the trees on the side of the highway towards the rendezvous point and directly through the area we were hiding in. It was tense because we thought he was going to step right on one of us and the whole job would have been blown. Incredibly, he ambled along, then stopped to take a piss and urinated right on one of the guys. He actually pissed on him and had no idea! He then kept walking, completely unaware of what he'd done.

—

With the OP watching carefully from a distance and confident that the SOG's cover hadn't been blown despite the hiccup, the call was made to continue with the drug deal. From a distance and out of view, SOG snipers covered the undercover agent in case the bikie tried anything untoward.

DANE: To our surprise, he continued on his merry way and went and did the buy. Then the trees came alive and the grass rose up from behind him and we made the all-important arrest. Not much went right on that job but we had to stay on course, despite all the mix-ups and someone getting pissed on.

—

Quick thinking also enabled SOG members to avoid situations that would have haunted them for the rest of their lives.

OSCAR: On one raid, we burst into the bedroom of an offender, and he sat bolt upright in bed. For some reason that baffles me to this day, he stretched his right arm out towards us and formed the shape of a gun with his hand and fingers and pretended to shoot at us. That instant when you enter a room is so tense, because you're looking for a weapon and also making numerous split-second decisions with all the information that you're processing that's in front of you. He's lucky one of the guys or I didn't react to his shooting gesture. I mean, imagine if we had fired a shot because of his stupid action. We look for hands because hands kill.

MOUSE: We're trained to look for weapons – that's why a lot of offenders get shot in the hands. When people have been shot by us, their hands or fingers are usually peppered. It's not that we're specifically aiming for their hands; it's just that we instinctively shoot at whatever the danger or biggest threat is. Our rule was never close with people until it was deemed safe. If you closed too early, you could end up in a shit-fight with someone you don't really want to be in a shit-fight with. We'd always keep our distance, because that would mean they had to get to us and we'd maintain control that way. You would just stand back and have your gun on them, and if they tried anything, you'd have the drop on them.

—

Confronting offenders who were trying to get themselves killed via 'suicide by cop' was another scenario that posed serious challenges. During a raid in Footscray, the SOG came face to face with a sixteen-year-old with a death wish.

RAYDEN: He had barricaded himself inside a house with a gun and was firing off rounds sporadically. Apparently, ten years prior, almost to the day, his own father had been shot and killed by police in a similar situation. This night, the kid wanted to die just like his dad, and all that crap. There was no one else in the house, so we were just negotiating with him and trying to get him to come out. We could have gone forward and given him his wish for a confrontation, but we would have come under severe criticism and he could have killed one of us. I mean, my thoughts were, 'If you want to top yourself, then top yourself, but don't involve us.' But most people, like this bloke, don't have the balls to do that, so they try and create a situation where the police will be forced to end their life for them. He wanted us to shoot him. He wanted to go out suicide by cop, just like Daddy.

—

With no pressing need to enact a raid, Rayden and the SOG explored other ways to end the siege.

RAYDEN: What pissed me off was that the dog squad handler refused to put his dog in the house in case it got shot – it could have cleared the house and attacked the kid and we would have gone in straight after. I was like, 'So you're happy for us to go in and get shot, but not your dog? Are you serious?' We didn't have a great rapport with the dog squad for a short time after that job, because we were like, 'Well, fuck off, then. You're no use to us if we can't use you.'

—

Having ruled out a gas plan, the SOG sent in its bomb robot with a shotgun attached to its mechanical arm.

RAYDEN: We pushed the robot right through a window and swung the arm around to ream out all the glass. On the robot's camera, you could see the kid cowering in the corner, so we pointed the gun at him and waved it around. It was enough to intimidate him and he eventually decided to come out. It's like a game of chess – you have all the pieces available on the board but it's a matter of which one to play and at what time. You play to win, not to lose. The best chess players won't even sacrifice a pawn, but they'll still smash their opponent. It's the same in the SOG.

Intelligence is paramount; that's what it's all about. If you've got a lone gunman in a house, there's usually no reason to go in and get them, but we assess each job on its merits and with the information available to us.

—

Despite his declaration of surrender, the teenager wasn't finished playing his deadly game with the SOG. He was still intent on making police use lethal force against him.

RAYDEN: He came out of the house but had his hand up his jumper, acting like he had a gun up there. We knew he had no long-arm rifle or anything, but as for what he was hiding up his jumper? We didn't know. He could have had a handgun or a knife.

—

The SOG cautiously surrounded the young offender and brought him out into the middle of the street. When they commanded him to put both his hands in the air and then lie on the ground, he made a final dangerous move.

RAYDEN: All of a sudden, he ripped his hand out from underneath his jumper in a really fast action. It was clear that he was trying to make us think he was about to pull out a gun. Someone could have easily reacted to that and shot him. He was just being a smartarse. In those circumstances, I don't think you could have blamed any of us for reacting with a pull of the trigger.

—

Despite the boy's desperate attempts to coerce the SOG, no harm came to him and he was safely arrested and processed. Overcoming all sorts of obstacles required great skill and dedication, but one in particular regularly encountered by the SOG often demanded patience and a tender touch.

OSCAR: Guard dogs were always an issue for us on jobs. When we did a recce and saw a dog or dogs on the property or in the house, it would always add an extra element in terms of our planning. Dogs posed all kinds of problems for us. If we were doing a drug raid and a dog started barking because it could hear us approaching, the crook might panic and flush the evidence down the toilet. Other offenders might grab a firearm and arm themselves when a dog is alarmed. A lot of crooks are pretty jumpy characters, and it doesn't take much to get them all wound up and on the defensive.

—

If given enough time and the ability to get sufficiently close, members have been known to win guard dogs over. During a reconnaissance mission of a large hydroponic set-up in a shed in a rural backyard, Tango encountered a large Rottweiler.

TANGO: The place was surrounded with cyclone fencing so I thought this dog would be pretty fierce. On the first night, the dog went berserk at us. It could sense or probably smell that we were there, just over the fence in the neighbour's yard. We went back a second time and I took some dog biscuits with me and threw them over the fence. We stayed for a few hours and I gradually got closer and closer – close enough to pass the biscuits through the fence to him. By the third night, I felt confident – or crazy – enough to climb over the fence and get in the yard with the dog. Luckily, my instincts were right, because after a few minutes and a heap more biscuits, I was scratching his neck and rubbing his tummy. He was making so much noise, enjoying my attention, that the surveillance techs were telling me to shut him up because they thought the crook was going to come out to see what all the sounds were about.

—

While Tango had the supposed guard dog occupied, the SOG assault team was able to follow him into the yard and complete the job without any trouble.

TANGO: Surprisingly, on most occasions even the most aggressive-looking and acting dogs will be more afraid of us than we are of them on a raid. I mean, if you've got six to eight guys with the adrenaline pumping, dressed in black, all crashing through various doors and windows or jumping over fences and yelling out orders of 'Police! Don't move!' It's a scary scenario, even for the dogs. I've seen dogs open their bowels. They've run between guys' legs to get out of the place because we hit houses so hard. We've seen dogs scale fences that they wouldn't normally be able to climb.

We hate to ever hurt a dog, so on occasions we'll lock them in wardrobes and leave them for the detectives to deal with. They come in after a raid and ask, 'Are there any dogs in the house?' and on our way out we just reply, 'Yeah, you'll find them sooner or later.'

OSCAR: I jumped a fence once and landed right between two big Dobermans. I didn't flinch and they both shit themselves and ran off. When the rest of the men came over the fence, they stood in the shit and we *accidentally* trampled it through the crook's house and all over his white carpet.

—

Fortified houses also create headaches, but criminals have learnt that there is no stopping the SOG from getting into a house, building or property, no matter how strong the barricades are or level of resistance is.

LIMA: We had been called in to arrest a crook and the detectives did the recce on his house. They told us his place had a standard door and it was the first one at the top of the first flight of stairs. I was the MOE [method of entry] man, and luckily I'd taken one of the biggest sledgehammers we had. When we got to the door, I remember thinking, 'This is no standard door!' It was a standard fire door, though, with a steel jamb and steel skin, and filled with concrete. I took a big swing, knowing I would have to hit it fucking hard, but the first impact didn't even leave a mark. The sledge just bounced off and the noise of the hit echoed throughout the building.

—

Displaying the persistence that SOG members are famous for, Lima refused to give up, despite knowing the element of surprise was well and truly gone.

LIMA: After that first hit, we were burnt anyway. The crook knew we were there. After fifty-five more hits, I turned around to see the assault team backing away down the staircase behind me. They were making rooster noises at me to indicate that it was nearly sunrise because it was taking so long: 'Cock-a-doodle-doo!'

I was exhausted, and, seeing that I was almost done, Papa stepped forwards and took over. I stepped away and was heaving – almost hyperventilating. After thirteen more hits, the frame around the door started to give way, not the door itself. It was all beginning to crack and then the entire wall fell in. 'Shit!' The potential for the criminal to be armed now was very high, so we didn't just storm in there. We just called him out, and thankfully he surrendered peacefully.

In our debrief, the gloves were off. That's the one thing about the SOG: we are more critical of ourselves than anyone else could possibly be. We don't tolerate mistakes, and if any are made, we must learn from them in order to do things better next time. Our main mistake on this occasion was accepting the detectives' information and not doing the recce ourselves. I was furious. It should have been a 'one hit and in' job. It was a fuck-up, and someone could have been killed.

–

One of the group's most famous raids involved an illegal casino that was operating on the seventeenth storey of an apartment block in the city.

OSCAR: The crooks had installed a heavy steel door at the front so whenever detectives turned up unexpectedly to do a search, they had time to clean everything up. When the police eventually got inside, all they'd find was a group of blokes sitting around some tables having a drink or a smoke – so nothing illegal.

–

Not to be outsmarted, detectives called in the SOG, but breaching the steel door wasn't a possibility. There was another way, however.

LIMA: We had to go into the building one by one over the course of a twelve-hour period. We couldn't afford to be seen going in as one big group. So each guy would walk in through the foyer in plain clothes with a bag full of kit and head to the top of the building.

ROGUE: The joint was almost impenetrable – *almost*. We got there really early and hid in the lift well. It was so cramped in there we had to take it in turns to lie down and curl up to get some rest. The casino didn't open until 1.00 am, so we had to wait for several hours because we couldn't afford to let anyone see us who might tip off the casino operators and blow the op.

–

The SOG's daring plan to raid the casino had to be executed to perfection, because there was no room for error. The assault team decided that roping off the top of the complex and abseiling down to the casino level a few storeys below was the only way to catch the crooks and gamblers in the act.

LIMA: It had a flat roof with a few square structures that housed the elevator mechanisms but was very difficult to rope off. It was very technical, being our first roping job, and we had two rappelling teams going down opposite sides of the building, but there were no decent anchor points. All the roping experts were there, including Papa, and they devised an incredible system where they triangulated our ropes so we would bear each other's weight and rope down at the same time. So we were anchoring off each other.

It was pure genius, but you had to be a roping bloke to appreciate and understand how safe it was. Unfortunately, I wasn't one of them and wasn't that keen on the idea. I mean, we were a long way up and I'm like, 'So, what are we tying off on?' And when Papa replied, 'Each other,' I said, 'Um, can I please ask a few questions before we actually do this?' I was quickly told to shut up and just get on with it.

ROGUE: I spent a lot of that day on top of that building formulating the roping plan. We used a leg rope, which basically involves a bag that holds all your rope and attaches to your calf. Using a leg rope meant we didn't have to throw a line over the edge of the building to slide down. There's nothing below you as you rappel down; the rope just uncoils from the bag. That way, the people in the casino below wouldn't see all these ropes suddenly appear over the side of the building outside the balcony window.

We had to be on guard in case someone was armed, but the intel we'd received was pretty good, and detectives told us that there was a slim chance that any of the card players or crooks inside would have any guns. So we were confident that no one was going to shoot at us or anything. There was a very different level of anticipation with this job, because we were all really excited about it and saw it as a bit of fun – the mood was very jovial throughout the day and night. The main danger was in our descent, because we had about a two-metre fall before we could make contact with the walls of the building with our feet again.

—

In the early hours of the morning and when the illegal casino was in full swing, the SOG roping and assault teams made their move.

LIMA: We had a pretty big team of Soggies all creeping around on the roof in heavy GP boots, so it wasn't easy to move around up there quietly. We set up and shifted to our move-off points. I shuffled out to the edge of the roof and leant back into my harness. It was a magnificent view. You could see the city lights gleaming in the distance, and the bay was perfectly still and looked like glass. My feet were the only part of me in contact with the building, and I was waiting for the green light to go – keeping in mind we all had to go at exactly the same time for the anchoring to work properly. Just when we were about to push off, I heard a noise from below. A few crooks had gone out onto the balcony below us for a smoke and we could hear them talking.

—

At risk of being burnt by the men on the balcony, who could have alerted the casino operators and given them a chance to destroy any evidence, the call was made to 'GO! GO! GO!' The SOG ropers on Lima's side landed quietly on the balcony outside the gaming room, but one of the men on the other side with Rogue had a mishap and landed one floor further down.

ROGUE: He got hooked up, flipped upside down and couldn't stop where he was supposed to. He overshot the mark and landed one storey too far down. He ended up having to knock on the door of the apartment attached to the balcony below and had to ask the residents to let him in.

LIMA: As soon as we jumped off the building, we had to whack the brake on. It was a really hard manoeuvre to pull off. I landed on the casino-floor balcony right next to one of the crooks, and let's just say he got absolutely flattened. He got hit real hard.

I don't think he was expecting a couple of big, heavily armed police to fall out of the sky that night.

—

Despite being a member down, the mission continued. Rogue took out a reamer and smashed through the locked glass doors on the balcony.

ROGUE: A reamer is like a sabre – a long, thin rod about two inches [fifty millimetres] thick made of metal and filled with lead. It's got a guard that goes over your hand like a jousting stick, and it's heavily weighted at the other end. You basically thrust it into a glass pane or window and sweep diagonally from top to bottom, then pull it up across the sides of the frame and clear out the glass. It takes only a few seconds and you're in.

—

Once he removed all the remaining shards of glass, Rogue stood to the side as the other SOG members poured into the room.

ROGUE: It was mayhem inside that room. They were all sitting there gambling and playing cards and were absolutely shocked to see us stream in with our guns up, standing there in the room with them all of a sudden. We strapped a lot of the blokes in there, but, to be honest, we didn't go as hard as we normally did with our arrests of other crooks. It wasn't a high-powered job, so we took it a bit easier on them. We weren't throwing them through the ground like we normally would because the main aim was to catch them in the act and prevent them from destroying any debts or gambling receipts. They used to write their records on rice paper and throw them in water at the first sign of trouble back in the day, so we had to prevent that from happening. So we caught them all in the act, including some very well-known sporting identities and celebrities, I might add.

—

Whether it was doors, windows, fences or even roof tiles, no impediment could keep out the SOG, as notorious crime family matriarch Kathleen Pettingill once found out the hard way.

DANE: She was standing behind her security door screaming at me, 'Ahhh! Youz fucken coppas. Ya bunch a fucken maggots!' I was standing there copping all this abuse, telling her to get out of the way, but she wouldn't listen. 'We're coming in! Get out of the way!' I told her. After a few warnings, I couldn't wait any longer, so I broke the door down and it fell right on top of her. That changed her tune pretty quickly. I was on the other side of it and she started pleading, 'Oh! Please don't hurt me! I've got arthritis! I've got arthritis!'

—

Bikie headquarters are notorious for their heavy layers of fortification, but while the modifications to the building might keep their enemies out, they just made life more interesting for the SOG.

ROGUE: We had to raid a bikie stronghold once, and this particular joint was seriously fortified with steel mesh fencing all the way around. We attached a chain to the front of the four-wheel drive and wrapped it around the mesh. We reversed the car and just yanked about forty metres of fencing away.

—

When the large section of fence was cleared, teams of SOG members stormed the property armed with ladders.

ROGUE: The fence was just one obstacle. This joint had security cages on the doors and steel shutters on all the windows, so we had to go in through the roof. We smashed through the tiles on the roof and jumped down between the rafters. I landed on a bed and there was a bloke in there – he had the surprise of his life. We arrested two or three blokes and a couple of bikie moles – that was a really good job.

–

While it was very rare, operator error sometimes affected the smooth running of some SOG tasks. During a house raid, one tactical team member, who won't be named for reasons of sheer embarrassment, struggled to break a pane of glass with a ram.

MOUSE: At the time, this particular incident wasn't funny, but in hindsight we can afford to laugh about it. We'd lined up outside a sliding door, and our entry man had the ram and threw it at the glass pane. Instead of smashing it, though, it rebounded off and came back and hit him square in the head.

–

Momentarily dazed and confused, the SOG member dropped the ram, leaving it for another member to take over.

MOUSE: Without hesitating, the second man in the entry line picked up the ram. His hit was right in the sweet spot and the glass came crashing down. We all just pushed our dizzy friend aside and went on in and got the job done. Aside from that minor setback, the rest of the operation went as planned, and no one was the wiser. Looking back, it was the funniest incident I'd witnessed.

–

Trust in the training, planning and equipment was integral for the SOG, especially in the most heated situations. When an armed man opened fire on two members in a suburban street, they had to bunker down and hope their protective gear would save them.

DANE: We'd evacuated all the houses in and around the area. We had the white side [front] of the property and had taken refuge behind a small brick fence across the street. The problem was it was only about four or five bricks high. This bloke came out the front with a shotgun and started firing into the street. BOOM! BOOM! BOOM! There was a car parked right behind us and you could hear it getting peppered with shotgun pellets. We actually had one or two pellets skip off the top of our helmets and into the car behind us.

—

Ironically, it was Dane's ballistic vest that almost got him killed.

DANE: The vest was stopping me from getting any lower to the ground and the wall wasn't very high at all, so my helmet was poking over the top. I was sure he wasn't gonna get me. If he had different-calibre ammo, we wouldn't have been so comfortable there. If we'd heard a WHACK sound or the pitch of a higher-calibre rifle instead of the distinguishable BOOM from a shotty, then the brick wall and my helmet . . . nah; I'm not happy with that scenario. We would have rolled out from behind the wall and brassed him, and he wouldn't have seen the next day.

—

Dane's instincts served him well. He was able to remain safe enough in that position to wait it out. The gunman went back inside the house and eventually gave up. He was charged with reckless conduct endangering life but was found not guilty in the County Court on the grounds of mental impairment.

DANE: For me, this incident and many others like it show the other side of the story that is never presented to the public. The media only likes to report on the rare occasions where someone gets killed or injured by the SOG. As far as they're concerned, we get turned to jobs and shoot people. There are hundreds of jobs we do each year that have peaceful outcomes, but the public never hears about them.

Forty years have passed since Mick Miller formed the SOG and history has somewhat repeated. Just like in 1977, terrorism looms large over our way of life and poses a real threat to our safety. I was lucky enough to have been granted an interview with Police Chief Graham Ashton, who revealed to me that in many ways he had to follow in Miller's footsteps.

When he took over as chief in 2015, Ashton immediately saw the need for rejuvenation within the SOG. 'When I saw what capability existed overseas, particularly in Europe, we were well behind,' Ashton said. 'In terms of capability, equipment, training and even numbers . . . we had dropped significantly compared to our interstate counterparts, so we really needed to invest and ramp that back up.'

Like Miller, Ashton said he made the SOG his number-one focus and secured much-needed funding to 'almost restart' the group. 'We went through a period of about three to four years where we invested a lot in family violence because it's such a large part of what we do,' he explained. 'When I got in this role,

I talked about some key priorities and one of those was deterio-
rating public order and having to do something about that. We
needed a response to that. With the first round of investments
from government, I was able to steer in this direction. I prioritised this first. That was to better equip us to provide a specialist
response to all those phenomenon – that includes your active
shooter, active armed offender, whether that person is armed with
a rifle or a car.'

Ashton said the police needed a much more specialist capability so he moved to invest, first of all, in the first layer of
specialty – that being the ORU (Operations Response Unit), the
CIRT (Critical Incident Response Team) and the PORT (Public
Order Response Team). 'But at the most elite end is the Special
Operations Group,' he continued. 'That investment into the SOG
is still underway and we've put a lot of money into new equipment
for the group, we've increased the FTE [full-time equivalent] so
they can bring in additional operatives. I knew there'd be lead-
times required because you can't train people overnight and we
were already behind the eight ball, but we've quickly caught up
again.'

Ashton strongly believes the SOG is more critical than ever.
'There's a "nationalist" mood sweeping through society, which
creates challenges for us with respect to social cohesion,' he
stated. 'The other arm is the terrorism overlay that makes it even
more fractious. The incident of people escalating their behaviour
to a very violent level, whether it be because of drugs, mental
illness or other factors, is right there in front of us today, more
than it's ever been.'

Significantly, the SOG looked overseas to bolster its capabilities
and Ashton led the way by helping to establish a critical relationship with the world leaders in tactical policing. 'The French
are traditionally a hard country to "get in" with operationally, but

I went over there with a member of the SOG and met with them and I was surprised with how forthcoming they actually were,' Ashton revealed. 'We formed a great relationship with the French equivalent of the SOG called RAID [Recherche, Assistance, Intervention, Dissuasion] because they have specific expertise in active shooter and counter-terrorism. I think because they had been smashed so bad in the previous couple of years with various terrorist incidents they let the walls come down a bit. Our members have been to France several times and we've had the French out here to share best practice. I'm keen to develop that relationship even more into personnel exchanges and things like that as we go into the future. They certainly are at the cutting edge and I think we should be as close to that as we can get.'

According to Ashton, exposure to the RAID has been invaluable to the SOG. 'The French are constantly confronted with some of the most dangerous situations, their officers are shot and slain in the street, and some of the jobs the RAID has to do are just horrendous and against offenders who are willing to kill as many people as they can without concern for their own survival. The RAID members are walking into situations where they're facing very large calibre weapons, so they're having to upgrade their own weaponry. So through our relationship with them, we can see what the latest equipment, weaponry and tactics look like well in advance. We've just got to keep making sure we can support the requests for new gear and resources. Fortunately, it's an easy investment to make because we're not buying hundreds of weapons each time.'

Although refreshingly candid when talking to me about the SOG, Ashton maintained a high level of secrecy and was careful not to give away too much, and for good reason. 'I think there's something in the mystery that's important to maintain,' he explained. 'Not so much for the community but for the potential offenders out there. If you remove all that mystery around the SOG, it makes the group less threatening to offenders or people who might be thinking about acting badly. It's about having people know there's this thing out there that's above everything else, that we can call in as a last resort, plus there's a bit of us saying, "You're not going to like it if the SOG is called into action". To me there's something in that, and when the community see specialist resources like the SOG arrive on a scene, I believe there's a general feeling of, "Everything's now going to be okay".'

In an ideal world, the SOG would have been deployed to stop a man from using his car as a weapon and ploughing through pedestrians at lunchtime in Melbourne's busy Bourke Street Mall in January 2017. But in reality, Ashton says it wasn't possible to call in the group working with the information police had at the time. Before the offender escalated his threat, police felt they had the situation under control. 'You can only rely on your people to make the best decisions they can as things transpire,' Ashton said, throwing his full support behind his troops.

More than terrorism and violent crimes, Ashton revealed that drugs, and in particular ICE, are an epidemic keeping the SOG occupied above and beyond any other issue or crime. 'A lot of the jobs the SOG do are on people that are using ICE and are really dangerous people,' Ashton said. 'That's most of their work – this ICE epidemic or drug-affected persons or drug-assisted offending. They're often too dangerous for even the CIRT to arrest, so we need to call the SOG to come and get them.'

As I began to wrap up the interview, I asked Ashton if there was anything else he'd like to add. He sat back in his chair and brought his hand up to his chin, striking that familiar thinking-man pose and barely hesitated before accepting my offer.

'Yes, there's one other thing that often comes up,' he said. 'I've been asked a lot lately about the Lindt cafe siege in Sydney and if we had a similar scenario here, would I call in the army to take over? There's always this suggestion that the police were out of their depth.' I could tell it was a subject that annoyed him. 'The danger of seeing those things in the prism of hindsight is very problematic and this question also dilutes the capabilities of the various state's tactical teams,' he continued. 'Legally there is a mechanism where I can in fact call in the military but it fails to recognise the threat we are dealing with. It is sometimes an instantaneous threat, a quick threat [clicks fingers]. Getting the military in can take a day or more, whereas the SOG are here on the ground and can be deployed within an hour or sometimes less to an event.'

During the Lindt cafe siege in Sydney in 2014, an armed man thought to be a terrorist held eighteen people hostage for sixteen hours. Two of the hostages were killed as well as the gunman after the New South Wales Tactical Operations Unit stormed the building. Without knowing all the details, Ashton suggests that the outcome would have been the same regardless of whether the SAS had been requested. 'The work that we're doing with our SOG – they're operating on the same level as the SAS and they currently train very closely with the SAS,' Ashton added. 'It's interesting that anyone would suggest calling in the army and only goes to show what little understanding they have about how good our SOG members really are. The military might be training this stuff every day, whereas our SOG is actually *doing it* every day – it doesn't make any sense to me. Some people want to keep pushing that line but it's to the detriment of the SOG and for no good reason.'

It's at this time I realise Ashton is as passionate about the SOG and its role within the force as Miller. He shares Miller's enormous pride in the group and respects the bravery of the members just as much. 'It is very specialist in nature, it requires very specialist skill sets and it's often pretty tough work every time they're called out,' Ashton said. 'If a job reaches the stage where we are calling the SOG out, it's a serious job and they're mostly going to get pressed into action. They have my utmost admiration and great respect. I see the detail in which they plan and train, and it's world standard. I don't think we could have put our hand on our heart a few years ago and said that. But I think we're well on the way to saying that now.'

Ashton is building and leading a reformed SOG that is more superior and advanced in both its capabilities and size than ever before. The result of which, it is hoped, will spawn a surge in interest from wannabe Soggies from within Victoria and around the country. 'If we were sitting here in two years time, I'm sure we'd be talking about one of the world's most elite units.'

In 1998, my father decided to leave the SOG. He found the decision incredibly tough to make. If members of the group weren't dragged out kicking and screaming, no one would leave. For Dad, it was his future that could have suffered had he stayed any longer. 'Two assistant commissioners spoke to me and said that I would never be promoted above the level of chief inspector if I stayed in the group much longer,' he explained to me. 'I had been there for eighteen years and it was by far the best time of my professional life. At the time, I couldn't comprehend walking away from the best job in the entire police organisation. But all good things must come to an end, and if the SOG had taught me anything, it was that nothing is forever.

'While it surprised me to hear that I could do more harm than good to my career by staying in the group, there was no point arguing with my superiors or dwelling on it. I never wanted to

become stale in the job or be seen as a dinosaur, so I decided to embrace the challenge of moving to a different department and set out to use all the things I'd learnt in the SOG to help improve another area of the force. I don't regret the decision, but I did miss being in the group and took a lot of time to adjust.'

While working on this book with my father and encouraging him to relive all the memories and scenarios from his near two decades in the SOG, I saw a familiar spark return to his eyes. My mum saw it too, and it prompted her to pose a hypothetical situation to him. She asked him, 'If someone from Force Command came along and wanted to lure you out of retirement to head up the SOG again, would you do it?'

Dad didn't take long to consider his answer, and Mum said she knew what was coming. At sixty-six years of age, he just smiled back at her and said, 'Yep!' and laughed. While it would be somewhat of a dream come true for him, I'm not sure history will repeat again.

ACKNOWLEDGEMENTS

To my inspirational father, Doug, it's needless to say that I wouldn't have been able to write this book without you. Your reassurance and guidance gave me the confidence and belief I needed to fulfil my ambition to tell the real story of the SOG – not the often negative one perpetuated by the mainstream media and others who have anti-police agendas. But most importantly, only through the respect you gained as a member and boss of the SOG, and as an outstanding 47-year police officer, was I able to ask for other members of the group to trust and confide in me. Being 'Doug O'Loughlin's son' opened up more doors and opportunities for me than I could ever have imagined, and that is a credit to you alone. After spending time with your 'men' from the SOG, it is clear that they all love and admire you for all the same reasons I do. Even those that initially disliked your hard-line stance and uncompromising rules when you took over as Inspector and Chief Inspector of the group now have nothing but respect and admiration for you. To a man, they have all come to understand and appreciate why you did what you did and why certain things had to change within the unit. You are a person of the highest quality and because of your strong character and care for those closest to you – people have always sought your approval and have always wanted to make you proud of them. I too have always sought those things, but having learnt so much more about you in writing these pages and hearing what you went through, I'd like to tell you that as your son I am so proud of you and what you achieved. You are my one and only hero – this will never change.

Being surrounded by people in law enforcement for my entire life has allowed me to always feel safe, secure and confident whenever I step outside – but I know that's not the case for everyone. In writing this book, I truly hope that readers will get a better understanding of the calibre of the people who are out there, fighting for their rights and safety every day. With the SOG, the public can rest assured knowing the community has a level of protection superior to any other, for the SOG are a team of men who are more capable, wiser and courageous than any criminal could ever hope to be. I believe any law-abiding citizen should be proud of the fact that their SOG is truly feared among criminals, and if the innocent are ever at risk of being harmed, injured or killed then – just like a big brother – the SOG is always there to step in and save the day. You couldn't find a group of men more stoic and proud of what they've achieved in keeping the public safe, yet more reluctant to take any credit. Perhaps it's time to use them more often and strike some fear back into the hearts of those making our communities unsafe and harming innocent citizens. This year marks the fortieth anniversary since Mick Miller created the SOG and a gathering of members past and present will be an occasion to celebrate and commemorate. We should all raise a glass and toast these incredible men.

To all the brave members of the SOG who took the time to speak to me about their experiences, memories and the challenges they faced, thank you for honesty and courage in breaking a long-standing code of silence. Your remarkable stories had to be told. It was a privilege to sit down with you all and know you placed your trust in me to tell your side of things. It has been an absolute honour and something I will hold dear forever.

To Rogue, Rayden, Oscar, Sierra, Haze and Sarge in particular – thank you for encouraging me to write this book and for all your support and assistance. You all went the extra mile and way over and above to make this book a reality, and without your generosity, time and help, I could not have accomplished anything close to the end result. I truly hope this book hits the mark and is something you can take pride in too. To those who didn't want to speak this time around, I hope there will be another opportunity for us to work together sooner rather than later, as there are many more incredible stories to tell.

To the wonderfully talented team at Pan Macmillan – especially my publisher Angus Fontaine, and editor Alex Lloyd, you both approached this project as if it was your own and matched my enthusiasm and passion for the SOG and its members. You allowed me just the right amount of control over this project, while also providing timely and expert guidance, advice and direction. To Angus, thank you for having the faith in me to pull this off and for recognising that this book needed to be written. From the first day I mentioned *Sons of God* to you, even as a relatively untried author, you never hesitated and backed me 100 per cent. I hope we can work on many more projects together. To Alex, having you there on the end of the phone or answering my emails was a tremendous support. I admire the level of detail you have to drill down to with each manuscript you receive, and recognise that yours is sometimes a thankless task. To Rebecca Hamilton and Kevin O'Brien, thanks for all your hard work in helping to get this book on the shelves.

To my beautiful wife Erika, you've been so understanding and supportive throughout my lengthy writing process. You tolerated crime scene photos being strewn about the house, and allowed me the time and space I needed to commit to this book. Thank you for all your encouragement and love – I'll never take you for granted and know how special you are.

To my mum, Linda, you and all the wives and partners of SOG members over the past four decades have so much to be proud of. The support and love you gave Dad in the face of some serious adversity and stressful events cannot be underestimated. You did this while providing a safe and loving home for Ben and me. Words cannot express what you mean to me.

To the supremely talented and hard-working John Silvester, your endorsement at the front of this book along with your work as a journalist and true crime author is an inspiration. Thank you for meeting me all those years ago about this project and for steering me in the right direction.

To the Victoria Police Force, Chief Commissioner Graham Ashton and David Spencer, your time and cooperation was greatly appreciated.

Many others contributed in many significant ways but I do not have enough pages here to list you all. You know who you are and how thankful I am.

I sincerely hope any officers battling demons that may have been incurred from past experiences or trauma while in the police force are able to find a way to some peace and comfort. You have one of the hardest jobs in the world.

The Victoria Police Blue Ribbon Foundation commemorates the memory of members of police killed in the line of duty by support-ing worthwhile community projects. In total, 159 Victoria Police members have been killed, of which 30 were murdered. For more information or to donate www.remember.org.au.

GLOSSARY

9-mm: a handgun or pistol with a 9-mm case length

A/C: assistant commissioner

Accurised: a firearm specifically built for accuracy

ADT: Active Duty Team

AFP: Australian Federal Police

AR-15: Armalite semi-automatic rifle

ARS: Armed Robbery Squad

Black side: the back of a house or building

Bomb-up: load cartridges into a magazine

Brevet: when an officer is promoted to a higher rank as a reward but without the corresponding pay

Buy/Bust: an exchange by undercover police where a drug deal or illegal exchange of goods is made followed by an arrest

Calibre: the internal diameter of a gun barrel/the external diameter of a projectile

Call on: order a person/offender to obey a specific command (i.e. 'Police! Don't move!')

Call out: deploy a team or group in response to an incident, event or offence

Cam: camouflage

Cammed up: camouflaged

CHOGM: Commonwealth Heads of Government Meeting

CHOGRM: Commonwealth Heads of Government Regional Meeting

CIB: Criminal Investigations Bureau

Close: close the gap on an offender or approach an offender to make an arrest

Cordite: a smokeless propellant developed to replace gunpowder

Cowabunga: a code word often used by the SOG instead of the word 'Go'

CTS: Counter-Terrorist Squad

Cut-off: a team or individual used to stop an offender escaping from a raid

De-bomb: unload cartridges from a magazine

Dogs: another name for members in a surveillance unit

Double tap: two shots in quick succession, usually meant as two bullets between a target's eyes

Dropped shot: a gunshot that missed its intended target

Evac: evacuation

Flash-bang grenade: a distraction grenade that doesn't throw out shrapnel

FX-rounds: non-lethal bullets used during training exercises. Each round has a tip filled with paint, and leaves a mark like a round from a paintball gun

Gas plan: a tactical method that utilises various forms of gas to enact an arrest or force a resolution to a siege

Ghillie suit: a heavily camouflaged outfit designed to hide snipers and infantry among heavy foliage

GP: general purpose

Green side: the left side of a house or building

The Group: a term used to refer to the SOG

GSR: gunshot residue

Heavy arrest: when an offender is deliberately made to feel the physical force of an SOG member while being taken under arrest

Hog-tied: when a person's hands and feet are tied behind their back during an arrest

IED: improvised explosive device

Intel: intelligence

Locked and loaded: a weapon that's been adjusted and put in a firing mode

Mag: magazine (a metal box of cartridges inserted into an automatic weapon as ammunition)

Muzzle flash: the visible light or blast from the barrel of a firearm when it is fired

Nine-banger: a distraction grenade that explodes nine times but throws out no shrapnel

Obs: observation

OC: capsicum spray

On call: off-duty but available for work if required

Op: operation

OP: observation post

Pincer movement: a military action in which forces simultaneously attack both sides of an enemy formation or stronghold

PT: personal training (or physical training)

PTSD: post-traumatic stress disorder

Ram: a heavy instrument, usually made of metal, used to breach a door or smash through a window to create an entry point

Reamer: a metal rod specially designed for smashing and clearing glass out of a window or door

RDT: Reserve Duty Team

Recce: reconnaissance of a house or building before a raid (pronounced 'recky')

Red side: the right side of a house or building

Ruger: a weapons manufacturing company

Sabot rounds: firearm shot or pellets encased in brass or copper

SAS: Special Air Service

Sawn-off: a rifle or shotgun that has had its barrel cut down in length, mainly to facilitate easier concealment

SG: small game/grape

Shotty: an abbreviation of 'shotgun'

SLR: self-loading rifle

SOG: Special Operations Group/Sons of God/an individual member of the Special Operations Group

Soggies: another name for members of the SOG

SSG: shaved small game/grape

Steyr: a brand of semi-automatic rifle

Stoppage: an empty magazine or a jammed weapon

Stovepipe: a jammed bullet

Strapped: handcuffed temporarily with plastic ties

SWAT: special weapons and tactics

Tooled up: armed with a weapon

TRU: Canadian Tactical Response Unit

UC: undercover police

White side: the front of a house or building